OFF THE
CHARTS

OFF THE CHARTS

RUTHLESS DAYS AND RECKLESS NIGHTS INSIDE THE MUSIC INDUSTRY

BRUCE HARING

A BIRCH LANE PRESS BOOK
Published by Carol Publishing Group

A Birch Lane Press Book
Published by Carol Publishing Group
Birch Lane Press is a registered trademark of
Carol Communications, Inc.
Editorial Offices: 600 Madison Avenue, New York, N.Y. 10022
Sales and Distribution Offices: 120 Enterprise Avenue,
Secaucus, N.J. 07094
In Canada: Canadian Manda Group, One Atlantic Avenue, Suite 105,
Toronto, Ontario M6K 3E7
Queries regarding rights and permissions should be addressed to
Carol Publishing Group, 600 Madison Avenue, New York, N.Y 10022

Carol Publishing Group books are available at special discounts for
bulk purchases, sales promotion, fund-raising, or educational
purposes. Special editions can be created to specifications. For
details, contact: Special Sales Department, Carol Publishing Group,
120 Enterprise Avenue, Secaucus, N.J. 07094

Manufactured in the United States of America
10 9 8 7 6 5 4 3 2 1

Library of Congress Cataloging-in-Publication Data
Haring, Bruce
Off the charts: ruthless days and reckless nights inside the music
industry / Bruce Haring.
                                p.   cm.
'APR (1) 2000'   Includes index.
                            ISBN 1-55972-316-5
    1. Music trade—United States.   2. Music—Economic aspects.
3. Sound recordings—Industry and trade—United States.   I. Title.
                        ML3790.H348   1995
338.4'778'0973—dc20   95-9358
                                                         CIP
                                                         MN

To my sister, Diane Cornell,
whose advice and counsel made it all happen.

CONTENTS

ACKNOWLEDGMENTS

This book began over fifty interviews ago because of the questions and problems I had with today's music business, concerns shared by individuals inside and outside the industry. There were many people extremely helpful in obtaining information and photos and setting up interviews, and I would like to thank them collectively for their assistance. Because whistle-blowers are not highly prized by multinational corporations, I will respect their privacy.

I salute everyone who had the courage to go on the record with his or her beliefs. Although we may philosophically disagree, I am grateful they took the time to answer my challenges.

Peter Levinson, an extraordinary publicist in Los Angeles, planted the seeds that made this book grow. Without his support and encouragement, it would not exist. I would also like to acknowledge the inspiration of my friend and colleague Fredric Dannen, whose bestselling *Hit Men* is the template for all music industry books.

Thanks go out to the professional support team for this project: my attorney, Pamela Koslyn of Los Angeles; Peter Sawyer, my agent at the Fifi Oscard Agency in New York; and particularly the editors who helped make water into wine, Hillel Black and Bruce Shostak at Carol Publishing.

The support and love of my family is also one of the reasons this book exists. I'd like to thank my mother, Ann Haring; my sister, Diane Haring Cornell; my brother-in-law, Phil Cornell; and my uncle, Edward Usiak, for their time, attention, and professional direction throughout my career. Special thanks go to Lila Williams, whose support was crucial at the beginning of it all.

My friends made the long and lonely task of compiling and writing this book much easier. My eternal gratitude to Maria Armoudian, executive editor of the Global Network News, for her faith and inspiration; Tess Taylor and Kelly Rush, for phone and e-mail support; Edna Gundersen for her insight and professional assistance; Ethlie Ann Vare, for sharing her book-writing experiences; Al Stewart, for his support and particularly for hauling boxes of magazines down from his penthouse and shipping them cross-country; Tim and Nancy Ryan for their continuing friendship and creating a West Coast sense of family for me; Rich Martini for his constant enthusiasm and fine piano playing; Lena Michals, whose support and friendship made the final crunch bearable; Bob Benjamin, a marketing expert and wise counsel; and Cathy Davis, whose constant good cheer and attention to detail saved the ranch.

Special thanks go to Chuck Phillips of the *Los Angeles Times*, Adam Sandler and Phil Gallo of *Daily Variety*, Bill Holdship of *BAM*, and Ava Berman, the queen of Los Angeles nightlife, all of whom took time out of their extremely busy schedules to help me. Valerie Keith gets my thanks for transcribing many of the interviews that form the backbone of this book.

I'd be remiss not to thank the editors who helped me discover the nuances of the music industry and show business: Ken Schlager, Ken Terry, Geoff Mayfield, Ed Christman, and Melinda Newman of *Billboard*; Rich Bozanich, Pete Pryor, Jonathan Taylor, and Kinsey Lowe of *Daily Variety*; George Kanzler and Jay Lustig of the *Newark Star-Ledger*; Claude Deltieure of *The Record*; Lydia DeFretos of the *Aquarian Weekly*; Robert Hilburn and Steve Hochman of the *Los Angeles Times*; Susan Weiss and Bruce Schwartz of *USA Today*; and Paul Sweeting of *Video Software*.

PROLOGUE

Since the dawn of the rock age, the fourth year of every decade has been the defining point of the music we will most remember from that period.

In 1954, there was Elvis Presley, who adopted elements of black R&B and brought it into the mainstream. In 1964, the Beatles and other members of the British Invasion ruled. In 1974, the first stirrings of the punk and new wave movements were breaking. And in 1984, MTV confirmed itself as the unrivaled promotional vehicle of the decade as it helped fuel the compact disc boom and propelled Michael Jackson's *Thriller* to a sales record that still stands.

But by 1994, the defining trend of the moment was not music but its marketing. After a decade of growth and consolidation, over 90 percent of the nation's music distribution was in the hands of six multinational companies. Rock 'n' roll had grown up, bought a proper suit, and gone to work at a big corporation.

While music has been big business for some time, it is only now entering a period where its business methodology has caught up with that of other multinational industries. Consider that most record companies had only a vague idea of their sales until 1992 when SoundScan, the company that provides information for *Billboard* magazine's record charts, eliminated most of the hype that allowed albums to stay at No. 1 for weeks on end. Similarly, the electronic radio monitoring of Broadcast Data Systems, which automatically calculated radio airplay, finally gave everyone a more accurate look at just what was being played over the nation's airwaves.

With new information systems providing the first clear indication of what's actually doing well in the market, it's no accident that alternative music, country, and rap, three genres given short shrift on the charts at the beginning of the 1990s, are suddenly defining the mainstream. That's the good news.

The bad news is that the refinement and precision that have entered the business have made it much easier to sell rebellion, all pre-packaged and ready for home consumption. Case in point: the generally bland Woodstock Festival and the even lamer Lollapalooza '94.

From 1981, which marked the birth of MTV and the compact disc, through today, a battle has been raging within the executive office suites of the world's record companies between the old way of doing business and the new approach to multinational musicmaking. While executives like Hale Milgrim and Joe Smith and artists like George Michael and Prince (sometimes referred to as "The Artist Formerly Known As Prince") maintain that unwillingness to let business-oriented bosses put bottom-line interests before the music, they are a dying breed. As a result, music, the purest form of artistic expression we have in the mass media, is being homogenized in unprecedented ways by corporate culture.

While some of the old guard fought the corporate battles and lost, others managed to adapt with the times. They took some of the early, street-smart ways and managed to triumph in the modern age. The best example of those survivors is Charles Koppelman, a song-writing contemporary of such giants as Carole King and Neil Sedaka who went on to become chairman/CEO of EMI Records Group North America, which made him one of the most powerful record executives in the world.

While Koppelman became an enormously wealthy man by taking advantage of the new business climate created by the advent of multinational corporate music—a blockbuster mentality whose hunger for hits sometimes went beyond financial reason—the art of music has suffered in a world dominated by MTV, a handful of radio consultants, and six multinational corporations. This book will attempt to explain how we came to that state.

OFF THE
CHARTS

THE SUITS IN THE SUITES

Joe Smith gazed at the Hollywood sprawl from his E floor office, the highest level of the Capitol Tower. It was a fine morning, but it was not a happy day. It was his last as president-CEO of Capitol-EMI Music.

After seven years as leader of one of the world's top music companies, Smith was stepping aside just before the start of the 1994 fiscal year in favor of an East Coast rival. His reward for helping to revive a company many considered moribund was, in industry parlance, a chance to "seek new opportunities."

Smith denied that he was the victim of a palace coup. At least that was the way they were officially playing it. But to believe that, you would have to buy the notion that Smith, a former disc jockey known as much for his restaurants, toastmaster skills, and courtside Lakers tickets as for his business instincts, was capable of quietly giving up a lifelong record industry ride and slipping gently into the night.

Smith was one of the remaining old guard Hollywood music moguls, as much a star in his own world as his performers were in theirs, a man who preferred table hopping at Morton's to budgeting and planning. "We created this business and made it up as we went along because we didn't understand all the things happening around us," he once said of his business methodology. Apparently, it worked.

Smith was part of a team that turned Capitol around from a division that lost $30 million the year before his arrival to one that made a profit.

Yet the business was changing. "I began to realize how administrative this job had become, so involved with numbers and logistics," he said on the day his departure was announced. "I didn't want to do that for a long-term future."

Some two years after Smith's departure, another occurred that was a lot bloodier. Mo Ostin, once the leader of the "Mo and Joe Show" when he and Smith were teamed at Warner Bros., had been venerated as one of the industry's legends by making Warner Bros. Records a haven for artist development. Despite growing the label from the low $100 millions to a billion-dollar business, Ostin was forced out the door by a corporate battle between the old way of doing business and the new school.

Ostin had fought his ouster, hammering away at his chief rival, Robert Morgado, a former assistant to New York governor Hugh Carey, who had been brought into the Time Warner system in the early 1980s by Warner boss Steve Ross. Morgado was good at his job, managing to trim corporate overhead by over $60 million in three years. He was rewarded by being named head of all of Warner's recording and publishing ventures in 1985.

Although Morgado was named chairman of the Warner Music Group in 1990, Ostin never gave up his old habit of reporting directly to the head of Time Warner, as he had done for years with Ross. Ostin was part of the Time Warner culture, but it was the culture that Steve Ross had led.

Ross's death on December 20, 1992, from prostate cancer gave Morgado the green light to assert his authority. On a July 1994 morning, Ostin, widely regarded in the music industry as an untouchable icon, and Bob Krasnow, a respected record man who helped build Elektra into an industry power, were startled to find that they now had to report to Doug Morris, formerly an equal but now the new CEO of the Warner Music U.S. operations.

Ostin and Krasnow received the ultimate corporate slap in the face that day. After years of spectacular success in the record industry, they were being asked to kneel before someone not just beneath the level of chairman on the Time Warner totem pole, but beneath the level of chairman of the Music Group as well.

The official spin on the situation was that Krasnow could not endure the new circumstances of his job description. He purportedly resigned the day following Morris's appointment but, in fact, was fired by Morris because of the lack of hits at Elektra over the preceding year and a half and the perception that things were "spiraling out of control," according to one senior executive within Warner Music Group.

Ostin, after contemplating his actions, finally decided to exit at the end of 1994. Asked about his decision, Ostin was blunt, telling the *Wall Street Journal* that "the environment inside the company had changed, and I no longer felt comfortable there."

On December 21, 1994, Ostin's last day on the job, employees lined up outside the wood-paneled Warner Bros. headquarters, applauding and crying as their boss made his final exit from the building.

The passing of Joe Smith and Mo Ostin from the scene was a by-product of the record industry's growth from relative mom-and-pop status to big business.

By the early 1990s, the record industry had evolved from a business run by creative people to one whose structure, financing, and direction were the concern of six multinational corporations—Time Warner, Bertelsmann, Matsushita, Thorn EMI, Philips, and Sony—whose primary businesses were, for the most part, devoted to concerns outside the music industry. Those six major distributors, which account for 90 percent of the record business, dealt in such nonmusic products as refrigerator rentals, electronic hardware, and book clubs.

Moreover, the new breed of employee mirrored the corporate image. Gone, in many cases, were the free-spirited, music-loving entrepreneurs who had built the business. In their place came suit-armored careerists in offices whose motif was early IBM.

Of course, none of the CEOs running the multinationals came

from the creative world. They, too, were a new breed—executives whose background and training were far removed from the days when a record label head would have worked in the studio, driven the truck, and opened the cash drawer to pay the artist. And while some of the music divisions were run by executives with direct, street-level music business experience, those heads took their marching orders directly from the top of the corporations, where it was clearly neither sentiment nor concern for art that drove financial and marketing considerations.

In a business where perception is king, none of the CEOs of those six major corporate music divisions would ever admit that they were what the beat generation used to call squares and what modern-day record industry hipsters referred to as "suits." Instead, press releases trumpeted their stereo systems, their key role in signing new talent (a task done on the backs of junior executives who did most of the work), and their boasts of friendships with artists—relationships that were largely figments of the imagination. In effect, they were the ultimate geeks hanging out with the cool kids, buying the drinks in the hopes of acquiring a hipness that never could be purchased.

One thing they could buy, though, was market share. And so, beginning at the start of the 1980s, they engaged in a feeding frenzy of signings, label acquisitions, and new record label startups, all in the name of getting a bigger slice of a business that had exploded to over $30 billion in sales per year by 1995, a phenomenon largely fueled by the record companies' artificially induced switch from vinyl albums to compact discs.

In the process of that great expansion, something intangible was lost. It wasn't that the record industry was churning out less music. In fact, the number of acts being signed and the number of executives working in and around the business were greater than ever. The missing element was that some of the romance vanished. Bands were being signed and then discarded at a faster and faster pace as the record companies searched for the one out of twenty whose sales pace would justify all the losers and keep the bottom line healthy. No more waiting while an artist piddled and experimented for several albums. The economics of breaking an act were just too costly.

Moreover, there weren't many executives with stable jobs who could be patient. Support an act that wasn't returning profits, and you could lose that cushy office and expense account. Better to follow the pack and sponsor a band so safe, so homogenous, that you couldn't be blamed if it crashed and burned. There was plenty of time to hop on the bandwagon if a group like Nine Inch Nails happened to begin attracting attention.

Adding to the problem of the industry's expansion was the contraction and concentration of retail and radio, as well as the development of MTV into the nation's radio station. Despite the consolidation, there was an added number of bands. Given that there were still only two hundred positions on the *Billboard* 200 album charts on any given week, competition for those coveted slots intensified, with the Big Six distributors resembling six wolves fighting over a pork chop.

All of which left the six multinationals little choice: Every label and artist that potentially could increase your percentage of those two hundred positions on the *Billboard* chart was fair game. Projecting their returns on investment over ten years, including hoped-for returns on albums yet to be recorded, the six multinationals were each betting that a new Nirvana would emerge from the pack.

Why was the record industry so attractive to these big corporations? Potentially huge return for very little investment. With strict cost controls on recording and overhead, some 60 percent of records recoup their costs for the company (some 95 percent of artists never make any money beyond their advance, which is most often eaten up with recording costs and day-to-day living expenses). Unlike the millions squandered in pursuit of a hit film or television show, a recording can be made for several thousand dollars. And at a $10 to $12 wholesale cost for a compact disc, it can contribute millions to the bottom line.

Over the period 1983–1987 (not the greatest era for the record industry), a report by the consulting firm Veronis, Suhler & Associates charted the financial performance of nine major entertainment industry sectors. In its look at music, the report found that Warner

Communications, Thorn EMI, CBS, MCA, Jem Records, and K-Tel had a 28.6 percent compound annual operating income growth rate, and a 26.1 percent compound annual cash flow growth rate. The average suggested retail unit price for recorded music rose from $6.50 to $8, as recorded music enjoyed the highest rate of pretax operating income growth of any communications industry, most of it in CDs. CBS Records (later Sony) and Warner Communications Inc. (later to be Time Warner) were the twin boomers of the lot. They and the other majors accounted for the growth, as independents Jem and K-Tel each filed for bankruptcy.

Of course, getting a hit is a pressure-filled endeavor, and there is little doubt the record business of the 1990s was not as fun a place to work as it used to be. Which is not to say that there still weren't rewards.

Smith, for one, had wanted to continue his grand adventure for at least a few more years. Like such social lions as Ahmet Ertegun and Walter Yetnikoff, he enjoyed the wheeling and dealing of the industry's elite in Hollywood and New York, the power that comes with being able to sign the checks. And there was little doubt that Ostin, despite being a longtime employee, had every right to feel that Warner Bros. Records was "his" company.

Yet Smith and Ostin were both forced out in rather unceremonious fashion. Certainly, in such a cyclical business as the record industry, they could be forgiven if their labels weren't the hottest in the business at the time of their departure. But the record industry they were leaving was not the record industry they had entered, a business that was built through entrepreneurship, gut instincts, and a big dollop of old-fashioned networking.

A typical example of the new type of company entering the music business came in 1979, when the stodgy British company Thorn decided to diversify by using a combination of cash and stock to merge with EMI Music. It was an odd marriage: Thorn, a defense company with interests in other areas, hooking up with the world of rock 'n' roll.

EMI Music—Electric & Musical Industries Ltd. of Great Britain—was one of the oldest music companies in the world, starting back in the 1870s as a printer of sheet music and expanding into recorded music. The company entered the American music market in 1955 with its purchase of a majority interest in Capitol Records.

The following year, the company moved into the landmark Capitol Tower on Vine Street in Hollywood. Although it has been fervently denied by company officials throughout the years, the building resembles a thirteen-story stack of records, each floor of the cylindrical tower encircled by a giant steel rim, topped by a needle.

Capitol Records was founded by singer/songwriter Johnny Mercer, music store owner Glenn Wallichs, and motion picture producer B. G. "Buddy" DeSylva in June 1942. Mercer, a top songwriter of his time, was unhappy with the status quo of the industry, arguing that recording artists were rarely treated with proper respect by their labels. As most big-name artists were already signed to other labels, Capitol Records set about signing and developing its own stable of acts.

The label had hits by Nat King Cole, Stan Kenton, Peggy Lee, Ella Mae Morse, and Margaret Whiting. Capitol opened a new era in record promotion in 1942 by becoming the first label to provide disc jockeys with complimentary copies of its product. The company also achieved another first when in 1949 it began manufacturing records in all three speeds—45, 33⅓, and 78 rpm.

Despite the apparent artistic success, EMI had a prudent reason for accepting Thorn's proposal in the late seventies. "Certainly, EMI was in trouble at that time," said a senior executive at the company who was intimately familar with its financials. A medical electronics division of EMI had fallen into trouble over a patent infringement suit on a brain and body scanner. Thorn's industrial logic in buying EMI "was, in a sense, not dissimilar to Sony's when acquiring Columbia Pictures and Matsushita's when purchasing MCA. Thorn had a strong position in the hardware business as a powerhouse in the United Kingdom in the rental of that equipment.

So there were some strategic strengths in the hardware company gaining a presence in the software business."

Thorn immediately sized up what it had bought. Like many new marriages, there were some second thoughts, based mainly on the unpredictable nature of music sales. "They may have had some concerns about whether they wanted to be in the [music] business," said the executive, whose contractual obligations to the company prevent him from revealing his identity. "In the first few months, there was some consideration to selling all or part of it. That passed very soon."

The record business, as it turned out, was the only media business Thorn EMI would stay in. During a decade when media empires were expanding into different fields, Thorn took the opposite tactic, divesting itself of the film and television businesses that were subsidiaries of EMI. "There was no question that Thorn had an almost intellectual inability to understand the culture of the film business," said the senior executive. "With the record business, they did have an understanding of the underlying value of copyrights. But with the film business, the investment factor was so high on every risk that you took, and the box office didn't happen. The film business was too rich for their blood."

The spirit of avoiding adventure also infiltrated the workaday world of the company's employees. The corporate culture of EMI Music was a reflection of the quaint British system. "It was like a civil service job," recalled Nick Gatfield, who from 1985 to 1992 headed the U.K.'s Artist & Repertoire division, which finds and nurtures new acts. "You could have a job for life as long as you didn't fuck up too badly. There was one guy in A&R when I got there who started in 1957. He was in charge of MOR, or middle-of-the-road music, of which there wasn't any, but he was still there. But that was part of the charm of the company." Gatfield recalled that Bhaskar Menon, the worldwide chairman of EMI Music, once jokingly advised his troops that they should not be afraid to make a profit, "just make one that was not too obscene."

It wasn't until the late 1980s that Thorn began to pay serious attention to its music business. It appeared that it finally took a hard look at what some of the other record companies were doing. The result was that Thorn EMI ceased to be the genteel men's club that it had been in the past.

Two years after his abrupt exit, Joe Smith expanded upon his views of the record industry with remarks that cut to the core of what the business had become, and in particular what Thorn EMI was like to work for.

"At no point during those growing years were Mo Ostin and myself ever concerned with return on sales, what percentage of profit," Smith said, leaning back into the sofa at a private office he maintained in Century City, California. "What you were trying to do was build, just keep building and not lose money. The understanding was that some years of business you spend money, but there were no quarterly meetings dealing with return on sales. While we were part of Warners, it was never, 'This division's losing money so you guys got to make more money.' There was never that kind of pressure to put out more records."

However, that changed with the industry's expansion, Smith explained. "As these companies got absorbed by larger and larger companies, you became a division of a major company and there were financial standards set for everybody. You had to get a certain return on sales, and anything else was not acceptable. You could be making profit, but you were not delivering enough profit based on your revenue. And that mentality meant that, well, I'd better do more sure things. It's somewhat akin to the motion picture industry betting on Clint Eastwood and Steven Spielberg rather than on something new."

Smith, in his role as CEO of Capitol-EMI, was required to explain the business side to the London home office two times a year. "And I stood up and did my North America song and dance. Nobody ever asked me, 'What artist are you developing? Where's the music going? How do you intend to buy into that?' It was, 'What are your day's credit outstanding? How fast can you turn around your manufacturing plant?' I'm not saying that shouldn't be a part of the business. But it seems to me that the creative side should lead the way and the other side should be the support. And so it seems to me that as this business is structured now, if Berry Gordy was still running Motown and then sold it, he would be an employee of Matsushita and have to deliver certain amounts of profit in a year or there'd be some severe meetings with Berry Gordy. Gordy didn't have to do that when he was building his company, and he made money every year."

The results of such thinking were hard to quantify, given that Thorn's reports usually showed an increase in profits and sales. However, the results of the financials were never broken out in a way that made them obvious. The North American part of Thorn EMI, which accounts for many of the new acts that provide vitality, was struggling by the 1990s, leaving the company to rely almost solely on its catalog—sales of albums released in the past rather than current product. It was an unhealthy situation for any record company hoping for long-term success, which is built upon developing new artists that will generate new revenues and, in turn, catalog. Moreover, expansion into international territories, where music could be sold at a higher price, helped pump up the volume with little additional development cost. Thus, Thorn EMI looked on paper to be a fat and happy company.

More was at stake, however, than the bottom line. Although not pining for the days when deals were done on the back of an envelope, Smith felt that the glamour had fled with the arrival of the suits to the suites.

"Any deal that was made during my time at Capitol went through glorious Lotus 1-2-3's, you know, and put up on the board and should we buy this based on that. So that the much maligned phrase 'gut feeling,' the intuitive sense of people like Ahmet Ertegun, Jerry Wexler, the Chess Brothers, people like that, that is not welcome in companies now. They say they want to get ahead creatively, but they really want a businesslike operation that delivers the right return on sales, and all these companies are under constant pressure, because the way we do business is quarter to quarter, and that just did not exist as this business was growing."

However, such corporate maneuvering has ramifications to its artists as well as its executives. The street-level talent scouts that find new bands and songwriters, as well as the promotion people who must convince radio of a product's worthiness, are also aware of a company's bottom-line concerns.

"A good executive keeps [the influence] away from them," Smith said. "But when it's turning bad, then the pressures [start]. There's been much more of that over the last eight, nine years than there ever was before. Normally a promotion person who has the attention span of a flea and the interest of a Bartlett pear in anything else besides what they do, they're not involved. I remember Hale Milgrim at Capitol, when Capitol had a tough year, just beating up the staff. He had to do it because pressure came from [Thorn EMI corporate headquarters in] England to [EMI music CEO] Jim Fifield. There is a financial mentality that runs in the entertainment industry now—there's no question about it."

The pressure on the bottom line was increased during the 1980s at Thorn EMI by its huge acquisitions: Chrysalis, Enigma, IRS, SBK, and ultimately Virgin Records—they all filled the need to expand the company's market shares. The idea, as Smith explains it, is volume. And even if a deal will cost far more than it ever returns, you still make the deal. "You're figuring, I paid $300 million for this. It makes about $30 million or $20 million profit, so I'm [in essence] buying it fifteen times."

The problem is, a company may not be generating profits or is generating very tiny profits, as was the case with Virgin Records when it was purchased for close to a billion dollars. So upon buying that company, Thorn EMI was essentially purchasing an expanded market share, a way to keep the distribution and manufacturing divisions busy, and the chance to get lucky with a new group of artists and executives. Whether it was buying anything that would add much profit to the bottom line is dubious. Eventually the company must account to its shareholders. And that's where the real accounting magic comes into play.

"Okay, they spent four or five hundred million dollars," said Smith. "So what's the cost of the money? Cost of the money is 10 percent. You paid $600 million. [The company must generate] $60 million a year. A&M's never made $60 million profit."

Which results in write-offs and hidden costs. "They do all kinds of things. The write-offs that EMI took on Virgin, my God, I mean, it's stunning how they did it. You think Motown Records was worth $360 million? They had one act going and the catalog had been beaten up badly [a reference to Motown's penchant for releasing ad nauseum compilations of inferior quality]. We're ready to shoot the dice in the same deal, but I stopped. I said, 'That's not worth $316 million.'"

How did several of the multinational corporations find themselves in the predicament of paying outrageous sums for recording catalogs that likely would give only the illusion of progress?

The case of EMI Music, one of the most active acquirers in the '80s and '90s, is similar to that of others who played the game. EMI can blame its own internal failures. A look at the company's history details that it did not develop the corporate culture necessary to find and support new artists.

During the late 1950s and early '60s, Capitol was one of America's most successful record labels, with a reputation built on the creative works of Frank Sinatra and Nat King Cole, among others. By 1964, however, Capitol was sharing in the quantitative growth of the industry but had not yet embraced rock 'n' roll, which was dynamically affecting the market for popular music. The assumption by its executives, which proved to be false, was that annual dollar sales increases were sufficient indices of the long-term health of its record business. It was a wrong assumption and would haunt the company in the following years.

Organizationally, according to a senior executive familiar with the company, Capitol in the 1960s left key A&R and marketing positions in the hands of a generation of staid record men removed from the transformation that was taking place in the marketplace. The company itself had become established as one of the majors and already had taken its place in the sun along with the giants RCA, Columbia, and Decca. It had long since become professionally prestigious to be a vice president of Capitol Records. But Capitol's management during this period was ill equipped psychologically to perceive the need for creating a climate within the corporation that was hospitable to discovering new contemporary performers. Thus, Capitol Records was rendered virtually incapable of operating competitively within the crucial area of finding and breaking its own new stars.

The company's survival during this period of internal creative decline was substantially assisted by the accidental phenomenon of the Beatles, at first a band no one within the company wanted to sign but whose contribution to Capitol's total sales from 1964 to 1971 represented nearly 30 percent of the company's volume. Although Capitol staffers found it difficult to recognize the uniqueness of the Beatles, the company continued for an unreasonably long period of time to equate Beatles sales success with its own internal professional capabilities.

In 1969, a new management team was imported from the outside to bring Capitol back into the mainstream. Immediately, the company's artist roster and the number of its monthly releases increased at an alarming rate, and Capitol's existing marketing force, which had little experience in successfully deploying contemporary products beyond the Beatles and Beach Boys, reacted with confusion to the sudden proliferation of product. Instead of focusing, the record company that in 1964, the first year of the Beatles at Capitol, had 1,700 employees, now swelled to over 4,700 people.

Beatles sales in fiscal 1971 were, by one insider's estimate, 41 percent lower than sales in the company's previous fiscal year. That fact, coupled with a series of internal mishaps, resulted in a loss for the year.

In April 1971, the company appointed Bhaskar Menon, the son of an Indian royal family, to take over its operation. Menon instituted a program of cost control and overhead reduction while streamlining the organization. He encouraged his executives to rejoin the contemporary record business, restoring credibility to the company's commercial practices. The process would be gradual. For the five years following 1971, the policy was to raise the company executives' credibility and skills to acceptable levels rather than drive for increased sales volume.

By 1977, Capitol felt confident in seeking higher market share and became more aggressive in acquiring and investing in talent. The establishment of the EMI America Record label and the purchase of United Artists Records were part of that strategy, resulting in an increase in sales and profits. United Artists' roster at the time included Kenny Rogers, Charlie Rich, Crystal Gayle, and Ike and Tina Turner. EMI Records included the J. Giels Band and Kim Carnes.

The American record market, which had registered spectacular growth throughout the '60s, continued to be extremely buoyant in the early '70s, registering an all-time high in industry volume levels in 1978, the year of the soundtracks to *Saturday Night Fever* and *Grease*. The record industry perceived its opportunities to be virtually limitless.

But for the next four years, industry volume continued to run well below 1978 peak levels. The growth of private home taping, substantial competition from video games and cable television, a high level of youth unemployment, and a radical change in pop radio programming formats that saw the rise of adult contemporary and country radio stations, both considered formats that, at the time, focused on an older, passive, non–record-buying audience, were among the reasons for the crash landing.

By the end of the 1970s, EMI Music was like most of the industry and watched as its returns, accounts receivables, and inventory levels rose to all-time highs. The American economy was in recession, with unprecedented unemployment and decreases in discretionary consumer spending. New artists from the expensive deals were simply not selling, yet even richer deals continued to be entered into in what by then the whole industry viewed as frenzied adventurism. That, and the demise of the Beatles as a group, left EMI in a bind.

The industry in general was caught unprepared by the market decline, particularly when it came so suddenly after the euphoria of 1978. CBS and Warners, the market leaders, were forced to cut back on their facilities and operating overheads, and both RCA and MCA were in serious financial trouble. Some independents like ABC, United Artists, Arista, and Casablanca were absorbed by larger entities, and the remaining indies—A&M, Chrysalis, and Motown—

had to seek refuge within the manufacturing, distribution, and sales umbrellas of the majors. At the same time, a number of important retail customers went out of business in the early '80s, while survivors came increasingly to rely on record company credit to maintain their inventory levels in the tough economic climate. The crunch hit the independent distribution network particularly hard, causing many of its main players to virtually disintegrate.

The worst victim of the overall bleak financial situation at the time was PolyGram, whose U.S. losses from 1980 to 1982 exceeded $200 million by some estimates, resulting in parent company Philips's trying several measures, including shopping 80 percent of its U.S. record operations and seeking a merger or joint distribution operation.

Total industry sales in 1979 declined 14 percent in value from $1.8 billion to $1.5 billion, and 11 percent in units from 438 million units to 389 million units. For the next four years, industry volume continued to run well below peak levels, reaching a low point in 1982, and even the apparent recovery in 1984 must be seen as illusory if viewed against the background of inflation, compact disc sales, and the unprecedented Michael Jackson *Thriller* phenomenon. In the following four years, from 1982 to 1986, failure to generate sufficient growth from EMI's own repertoire resources—let alone replace the licensed volume, which was relinquished voluntarily—resulted in a progressive decline of EMI Music's shares and leverage in every major market.

Surprisingly, EMI was not immediately affected by the down-swing, thanks to three unusual record releases that artificially insulated their labels from sharing the general industry experience in the early '80s.

First came the resurgence of Kenny Rogers after the release of his greatest-hits album in the autumn of 1980; then, a tragic and unexpected windfall, as a substantial increase in Beatles catalog sales followed John Lennon's assassination; and finally, the surprise smash success of Neil Diamond's *Jazz Singer* soundtrack, a stark contrast to the disappointing box office of the film itself. Those three products, which had low originational and royalty costs and required minimal promotion, contributed approximately 50 percent of Capitol's U.S. sales for fiscal 1981 and were also a solid source of revenue for several years thereafter.

Still, the company felt that a defensive posture was the correct approach to the shrinking record industry. To give an idea of how bad things were, consider that industry giant CBS Records described its experience in 1982 as almost a complete lack of business.

Thus, in early 1981, despite Capitol's excellent performance, major cost cuts were undertaken, including the closing of three manufacturing plants and two distribution centers. By the summer of 1982, some three years after the rest of the industry had fallen victim to recession, Capitol's turn came, as U.S. record sales were running 30 percent below those of the prior year, with growing evidence that Capitol's volume slippage now exceeded the market recession.

After three years of decline, Capitol's strategic policy shifted in 1984 to rebuilding product and marketing strength to substantial new investments in talent and promotion. Recognizing that time and expense would be required to achieve the expansionary volume objectives that had to be aborted in 1982 for short-term survival, Menon brought in new executives to head Manhattan Records, Angel Records, and Capitol Nashville. Continuing support was extended to the recovery of EMI America, which was slumping along with the sales of its chief artist, Kenny Rogers.

EMI's position, as earlier in the decade, stood again in contrast to the rest of the music industry in the mid-'80s. CBS from 1982 to 1986 increased its share of the world sales by 6 percent by growing its own talent in the United States and the United Kingdom, including Bruce Springsteen, Billy Joel and Wham!, adding to its own strength to such a degree that it was able to forgo renewal of its long-term license agreements with A&M Records outside North America and yet expand into new markets.

Thanks to its talent-nurturing environment, the other giant of the industry, WEA, the distribution arm for the Warner Bros., Elektra, and Atlantic Records family, was able to maintain a high level of success. Meanwhile, RCA and MCA also were active in increasing their volume through mergers and major distribution deals that helped to provide the profits and cash for rebuiliding their own repertoire sources. Even PolyGram managed to catapult itself out of decline by embracing the compact disc and becoming one of the cutting edge companies issuing the new technology. Meanwhile, EMI lagged, a fiscally conservative company perceived throughout the record industry as reluctant to invest in new-talent development and marketing.

Having weathered the decline, EMI was ready by 1985 to jump back into the game. Realizing how slow and expensive it would be to grow its own talent—a process that was not guaranteed—the company set out on a course that would quickly enable its market share to grow by absorbing or acquiring existing labels, while trying to set up exclusive national distribution and sales arrangements with labels it could not purchase.

The roster at that point included Power Station, Heart, Tina Turner, Freddie Jackson, Duran Duran, Corey Hart, Motels, Katrina & The Waves, Limahl, Kim Carnes, Belouise Some, John Waite, George Clinton, Marillion, Maze, Ashford & Simpson, Melba Moore, Boogie Boys, Brass Construction, Stanley Jordan, Sarah Brown, Marie Osmond, and Andrew Lloyd Webber. Most of them were career artists.

Still, PolyGram and EMI Music, the only non-American–controlled music companies, were like Third World record businesses battling for U.S. market position against the superpowers, CBS and Warners, as well as the second-level companies, MCA and RCA.

At that time, the company managers realized that long-term success in the record industry required high-volume market share. To get that, you needed to attract and retain artists and operating executives, a strategy requiring risk and high product investment until a decent level of volume could be attained.

The problems with that strategy were plentiful. Artists often missed their scheduled release dates or delivered albums that were substandard to previous releases, resulting in financial projections that could be incredibly inaccurate. However, that risk was not built into the inflexible financial picture.

Pressures increased at Capitol. Many Capitol artists were slow to write and record new albums; thus, sales and profit forecasts, which are based on estimates of how new albums (which frequently had not been written or recorded) will do in the marketplace, began to resemble science fiction, leaving accountants screaming for an answer to the shortfalls in projected income. Adding to the budgetary difficulties was the fact that substantial promotion and marketing expenses must be committed before and at the release time based on original sales projections, creating a further liability on the balance sheets.

Menon tried to get Thorn EMI to commit to supporting his goals of extended talent acquisition and delivery strategies in the United States, asking for a five-year period of investment in executive manpower, artist acquisition, and market support. He warned that backing off would leave the company with little room to maneuver, and he suggested that the company might consider selling if it was not willing to play the game.

Unfortunately, Menon was not given the time to complete his vision. Thorn EMI chairman Colin Southgate decided to bring in a new plan and a new leader, perhaps sensing that the entrenched bureaucracy at the company would not respond to this new call to arms without a shakeup.

Although still holding the title of chairman, Bhaskar Menon was, in effect, succeeded in 1987 as creative director of the company by Joe Smith, the former president of Elektra and Warner Bros. Records, who had actively sought one last hurrah in the record industry by becoming the first man to head three different record labels. The Capitol Records that Smith found when he arrived was moribund.

Smith was appalled at the lack of initiative among its employees when he arrived. He set to work swinging his hatchet. "I mean," he said, "I thought, 'Were you waiting for me to come in and do this? Why didn't somebody do this before?' So that was my task. And I looked around. I saw the business. Capitol could get going again. It had great values. It had a catalog. It had some artists, and they were aging, but there were other things. And I felt I could bring something to it if I brought in some other exciting people. So I got people with profiles. The company had to have a profile. If there's anything that still exists in this business, it's that there are stars out there in our own world. And that kind of has a subtle influence on talent, on radio stations. When Mo Ostin walks in, he would intimidate more artists than would intimidate Mo. They'd look at Mo Ostin and say, 'Hey, Christ. He signed Neil Young. He signed Madonna. He made the Sire Records deal.' Or they look at Ahmet Ertegun. 'My God, this guy brought in Ray Charles and Aretha Franklin.' When Capitol was trying to flash on an act, they'd bring me into the picture. And these kids knew that I had been with the Grateful Dead, or whatever the hell the story was. So that was the job at Capitol Records, and it was trying to inject personality. I fear everything's getting a little grayer now there too, and that's the corporate influence. There are fewer characters, a little less wildness, and a little less tumult that the record business always had. Conventions used to be wild and fun."

Smith, who has written his own music history book, summed up what the story of the 1980s had been, both for EMI and the industry in general. "I would just say it's the corporatization of the music business. The thrust of it is you have kind of sucked out a lot of the adventure, a lot of the charm, a lot of the distinctive nature and all that, and replaced it with better business practices, more order, more tools so people know what they're doing and what they've got. But there's a tradeoff in that. When you provide all that technology and all that business sense, you have now impacted what made it in the first place," which Smith termed, "fly by the seat of your pants, sign an artist based on just how the stars are."

Smith grimaced a bit as he recalled the new mentality. "So I would submit a five-year plan and I'd get a call from some technician in England saying, 'Joe, you have your market share going from 14 to

14.2.' I said, 'Wait a second. You really think they're real numbers? Future planning in this business is where we're going to lunch Thursday.

"Can you predict Garth Brooks would come along and make Nashville, which was limping along, all of a sudden the most profitable record company, maybe, in the entire industry? They're trying to make it more predictable, and when you try to make it more predictable then you take less chances. You know a Steven Spielberg picture will open big. You bet on Julia Roberts, because generally she opens big. You bet on Clint Eastwood, because he'll open big. You can always say, 'Well, Jesus, we went with Julia Roberts and it's not our fault.' And so companies will try to keep their executives in here, with just very occasional straying out there to do something off the wall. And I think that we'll get more and more involved with the technology of it and that will even drain more of the adventurous talent side of it too."

Jim Fifield, Smith's boss at EMI, had a different view of how the music world had changed. "The music industry was a little slow accepting what's been going on in other industries for fifteen, twenty years, even down to knowing what is sold every week by your major accounts," said Fifield, speaking from his antique-furnished office atop the Capitol Tower. "You're talking about people that are (in some cases) a four and a half billion dollar industry within a company. That's a big business. It requires, in my case, 8,500 employees. You've got a major business with a lot of variables and it's certainly not done intuitively and it's certainly not done off the seat of your pants in the back of a car. You're dealing with a very, very large asset base, and that does require different skills than calling on radio in 1958."

Fifield was a firm advocate of the industry's consolidation into six major bases. "I think consolidation was just a realization that the business was becoming a global business and that an entrepreneur with a $15 million to $20 million company who could be doing great things musically could just not exploit them nationally or much less internationally," he said. "My view was we laid down these machines, these distribution arms. You've got to put things through it. The entrepreneur with the localized companies, the Chrysalis, the Islands, and Virgin, they were having trouble competing and getting the right economies of scale. It's just too expensive to go out and try to set up twenty companies. MCA is doing it now. That's an expensive proposition to do. It's necessary for MCA. But other companies just couldn't make that investment."

As for the idea that big business practices sucked the creativity out of the music industry, Fifield scoffs that it's "all insane. I haven't seen any corporate dictum that's enveloped a company and all of a sudden made it from being a zebra into being a giraffe. Certainly, at EMI Music I'm sure you could talk to any of the companies that I've acquired and (they would admit) I've given them their autonomy. They would never say the success or their failure was due to EMI Music's 'corporate culture.' That's just insane to me. Just because you're big doesn't mean you're bad. You still have to sign good acts. You have to make great records. And then you've got to go out and exploit them with the right priority systems and the right marketing plans. Because consumers aren't brand loyal. They buy what they like. They buy with the artist. They don't buy the company. No one could care if Richard Marx is on Capitol Records or if he's on Warner Records. They're just going to buy Richard Marx's CD."

Unfortunately for Joe Smith, his insight into what the corporate culture had wrought probably came in hindsight. A man who worked in a record industry heavily reliant on promotion, he had failed to see that the world of self-marketing had changed.

Contacts along the old-boy network counted less in the record industry of the 1990s than the ability to think like an accountant. Long-term investment was the watchword, but the reality was instant heat, the better to pump up the perceived value of the company in a world ripe with multinational corporations eager for investment opportunities in entertainment. During the late '80s and early '90s, companies like Disney, Time Warner, and Bertelsmann all invested heavily in startup labels, while such millionaires as department store magnate Ted Field and Ticketmaster/Hyatt Hotel heir Daniel Pritzker also tried their hand at music.

Smith had built a strong following, but he had isolated himself from the corporate headquarters in New York, where a different attitude far removed from the glamorous life of Hollywood prevailed. It was an attitude shaped by Fifield, a deadpan executive whose business views were honed by a long career at General Mills, a company known for breakfast cereal, a dish not recently seen on the Morton's menu.

Fifield's connection to music was loudly trumpeted by P.R. people who regularly described with evangelical fervor his passion for rhythm and blues. However, he was no entrepreneur who had come up through the ranks. Fifield, whose yearly earnings from EMI reached $20 million, was charged with expanding the company, to the point where, some observers predicted, a spinoff stock offering or actual sale was possible.

Annual reports that proclaimed record sales and increased profits were used to bolster claims that growth was good, even though results were never specific enough to reveal exactly where the growth was coming from. Most likely, international expansion and Fifield's consolidations had increased the bottom line. There was no denying that the music division was healthy; its profits were one of the bright spots for parent corporation Thorn EMI, whose businesses included such esoterica as renting refrigerators to those too poor to afford their own. The company gradually divested itself of other media properties, which had lost millions of dollars. Gradually, it began to center its multinational activities on music and music retailing.

Fifield may not have been much of a music man, but he did have an eye for choosing executives who would work with him.

Two thousand miles to the east, on the day of Smith's exit, another man was contemplating the future. No one knows what thoughts were going through his head, but it's likely that Charles Koppelman, whose cigar-smoking habits were his music business trademark, was lighting up a fat one.

The *Los Angeles Times* called Koppelman "the most disliked mogul in the music industry," claiming he surpassed former MCA

Music head and Giant Records co-owner Irving Azoff for that dubious honor. It also took issue with his alleged habit of having his Bentley flown out to the West Coast whenever he was in town, despite having laid off hundreds of workers at his record label.

But Koppelman had clearly been playing the record industry game the right way. He had enriched himself by millions of dollars through a knack for buying and selling companies at the appropriate moment. After deposing Smith, he now ran the North American operations of one of the largest record companies in the world.

All of Koppelman's empire was created by spending money lavishly, to the point where profit hardly seemed to matter. But that was Koppelman's genius.

The attention span of the public had never been shorter, requiring record company promotion departments to spend huge amounts of money to create "artists" whose shelf life was not much longer than that of milk. The short-term result was hitting the top of the charts, if the game was played the right way.

As a music publishing veteran, Koppelman understood that songs were what the public remembered. The record industry of the 1990s and beyond had given up on creating long-term careers. In the video age, where attention spans rivaled those of houseflies, instant heat was the name of the game. Get a song on the charts and everyone will assume an artist's career—not to mention the record company sponsoring it—was financially healthy.

Koppelman knew that he could virtually forget about the cost. The new name of the game in the multinational world of music was not instant profits but the impression of success. Create enough heat, however brief, and the deep pockets of the corporate machines that now ruled the music industry would fight to feed your software to the ever-hungry hardware monster. Businesses like Thorn EMI, Sony, PolyGram, Matsushita, Time Warner, and Bertelsmann would seek an elusive quality called "synergy" between their recordings and other properties. The goal was particularly desired by companies that actually manufactured the stereos, portable cassette players, VCRs, and other devices for listening and/or viewing.

The companies involved in the growing business claimed they

were looking toward the future: music video, compact disc players, CD-ROM—the profit potential seemed so limitless that the short-term results could be forgiven. But what they were essentially betting on was that someone, somewhere, would care to buy the music of Vanilla Ice, Marky Mark, Wilson Phillips, and Gerardo twenty years down the road, making the huge investment in the marketing of such recordings questionable at best.

In many ways, despite growing into big business, the music industry remained a shell game played by hustlers—savvy, street-smart entrepreneurs—and Koppelman was one of the best. Unlike their predecessors, who primarily victimized artists by stealing royalties, Charles Koppelman, Island Records founder Chris Black-well, and A&M Records fathers Herb Alpert and Jerry Moss all are among the kings of the music industry hustlers of the 1990s who found a bigger mark—the multinational corporations of Thorn EMI and PolyGram.

Although the artistic nuances of the music industry were lost in the rush to growth, the biggest price was ultimately paid by consumers, who were forced to accept a switch to high-priced compact discs despite considerable evidence that a good portion of the world was not ready to end its love affair with vinyl recordings.

COMPACT DISS

Imagine waking up one morning and hearing the following announcement on the news: a new jet pack has been invented that will be better and faster than the automobile clogging your garage.

The new jet pack will cost more, and you'll need to buy special fuel for it, but it will revolutionize the way you travel. True, you won't have such luxuries as a stereo system, air conditioning, or your choice of color. But rest assured: This is the wave of the future.

Okay, you say. That's great for some people. But I have a reliable car and I intend to keep it.

Fine, say the jet pack people. But you'll have an increasingly hard time finding parts for your car, because we're switching auto manufacturing over to jet pack production. Perhaps you'd like to consider investing in our product—or give up your transportation habit.

That fantasy scenario, in effect, is how the music industry financed its explosive growth in the 1980s: by unilaterally declaring the death of the vinyl album in favor of the compact disc. The result was the greatest boom period in audio recording business history, most of it created by reselling the same music to the same people.

The vinyl album had been a good friend to the record industry. The long-playing, microgroove record was invented in 1947, displacing the 78 rpm record. In the mid-'50s, stereo sound came along.

Then came quadraphonic sound in the mid '70s—a dismal failure in its attempt to break monoaural sound into four distinct bandwidths—and digital albums in the late '70s, which basically put digital recording on a vinyl format, an odd combination that didn't work.

Although better audio quality and durability was the altruistic promise of the digital revolution that eventually resulted in the compact disc, the real sound sought by the music industry was the ring of the cash register.

The record industry in 1981 needed an injection, if only to put it out of its misery. Although the business stood at an overall $3.9 billion generated at retail, according to statistics compiled by the industry trade group known as the Recording Industry Association of America, much of that total came from artists who emerged in the late '60s and early '70s. Moreover, the blush of punk, new wave, and disco had ended, having spawned little in the way of bands that lasted beyond a single album.

MTV, which was to become a key promotional tool in breaking new talent by the end of the decade, was but a gleam in the eye of its creators in the beginning of the year, waiting to go on line in August 1981. Such "faceless" bands as Journey were the rock warhorses of the moment, creating a situation where the dull were getting duller.

A look at the bestselling songs of 1981 underlines the malaise. "Physical" by Olivia Newton John, "Endless Love" by Diana Ross and Lionel Richie, and "Bette Davis Eyes" by Kim Carnes were the type of middle-of-the-road ballads that were as dispassionate as their performers, creative death to a business that thrives on brash artistry and withers in its absence.

The lack of excitement was acutely reflected in the decline from 1981 to 1982. Total units shipped to stores, minus the product sent back to the manufacturer by the retailer, dropped precipitously, diving from 635.4 million units to 577.7 million units, according to the Recording Industry Association of America.

Worse, total dollar value of those shipments fell from $3.9 billion to $3.6 billion, showing that customers couldn't be lured back to the stores even with special sales gimmicks.

Solutions to the problem were both simple and complex. "Release better music" was undoubtedly the old guard solution, one easier said than done. More progressive thinkers might have been dreaming of new ways to market the sounds, but the multi-billion-dollar music industry generated surprisingly little marketing initiatives. A business that had largely been grown by savvy street hustlers still relied on the backslapping school of promotion and considered sticking a poster on a record store wall as marketing genius.

Where humans failed, technology entered. What if the record industry could find a way to resell the same music to consumers, obviating the need to develop a large number of new acts and perhaps reviving the enthusiasm of the record-collecting baby boomers?

Jim Fifield, president and CEO of EMI Music, explained the impact of the compact disc on the music industry.

"The music industry since 1945 has grown at a compound growth rate of over 10 percent a year," Fifield said, explaining that his research had been part of his learning curve about the music industry upon taking the job at EMI. "And you start looking at the components about why it grew and I came up with a number of factors, such as fashion, style...[but] economics definitely was a factor in the equation. When things are good, music sells more. And when things are tough, things are tough, especially on a global basis. There's definitely a correlation between per capita income and sales of prerecorded music."

But the biggest factor in growth, according to Fifield, was technology. "If you looked at where the big [growth] blips were, you saw that the advent of the cassette brought portability to the music industry. It took music out of the living room with Dad's stereo that was persona non grata. It allowed you to take it with you. And the Walkman was another derivative of mobile music. It was in the cars and then it was in the hand. A tremendous surge. And then here comes the CD, which is of superior quality with instant access to tracks, and it's relatively indestructible in nature. That's why EMI has always been supportive of new technology. Because if any of those new technologies grab hold, the music industry is going to go through another big boom."

Others were equally effusive in their praise for CDs. Like Fifield, they recognized the potential more with their fiscal eyes than with their ears.

"I remember when I first saw it, I was really excited," said Michael Dornemann, the chairman and CEO of Bertelsmann Music Group. "It was a must for the business. It was more than a savior. And for the music business, it came just at the right time. We had been in the recession, and suddenly you had this wonderful product, high-quality digital, appealing to everybody. So, yes, it did a lot of good for the economy. And it's still not over. The CD is still not only not over, it is still in the growing phase, because the world consists of more than five important countries, and the next twenty-five countries which are on the threshold all want to have music. We all listen to music. In Latin America you still have a very low CD player penetration. So we have a lot of growth yet in the traditional distribution channels and retail through CD. A lot of growth."

As with nuclear power, the benefits of compact discs were perhaps oversold. Consumers were promised a golden age of sound reproduction, one that would lift us from our mud huts into cities in the sky.

Unfortunately, the reality of the situation proved to be far less than the expectations. In fact, many of the first compact discs were created from monoaural recordings and, in many cases, sounded worse than their alleged inferiors, the vinyl albums. The further one goes back in time, the higher percentage of poor-sounding reissued CDs, mainly because the CD is only as good as the source tape from which it is mastered.

"The catch phrase when CDs were launched was very simple: 'Perfect sound forever,'" said Pete Howard, editor of the CD collector's newsletter *Ice*. "So what they summed up in those three words were yes, much better sound quality and no wear and tear. Of course, those three words don't cover the convenience factor either, which is a massive part of the CD success. The convenience of lightweight, small, compact, portable, and jumping around from track to track and rewinding and fast forwarding within a track—all those convenience factors played a very important role in the CD's success. But when it was launched—and even the staunchest proponents of CDs have admitted—it was hype and overstatement to say perfect sound forever."

Indeed, according to Howard, some early CDs were poorly manufactured or treated and have already begun deteriorating, with seals breaking on the edges of the discs, causing oxidization to the inner metal.

A compact disc is a thin polycarbonate wafer four and three-quarters inches in diameter, according to the Electronics Industry Association of America. Instead of the spiral groove on a vinyl long-playing record, a disc contains millions of microscopic pits in a highly reflective, smooth surface, covered by a coat of clear, protective plastic.

Each pit represents part of the music in the form of a binary digital code. Arranged in patterns on the surface of a CD, the pits are read by a low-power laser beam in the CD player. The laser reads from the center of the disc outward to the edge and converts the digital code into a digital signal, into electrical energy, and eventually into audible sound.

Since the laser beam does the tracking, no solid object comes into contract with the surface, and thus no distortion or wear and tear on the recording is caused. The idea is a clear, clean sound that breaks new sonic ground.

But even Howard, a CD proponent, admits, "It's a huge open argument about whether CDs sound as good as vinyl. To people with good stereos, and a very, very critical ear, there's no question you can take a stack of LPs and a stack of CDs, especially reissue CDs, and one half of one stack will sound better and the other half of the other stack will sound better. And even that can be for varying reasons, most importantly what source tape was used to make the CD. There's a saying: An old LP made from a good master tape will always beat a new CD made from a bad master tape."

Audiophiles attempted to circumvent this problem by resorting to such bizarre practices as drawing on the compact disc surface with green felt-tip markers, a tactic that, according to legend, would enhance the sound quality.

Sound professionals were also not convinced of digital recording superiority. "I used to love the sound of the stylus dropping on the disc and that rush," said Brooks Arthur, a Grammy-winning producer. "It's like opening up a party package and not knowing what's inside. I also miss the large graphics. But there's something about vinyl, about analog, that to me expresses warmth. The bass sounds warmer. I really hear the man's or woman's fingers articulating on the bass. I hear the hands of a percussionist really rapping nicely against the top of a conga drum. I get a different impression from a vinyl sound sonically than I do from a digital sound. I get a pristine, very clear sound, very distinct sound from the digital domain, CDs and digital audio tape, and I get a warmer, more textural feeling from vinyl."

Bruce Swedien, an engineer on Michael Jackson's *Thriller* and many other hit albums, was an early digital opponent. "It's like the difference between film and video," he told *Billboard*. "Improved dynamic range is not reason alone to go with digital. I hate what digital does to the human voice. It's almost as if a part of the sound were missing."

Such objections, however, came too late to stop the multinational corporate machines that were determined to make digital recording the music industry standard.

Digital technology had actually been around since the 1930s, when Bell Labs first dabbled in prerecorded sounds. NHK, Japan's broadcasting system, is generally credited with creating the first digital recordings in the late 1930s, which were used for broadcasting and the station archives.

Although Decca had experimented with digital sound in 1969, Sony is considered to have made the first commercial releases, a series of classical music audiophile albums issued in the early '70s by the Nippon/Columbia venture. It would soon be followed by other classical label digital products.

Philips Electronics of the Netherlands and Sony announced in 1978 that they were teaming up to develop the compact disc under a uniform standard. (In 1994, the U.S. Justice Department would investigate Sony Corp. and Philips Electronics for federal antitrust violations on the manufacturing and marketing of compact discs. Sony and Philips agreed in the 1970s to cross-license each other's patents on CD technology. But the Justice Department sent subpoenas to over a dozen companies to ask for details of their business relationships with Sony and Philips, seeking to find out whether licensing the technology violated federal antitrust laws.)

The agreement to seek common ground, however, did not mean that both companies had the same ideas. Sony favored a 12-inch format, whereas Philips, in turn, proposed a standard diameter of 12 centimeters. A Sony official later said that the 12-inch size, was chosen merely because it could contain the music to Beethoven's Ninth Symphony.

Finally, in 1982, the war was over. The companies announced a worldwide standard which ensured that all compact discs could be played on all CD players, an agreement that covered such esoterica as sampling rates, optical wavelengths, error correction, size, and frequency response.

The first commercially released compact disc was issued in Japan on October 1, 1982: Billy Joel's *52nd Street*. Two years later, in September 1984, Bruce Springsteen's *Born in the U.S.A.* became, appropriately, the first CD manufactured in the United States.

In truth, many record companies just didn't understand the potential goldmine that CDs offered. No one beyond CD inventors PolyGram and Sony were jumping to support the new format, perhaps recalling such disasters as 8-track tapes and quadraphonic sound. More likely, they were afraid that the lack of copy protection on a CD would enable consumers to create, in effect, their own master discs, which would last until the end of time, unlike vinyl, which eventually wore out.

Pete Howard of *Ice* explains their attitude. "The record companies had just been burned by quadraphonic and nobody really knew how [CDs were] going to do, so you're not going to put a whole lot of time and money into this new product until it starts to prove itself. And once it started to prove itself, obviously it became more and more apparent that time and money had to be put in. Actually, it's really a tribute to the CD's success that it succeeded like it did with all the poor-sounding early CDs."

In fact, sales of the CD hardware were slow at first. Cassette players and turntables continued to rule in all but audiophile households. Still, with plenty of money at stake, an industry coalition of hardware and software manufacturers known as the Compact Disc Group set to work to overcome objections. History records that it was not that hard a sell.

Overseas companies handled much of the early manufacturing. With few CD manufacturing plants open, many record labels were forced to carefully select which artists would be issued on CD first. Packaging issues also needed to be addressed. Although the jewel-box—the hard clam-shell outer casing for the CD—was readily accepted, retailers asked for something else to cover the casing, which could crack. Eventually, the industry standard became the 6 × 12 cardboard container known as the longbox, a size chosen because two CDs would fit side by side in standard 12 × 12 record bins, eliminating the need for retailers to refixture their stores.

(Later in the decade, these arguments for the 6 × 12 would be tossed aside, as ecologically-minded opponents of the 6 × 12 rightly pointed out the wastefulness of the additional paperboard and plastic wrapping. After months of intense but fruitless negotiations between retailers and manufacturers, and several attempts at developing earth-friendly alternative packaging, the record industry unilaterally ditched the longbox, offering a small rebate to retailers to ease the transition period.)

Once the CD and its wrapping were standardized, the hard part started. Consumers needed to be prodded to rush the cash register for a product many neither wanted nor needed.

The biggest barrier was the high price of both the hardware and the software. The first commercially available CD players were Sony's CDP-101, followed shortly by a Magnavox model, both retailing for around $1,000. Because of the lack of domestic CD manufacturing plants, the average retail price of a CD was $16 to $18, the high price in part justified by the need to import the product from Germany or

Japan. Naturally, the elevated costs kept the market isolated to what were termed "upscale audiophiles," with most early CDs issued in classical music.

In June 1983, the first U.S. CD releases were issued, including a dozen titles from CBS, thirty from Denon, and fifteen from Telarc. PolyGram followed in August with a hundred CD titles, eighty of them classical music.

But the real vehicle that would help kick CDs into the mass market had actually been around for two years, and it was only starting to gain momentum.

MTV took to the air at 12:01 A.M. on August 1, 1981, with an appropriate video by the Buggles, "Video Killed the Radio Star." It was an event witnessed outside the great media metros of New York and Los Angeles, cities in which MTV would not debut for another year.

The estimated audience of MTV is now 250 million households, and its international expansion plans could double that figure. All this from a service that many scoffed at when it started.

MTV and, to a lesser extent, its sister channel VH1 remain the most powerful sales forces in commercial music. Proposed competition from a consortium of EMI, Sony, PolyGram, Warner Music, Ticketmaster, and later Bertelsmann Music Group was first put on hold by a U.S. Justice Department investigation into the antitrust implications of the channel, and later dropped.

Although claims were made that the planned new video channel could not get enough access in the crowded U.S. cable market to justify its existence, the plan was shelved only in the wake of an agreement by MTV to drop an antitrust lawsuit it filed in British court, claiming it was paying too much for record company videos because the companies were negotiating as a group.

The implication of the horse-trading was obvious: MTV and the record companies were not rivals but partners. To underline that cozy relationship, PolyGram and MTV announced a deal in the summer of 1995 to co-own and operate two MTV channels in Asia.

Without the threat of competition from its chief suppliers, MTV sits fat and happy atop the music universe, with such outlets as The Box, BET, and assorted local cable programmers swarming around its feet like the broadcasting ants they are.

Although a gentlemanly business relationship apparently exists on the surface between MTV and its suppliers, MTV is clearly the absolute dictator when it comes to deciding the direction of popular music. It has grown from its beginnings as a friendly, somewhat underground guide to new bands into a corporate monolith that can make or break a band's career.

By extension, that large responsibility has MTV virtually controlling the fastest changing segment of popular culture, and in some ways, MTV has lived up to the challenge. Although it has vastly changed since its introduction, the video channel does continue to break selected new acts, has blazed new visual trails, and perhaps has subliminally speeded up society with its quick-cutting video effects. All of this spiced with a host of "good works," such as the antiracism "Free Your Mind" campaign, the get-out-the-vote "Choose or Lose," the Rock 'n' Jock Softball Challenge for T. J. Martell, its antiviolence messages, and other assorted charitable efforts.

Ironically, an institution that is now the most powerful tool in record promotion had little support from record companies when it first started.

Bob Pittman, former chief operating officer of the music channel, said that MTV was one of the ideas that had been bubbling around the music industry. "Others had tried in various forms—the Video Concert Hall National Network, Columbus Video Jukebox, the Album Tracks show and two or three other ideas. I pushed like hell at Warner Amex for a music service, but the board of directors said no."

A meeting was called with Warner chairman Steve Ross and American Express chief James Robinson. Pittman put on what he later described as a "big dog-and-pony show" to convince the executives that MTV was worth trying. Pittman won his argument.

Music video was considered by the labels to be a second-class form of promotion at the time. One veteran record industry marketer who was approached about the idea explained the climate they faced. "I felt it wasn't gonna work. I didn't think they were gonna have the inventory for twenty-four hours a day and at that point we made videos for the abroad markets and it was an excuse. Instead of doing the show live or doing a lip sync, it was second class, it was a cheap way of promoting an album. And so it was solely made for Europe. It wasn't shown in the United States because if you were going to promote something in the United States, you'd go do the show."

The record industry was also dubious that Americans would be satisfied with watching preprocessed, canned videos. "But they were right and we were wrong," admitted the marketer.

Fortunately, there was a ready supply of videos coming from young British bands who had quickly embraced video as a new artistic tool. Those videos initially filled the channel's need for programming.

A year after it began broadcasting, MTV was a hit with consumers, but it was a financial failure. Advertising was a major problem—big-ticket items such as automobiles and airlines were absent from the screen. The reason, according to several MTV sources, was that the old-line marketers who were selling the channel's advertising just didn't understand that MTV was a new product in the new medium of cable television and had to be sold in an entirely new way. Those in the ad sales department who didn't have the commitment or energy that startups require soon found themselves out the door.

In the early '80s, cable networks gave operators money to advertise their programming. MTV didn't, instead launching its own successful campaign, "I Want My MTV," using the Police, Pete Townsend, Pat Benatar, and other stars to promote the video channel. The subsequent consumer demand forced previously reluctant cable operators to carry the channel on their systems.

Instead of selling ratings, MTV approached advertisers and sold them on participation in big giveaways. "I would call on the big guys and have a great promotion, something we were doing better than anything, giving away an island, a house," Bob Pittman, the MTV chief operating officer, said. "I said, 'You can be the sponsor—and, oh, by the way, can you give two million in advertising? Once we got one category, others would come in. Pepsi and Roger Enrico were big supporters." When Manhattan finally turned on to MTV, "all the media buyers began to see it and press began to see it. Suddenly it was something they could feel and taste."

MTV was able to cite its teen and young adult demographics as a very favorable targeted buy. Slowly, the channel began to build momentum.

The record industry, perhaps owing to its history, was not really all that receptive, according to Pittman. "But they had hit the first downturn since the '60s, and they were desperate. Radio was so tight, they couldn't break any music. If we had come two years earlier, they would have told us to pound salt. Only a couple truly believed in the idea."

PolyGram and MCA were among the labels that didn't want to give MTV its videos for free. "So," Pittman said, "we went directly to the artists, and they had enough clout to make them give it to us."

Still, there was a shortage of product to go around, Pittman admitted. "We would play everything out there, but we only had 250 videos in house. We were playing Andrew Gold because we needed videos. Our calculated risk was that if we sold records, they would produce more videos. If they didn't, we would be out of business."

Pittman remembers the early signs that MTV was indeed having an effect on the record-buying public. "When we hit the air, we sent [executives] Tom Freston and John Sykes out to Tulsa, Oklahoma, the biggest market in which we were launched. Only a couple of stores had Buggles records [a video in heavy rotation] because they all blew off the shelf."

The advertising problems may have been solved. But the new medium that was being created presented challenges to performers that had previously been a hidden secret in the business.

"There are acts, MTV acts, that have been created by MTV and the like, that can't play," says one record label veteran who, like many who work with MTV, asked for anonymity in return for candor. "When I was at [a major label] in charge of artist development, we had an act which will remain nameless. They put together a record and it was a hard rock 'n' roll record, and I met with the band and we worked on the album cover and we worked on a bio and then we decided the best video for a rock 'n' roll band would be a performance video. We went ahead and we booked a very expensive video and we put it together and a couple days before the video was to be shot, we found out these guys had never played together before. They had absolutely no idea. They had never performed. There's no excuse and there's no substitution for the chops of doing live shows. You know, when you have several hundred shows under your belt, you can walk out there and if you're off that day or the sound was off, you can get by because you've done it time and time again. And what MTV created was acts that have no relationship to that. They've done a music video that has nothing to do with them performing in front of 15,000 people.

"It's getting more and more common every day. You still have successful bands, promoted via MTV, that never have performed. It's really broken into two categories. Where it used to be a record performer, more often than not they go out and promote their wares by doing live shows. But now, you can make a movie and then become a record star. It's a little like the 1950s, the TV stars, the Shelly Fabares's and the Paul Petersens, you know, they couldn't sing. They just went into the studio and created the magic of the studio and had hit records. It doesn't mean they're performers and they can do concerts."

Of course, not everthing made it onto MTV. The video channel had few if any black acts on display, until the day CBS Records CEO Walter Yetnikoff allegedly threatened to pull all of its videos unless Michael Jackson got on the air with videos from his album *Thriller*.

Pittman denies there was a problem. "It never got to me. No one made threats about anything. Before Jackson, it was Rick James, that we wouldn't play his video for the song 'Superfreak.' But unfortunately, many repeated the charge without looking into the facts. No one was making videos. There were plenty of black artists we weren't playing because they weren't making videos. Don't forget, Bruce Springsteen hadn't made videos. So we went on a crusade to find black artists to make videos. One of the obvious targets, having just come off *Off the Wall*, was Michael Jackson."

Pittman claims he "wined and dined" producer Quincy Jones in order to get Michael Jackson to make a video, resulting in the airing of "Billy Jean" on the vidchannel.

As for the genesis of the alleged CBS boycott story, according to Pittman, "Walter [Yetnikoff] probably went to Michael and said they didn't want to play your video. He was trying to make himself a hero to Michael. It's not the first time a record company or manager did that to us."

MTV continued to grow, changing its on-air cheerleaders, known as video jockeys or VJs for short. The channel also showed how powerful a force it was early in its career, dumping heavy metal videos in response to an outcry against their generally sexist content, virtually stopping that genre cold in the mid-'80s. The channel also became more and more important in breaking a record for the labels.

Pittman explains the whirlwind. "We made the decision very early on that we were going to be the voice of young America. If we were going to do that, we had to change constantly. No one would buy it if we looked like we were the previous generation's music channel."

Unfortunately, as the channel's power and reputation grew, so did record company perceptions of its arrogance. In the early days of MTV, there was no problem accommodating most of the industry's desire for a simple reason. "We had so few videos, we were able to take care of record companies and played more videos," Pittman admits. "We made a decision that we would play videos that didn't help us but would help companies, quid pro quo for their support. Now they are so flooded with videos, they have backed off. Folks there don't remember how hard it was at the startup."

Pittman insists that MTV does not have too much power. "Even when I was there they said that. It's not valid."

That simple conclusion has more than a few challengers, particularly from record company executives whose clip didn't make it on the air. Such clips, which often can cost $500,000, are then consigned to regional video shows and home video compilations, outlets whose impact is far less than MTV. Such misfortunes definitely do not enhance the long-term job prospects of the executive in charge, who must justify spending such enormous sums and getting little in return.

Each clip's content is examined on an individual basis, says MTV spokeswoman Linda Alexander. "We use the same guidelines the networks do." However, such strict standards, which prohibit nudity, profanity, and ethnic slurs, among other restrictions, can create questions about just what's being controlled and to what purpose.

Artists and labels are acutely aware of appeasing the gods of MTV standards and practices. So much so that even Mick Jagger and Keith Richards, those street-fighting men who have built a four-decades-long career on a rebellious image, thought it wise to check with MTV before releasing a video that showed them smoking and drinking.

According to *U.S. News & World Report*, one out of three videos accepted by MTV has been altered at the request of the channel's standards and practices department. Of the four nominees for best video for 1994's Video Music Awards—"Cryin'" by Aerosmith, "Everybody Hurts" by R.E.M., "Heart-Shaped Box" by Nirvana, and "Sabotage" by the Beastie Boys—at least two were rejected by the standards and practices department when they were first submitted. Scenes had to be removed, edited, or blurred before MTV would televise them, although which details were unacceptable are known only to the original editors and the MTV censors.

The practice of rejecting videos for content is growing. The one-in-three ratio is up from one-in-four the year before, according to *U.S. News & World Report*. In fact, the winner of the 1993 award for best video, Pearl Jam's "Jeremy," was allegedly sent back by standards and practices five times. The effect on the art? An "ambiguous and confusing" ending, according to the video's director, Mark Pellington.

"Everyone knows we're a basic-cable network and have standards that are difficult to explain," says MTV president Judy McGrath. "We try to do our best and live by them. When you apply a standard, it's not black and white. I wish it was. It's judgment, and whenever that enters the picture, you need to convince people you're exercising the right judgment. We're attempting to do a better job. We've invited people into the process. We have a point of view as to who we want to be in terms of standards. We're proud of the way MTV looks every day. Some things are not acceptable to us as a programmer; some things are not acceptable on basic cable. We're trying to talk about it more and more explicitly, make it quicker and easier for everyone.

"Look: MTV is something that lives in people's homes and living rooms," McGrath insists. "MTV is powerful: Music is powerful. In combination, it's extremely meaningful. There are other video music outlets. There are all kinds of choices to watch and listen to today. We've done a good job connecting with our viewers. That's something we share with our suppliers, the ultimate winners in this. It makes me happy that MTV is powerful. People are seeing these artists that they are not hearing on local radio and it's stimulating record sales, stimulating cultural change and thinking, the way music always has."

However, it seems that one of the standards being imposed for the majority of videos is that they must originate from a multinational corporation.

"MTV has the power to change so much," said one independent label owner, again begging for anonymity for fear of retaliation. "I just wish they'd be a little more adventurous."

The executive took issue with what MTV terms alternative music, pointing out that the definition changes as bands grow more influential. "'120 Minutes' [MTV's alternative music show] is like five minutes of alternative music," the executive said. If you look at the big artists that have really made it in the MTV era—alternative acts like the Cure, Depeche Mode—those aren't alternative artists anymore. They have roots in the alternative market, but they're selling millions of records. And it seems like there's so many great bands out there with so much talent that they could do a little more to help foster a whole new wave, a crop of bands. And to me that they devote two hours at midnight to 2 A.M. on a Sunday night is really lame."

San Francisco attorney Steven Ames Brown, who specializes in artists'-rights issues, is also no fan of the video channel.

"MTV should have apologized to the American public for Milli

Vanilli, for Black Box, C + C Music Factory," Brown said. "MTV should have taken some responsibility for cleaning them up. And they didn't. Their attitude is, 'Fuck you.' What has it done for artists'-rights enforcement, or artists' rights in general? I think it's made a lot of people second-class citizens. If you can't get your videos on MTV, you're in trouble unless you're Madonna, in which case you can turn it into a scandal and make an extra million bucks. But that's Madonna. I think that the leverage that a lot of new artists would have wanes considerably if they can't get MTV to play one of their first videos. I think [MTV] has a lot of clout in terms of inadvertent ability to ruin careers and an undeserved ability to make careers. Because there are plenty of pop artists who are terrible singers and great video artists. And it promotes their careers."

MTV, instead of being a conduit from record companies to the public, is now viewed as a dictator to its suppliers. As with many developments in the corporatization of the record industry, the concentration of power in one station has contributed to the ever-rising cost of doing business—be it in the actual video shot, its promotion, or its marketing—a cost that is invariably passed to the consumer in the higher prices of CDs.

One immediate effect of the CD revolution was that artists began making longer albums. Where once the forty-minute album was not uncommon, artists began adding more songs, resulting in an average ten-minute lengthening of albums since the advent of the CD.

Record company artist and repertoire departments, the talent scouts who ultimately have a large say in the sequence of tracks on an album, also began thinking in terms of continuous play on song selection and compilations. The first single didn't necessarily have to be the first song on side one or the second single the first song on side two. Plus, more songs could be added to the CD to make its purchase more attractive to consumers.

Sales of CD players did not reach a large percentage of the U.S. and worldwide audience until well after the hardware's introduction. To this day, the penetration of CD players in homes is nowhere near VCR levels. Clearly, it was the hardcore music fan who bought the first compact discs, and even more clearly, these buyers were repurchasing the same music they already had on vinyl.

At some indefinable point, a sense of desperation must have set in among those who had not bought compact disc players and compact discs. The music industry was pulling up the gangplank, and vinyl lovers were left waiting on the dock.

First, seven-inch vinyl singles were victimized. Once the lifeblood of the industry, singles had become annoyances that some contended actually cannibalized sales of more expensive albums by allowing consumers to pick and choose songs instead of purchasing the entire package.

As vinyl disappeared, the singles loyalists shifted to cassette singles. The record industry then began to eliminate the production of singles before demand was quenched, forcing those who wanted certain songs to buy the entire album.

The retail community realized what was going on.

"We get the cassette single going, and it's selling like crazy, and what are the record manufacturers doing?" Tower Records vice president Stan Goman told *Billboard*, "They're scared to death that they're cutting into album sales. Well, there aren't any vinyl album sales. So they must be cutting into CDs. Everyone and their mother has some kind of cassette player and they can get what they want at a cheap price. So what's the solution? The record companies raise the cassette single's price. It doesn't cut into CDs, but then nobody buys the cassette single."

But even retailers soon realized that they had an economic tiger by the tail, one that would allow them to ignore the fact that the music industry was relying on the same old formula of hit-or-miss marketing of new artists, cushioned by an explosion of catalog sales.

"It was a total, absolute manipulation by the record industry of the market," said Marty Levy, owner of Rockaway Records, at one time one of the largest independent stores in Los Angeles. "I would buy 100 copies of the new Milli Vanilli or whatever when it would come out, and I'd usually buy 30-some copies of the vinyl, 30 CDs and 30 cassettes. I would sell out of them, and I would go back to reorder, and I would never get the LP again. Ever. I could get CDs anytime I wanted. I could get the cassette anytime I would want it. And then I would be reading in *Billboard*, it would say Milli Vanilli sells 100,000 units of CD, and 240,000 units of cassettes, and 23,000 units of LP, further proving the decline of the LP. They were limiting the amount of vinyl sold, the best way they could do it, by only making a certain amount of vinyl. They were using their own statistics to manipulate statistics to prove it."

John Branca, one of the most powerful attorneys in the music business, agreed with that assessment. "There's much higher profit margin in CDs. So why sell something for $8.98 when you can sell it for $15.98? I represent many publishing companies, including Michael Jackson's ATV. Well, it was a huge windfall when everybody wanted to go out and buy all the Beatles albums again on CD."

Exacerbating the decline of vinyl was the institution by record companies of a one-way sale on vinyl singles, which meant that stores could not return unsold product. Further proving that vinyl's lack of popularity was not the reason for its demise, record companies began halting manufacturing on vinyl singles while some were still on the charts.

Indeed, many independent stores and one-stops (wholesalers used by independent stores and chains) reported a continued demand for vinyl, even as most major retail chains lowered their stock of vinyl albums, particularly in titles deleted from vinyl by the major labels.

Undoubtedly, the major labels had caught on to the fact that they could induce consumers to switch to the CD, a format that could be manufactured at the same cost as a vinyl album but sold at greater cost. Although CDs were introduced at a painful price, a core of strong audio enthusiasts bought the new configuration. Even when high price and a temporary lack of manufacturing capacity caused CD sales to stagnate, the industry executives recoiled at the notion that lowering the price might actually increase consumption. In the early 1980s, a brief flirtation with price experiments on front line, midline, and budget pricing saw some CDs drop to a suggested $12.98. However, the price soon rose again. (In 1995, huge electronics chains like Best Buy irritated retailers by selling CDs at loss-leader prices, hoping to build customer loyalty and sell higher-margin accessories. Many retailers suffered as consumers voted with their feet and deserted the national chains and local independent stores in favor of cheap CDs).

Unfortunately, recording artists were not the big beneficiaries of the new configuration. For most of the 1980s, artist royalties were paid on the basis of vinyl rates rather than the CD's higher wholesale or retail price (record companies have various accounting methods; some tie to wholesale prices, others to retail). Only superstars with huge clout could command their fair share of the pie. The cost of research and development was usually the reason given by record companies for taking advantage of the people who were providing them their lifeblood.

"When new technologies came out, major labels saw an opportunity to raise prices, which they previously believed wasn't raisable because of high consumer price resistance," said Thomas White, a Beverly Hills, California–based consultant to the record and music publishing industry. "Majors wanted to keep that margin between vinyl and CD [rather than pass it on to the artist]. And when vinyl was no longer the dominant configuration, they tied royalties to the price of a cassette."

In many cases, White says, labels still pay based on vinyl or cassette royalties. "There are plenty of recording artists whose contracts were entered into pre–CD technology. Many labels are still paying them based on the royalty rates in their contracts. They haven't raised the rates to a contemporary rate. Some royalty rates were expressed in pennies, so no matter how many times the price changed and the retail and wholesale price increased, they were on a penny rate rather than a percentage."

Today, even as manufacturing costs decline, new CD releases from superstar artists are starting to increase in retail price, as the astonishing growth of the record industry has made corporations happy with their rising incomes even more reluctant to lower CD prices, knowing that there is still a hard-core audience that will not give up its music, no matter the price. As proof, market penetration of CD players was still only 20 percent of total households in the U.S. by the end of the 1980s; yet compact discs at that point accounted for nearly 40 percent of the software sales. The audiophile was clearly on a buying binge.

Compact disc sales volume grew from a modest beginning in 1983 (the first year sales of the configuration were measured) of $17.2 million in retail sales to an estimated $2.69 billion by the end of 1989. Contrast that with vinyl's shrinkage: from a peak of $2.5 billion in 1978 to an estimated $232 million by the end of 1989, according to the Recording Industry Association of America—an estimated decrease of 92.7 percent in twelve years.

Europeans in particular were skeptical that the vinyl decrease was all market-driven, complaining vociferously in the trade press during the late '80s that vinyl was being prematurely killed by U.S. record companies. Still, consumers and retailers held out hope. The assumption by all concerned was that the CD price—as with almost every other home electronic innovation—would eventually be reduced as demand increased and manufacturing costs dropped. But the industry, having grown used to the fat profits being generated by the CD, stubbornly refused to bend on price. In fact, some labels claimed they needed the money from CDs to justify the dwindling income from vinyl!

Initially, record companies blamed the cost of CDs on the lack of sufficient manufacturing capacity in the United States. Between 1980—when the first disc was developed—and 1986, only one major CD pressing plant existed in the United States, the Sony-owned Digital Audio Disc in Terre Haute, Indiana.

Back then, the cost to manufacture a disc was much more than it was to manufacture vinyl. But as additional plants opened, the costs began dropping, to the point where a CD was comparable to a vinyl album.

Without the protective fig leaf of the manufacturing-capacity defense, the labels turned to another argument to explain the additional profit margin on compact discs: The additional monies were needed to support the new, massive infrastructure. Excess profits were being used to create new labels, in turn creating a need for more employees, with veterans commanding a premium price.

Adding labels and executives as the tide of high-priced CD sales artificially swelled the corporate coffers, the recording companies cited everything from higher advances on artist contracts (virtually all of which, incidentally, were recoupable) to recording studio fees, video production, independent promotion, marketing, and tour support.

The money, they said, was put into developing new acts, the so-called baby bands that usually didn't make any money. But because few of those bands received any substantial marketing or promotion, the income essentially pumped up the bottom line of the companies without any real innovation.

Not only were profit margins high, they were heading even higher. By the beginning of the 1990s, superstar CDs actually increased in price, rising to a suggested $17.98 in several cases.

By the early 1990s, the average cost to manufacture an album came to less than half the sale cost. The compact disc came to roughly $5.50 per package (marketing and promotion, of course, being extra), whereas a cassette was $4.75. But consumer prices remained high. Moreover, retailers—who traditionally had lobbied for decreased costs—were themselves victimized in part.

In the early days of the CD, the labels set wholesale prices in such a manner that CD list prices could leave merchants with a gross margin of about 36 percent for the CD, compared with a gross margin of nearly 42 percent on cassettes. By 1990, as the CD became a greater factor in the business, merchants were finding that profit was becoming a smaller percentage of total sales.

At that year's National Association of Recording Merchandisers convention, higher gross margins became the chief complaint for merchandisers. But manufacturers refused to give in to the pressure and noted that retailers were free to adjust their prices to increase their margins. They also noted that they would reissue more budget-priced and midline product, so-called because they featured catalog titles from older, in some cases less popular, artists that could be sold at a discount to consumers.

The winking message to merchants sent by the manufacturers was simple: Need more money? Then increase the price to consumers on these traditionally low-cost titles. Retailers needed little prodding.

Pete Howard, publisher of *Ice*, admitted the sorry state of affairs in a 1993 interview with the *Los Angeles Times*. "When the CD arrived on the scene, it was a risky and expensive technological gamble," Howard said. "Because nobody knew whether it would catch on or not, the companies had a legitimate reason to charge as much as they did. But in the past five years, demand has increased and manufacturing costs have dropped considerably. I think it's time for the record industry to pass some of those savings on to the consumer."

One theory on why the transparently excessive profits weren't being used to lower prices can be found in the business practices of the multinational corporations that owned the labels, according to Rob Simonds, an executive at Rykodisc Records.

"These giant corporations own other, non–music related businesses that regularly turn a specific margin of profit, and they expect the profit margins for records to live up to what their other ventures take in," Simonds told *Billboard*. "What you have to remember is that this industry wasn't always so profitable. In the '70s and '80s, the record business was in a very unhealthy economic state. But now, with CDs, the profit margin is finally more in line with what a business of their ilk should be commanding."

A few savvy businessmen had earlier realized the potential that the music market of the 1980s had for creating new businesses whose value could be inflated. Now, a new record company could produce vastly inflated gross numbers that could be used to paint a picture of vibrant growth, when, in fact, the public appetite for music was pretty much the same as it always was.

None of the executives who recognized the appeal of owning an entertainment company that looked like a cash cow played the game as well as the cigar-smoking, white-haired hustler named Charles Koppelman, who would become one of the most powerful—and disliked—men in the business by using the old-fashioned shell game of promotion to create instant stars and instant, if fleeting, profits.

THREE

THE HUSTLER

"I mean, he's a funny guy," said financier and **Spin** *magazine* publisher Stephen Swid, sitting in his imposing office on the fifty-Seventh floor of a Manhattan skyscraper. "I remember it was a very cold January day. I'll never forget this. Our office was on 53rd and Seventh, and we were having lunch in a restaurant between 52nd and 51st on Seventh. It was on the other side of the street.

"We go out and Charles has a limousine outside. I make a right to walk to the next block. And he says, 'Aren't you going to ride? Come on in. We'll ride.' I said, 'Charlie, it's one block. It's across Seventh Avenue.' It's about twenty yards across Seventh Avenue, but it's one block. I don't want to ride. He said, 'No, we'll ride, we'll ride.' I said, 'I'll meet you there.' He wanted to get in the limousine and ride and get off in front of the restaurant in a limousine. I mean, it was a different mindset."

Charles Koppelman was born March 30, 1940, in Laurelton, New York, the last town in the borough of Queens before Nassau County, the promised land of the post–World War II suburbs. The son of a printer and a secretary, Koppelman realized early that entrepreneurship was his ticket to the good life.

"When I was twelve I had a business card that said, 'We Mow Lawns, Inc.,'" Koppelman said. "I was mowing lawns. And then, as I got older, I always had the sense that I would want to be in my own business to somewhat guide my own destiny."

Koppelman claims that during his youth he carried the same attitude he has now. "When I was a kid, I either wanted to pitch or play shortstop. I only wanted to be in the action. If there were three seconds left in a basketball game, I wanted to take the shot. I might not make the shot, but I wanted to take the shot. Those are things that either you inherit, you develop, or hopefully you grow into them. So I still want to take the shot."

After high school, Koppelman matriculated at nearby Adelphi College, with the goal of becoming a gym teacher. There, at the Alpha Kappa fraternity, he met Don Rubin, a man who would later become his business partner and longtime friend.

"I used to sing and play guitar around campus," Rubin said. "And we became good friends during the year Charles was pledging. So one day the phone rings, and he said, 'I got this great idea. Let's start a singing group.' I didn't know he sang. I had another friend, Artie Berkowitz, who sang really well. So we all get together at Charles's mom's place in Laurelton."

The year was 1959, and thus was born the Ivy Three. Koppelman later admitted that he was really using the trio as a vehicle to bigger things. "I mean, I'm not a performer," he says. "Nor was I really a talented songwriter. It was more of a lark. When I was going to college I had two friends who were quite talented and I was kind of the third guy." It was the third guy, however, who got the group its first big break, as Rubin recalls.

"One day Charles calls and says we have an audition in the city, so I pack my guitar and me, Artie and Charles go heading into the city. We get to 1650 Broadway, one of the big music business kind of hot spots where a lot of record companies were located, similar to the Brill Building. Charles tells us to wait in the lobby; he will make sure everything is in order for our audition. So we wait a half hour, forty-five minutes, we can't figure out what happened. He comes back and says we're ready. We don't think anything of it. So we pass the audition and get the contract."

Six months later, the Ivy Three managed to record a Top 10

single, "Yogi," a novelty issued on Shell Records, and the truth came out. "He confided that we never did have an audition scheduled," Rubin said. "He went banging on doors in that building until he found someone who agreed to have us. That shows you early on the ambition and the drive that Charles had."

"Yogi" was something of a precursor to the rap era. Koppleman had the Yogi Bear accent down, as "I'm a Yogi" was recited in imitation of the cartoon character. "We were on Dick Clark three times, did a William Morris Tour," Rubin recalled.

The group later evolved into the Cardigan Brothers, featuring Koppelman and Rubin. But a gig at Grossinger's resort in the Catskills led them to Don Kirshner, who convinced the young performers that their future lay in songwriting and producing. Thus, Koppelman and Rubin signed in 1961 with Don Kirshner's Aldon Music, working in a songwriting factory that included such superstars as Gerry Goffin, Carole King, Barry Mann, and Cynthia Weil.

"It was one of those little cubicles of writers," recalled Brooks Arthur, a fellow songwriter and later a Grammy-winning producer and engineer. "It was a classic. Everybody would be in a room, writing. It was truly the new Tin Pan Alley. We were all in our teens or early twenties at that time, I might add."

"It was kind of like growing up together," added Arthur's wife, Marilyn, now a publicist at RCA Records' Nashville operation. "We'd all get in a car and sing songs on the radio, and funny enough, a lot of them were their songs. You know, we'd get in Neil Sedaka's car and there was Neil on the radio with 'Calendar Girl.'"

The competition was fierce to get songs recorded. "We'd all write for the same talent," said Brooks Arthur. "When Roy Orbison was up for a session or somebody was up for a date, we'd get the room from Donnie Kirshner and we'd all write for the Everly Brothers or for Bobby Darin, Connie Francis, the Drifters, Ben E. King or for whomever, and the best song won. It was like a contest."

But whether Koppelman and Rubin could have made a career as songwriters, even given that they were peers of a group considered among the best of that era, was open to question. Brooks Arthur believes, "When you're in the same room with Mann and Weil and

Neil Diamond and Carole Bayer Sager, Gerry Goffin, Carole King, and Neil Sedaka... I know that Charles and Don, with all the accolades and the standing ovations I will give to them as friends, allies, and superior executives... I think they made the wisest choice."

Koppelman himself admits that there's some truth to that assessment. "I learned real early to have tremendous respect for talent, because I wrote songs poorly. I learned how to edit songs, and because I had the experience of being next door to Barry Mann and Cynthia Weil or Carole King and Gerry Goffin, I learned the difference between great, good, and not so good. I learned that a word or a phrase there or changing a hook from one place to another could make a good song a great song. I'm a real good listener and I take it all in. All that stuff is invaluable."

When Aldon Music was sold to Columbia Pictures in 1964, the twenty-four-year old Koppelman became director of the resulting company, Screen Gems/Columbia Music. He left this position in 1965 to form Koppelman/Rubin Associates, an independent record production company and independent music publisher that discovered and nurtured the careers of the Lovin' Spoonful, Bobby Darin, the Turtles, and Tim Hardin. In 1968, when Commonwealth United purchased the company for $3 million, Koppelman and Rubin stayed on-to run the new music division.

However, not everyone had a pleasant experience. The Lovin' Spoonful later sued Koppelman and Rubin and claimed that they did not discover the act. In an interview in the magazine *Goldmine*, Lovin' Spoonful leader John Sebastian said record producer Phil Spector discovered the band, terming the rest of the pursuers "all the little weasels from 1650 Broadway, who were kind of following Phil around to find out what he did." Sebastian later in the interview referred to the duo in the interview as "Koppelthief and Robber." (In later years, Sebastian evidently had a change of heart. Charles Koppelman's son, Brian Koppelman, claims Sebastian verified to him that Koppelman and Rubin did indeed discover the band. Koppelman claims he voluntarily gave the Lovin' Spoonful back his producer royalty points, which he had never collected, to help them out with hard times.)

Koppelman had a strategy in mind while constructing his business. "I had started to sign record producers the way one would sign songwriters, so that I combined the two without having the risk of the record business," he said. "As I moved along—just to underscore my belief in music publishing—I had bought several music catalogs from record companies or guys who entered the record business and ended up losing all their money. And the only asset they had left that they could sell that could bail them out were their music publishing companies. I was able to buy some good catalogs.

"I've told this story before," Koppelman added. "It's a true one. When I was in my early twenties, I noticed when I would go to industry gatherings that the record company executives all were chain-smoking cigarettes. They all had very white pallors. They always looked like they were running from somewhere to somewhere. And I looked at the music publishers. They all had these great suntans and they were all smoking these Cuban cigars. So I said to myself, who do I want to be when I'm in my forties? And it was clear that I preferred to be the guy that had the suntan and the Cuban cigars. Now, being young at that time, I also wanted the action of the record business. I recognized that there was this great action that was going on, the creation of a hit, that immediate—somewhat immediate—gratification. So I combined record production and music publishing so that my first company, which was Koppelman/ Rubin, was a music publishing company, but we were also a record production company."

Koppelman and Rubin's first brief entry into the record business was, ironically, achieved with the same ingredient they used to get their first recording deal: chutzpah.

Rubin recalled the moment. "Shortly after we were in the publishing business and achieved success with the Lovin' Spoonful, we were in L.A. and having meetings, but there was a three-hour gap," he said. "So we left the hotel, and Charles had the idea to go over to Capitol Records to have a meeting with Alan Livingston, the president then, to see if we couldn't get into a label kind of situation.

I don't want to call it a lark, but we had some spare time. So sure enough, it was the first meeting that led toward a record company—Hot Biscuit Discs, an imprint that ran through Capitol from 1967 to 1968. We had one or two sort of minor successes, nothing major."

However, in 1969, the team was offered "a deal we couldn't refuse," by Commonwealth United, according to Rubin, and decided to sell Koppelman/Rubin. "It was the coming of age of all these conglomerate companies, and they wanted to start a music division. They were a film and real estate company, and music seemed a sort of allied business to be in."

Rubin left for the West Coast to spend ten years with the Charlie Daniels Band and as a consultant. Koppelman decided to leave the music business but had the foresight to buy back the copyrights that he had sold from Koppelman/Rubin Associates.

"I was really somewhat disillusioned by the music business," he says. "But I wanted to own all my songs. They were kind of like children. And the business at that time was taking a turn that wasn't very song-oriented. A lot of very heavy metal, a lot of very—to me—dissonant music. And I just didn't feel that I had the sense of it. So I kind of retired. I'd made a lot of money at that time for me."

The lure of entrepreneurship, however, was unabated. Charles Koppelman, music mogul, briefly became Charles Koppelman, head of his own home repair business.

"A friend of mine was complaining about how he couldn't get anyone to fix anything in his house. And I had a new house myself and I had the same problem," Koppelman recalled. "So we decided we would form a company that was called Homeowner's Emergency Services that was going to fix anything in anyone's house within ninety minutes. And I put up my own money and I hired all these off-duty firemen and policemen because I figured these guys can't afford to call a plumber. They must know how to fix their houses. And we bought all the state-of-the-art equipment and I went on an advertising campaign and I took out all these great full-page ads all over Long Island. I went on *To Tell the Truth* and talked about it—I was the real Charles Koppelman, by the way—and it was a landslide. We had more people calling us for subscriptions. It was going to be like the AAA for homes. We had a zillion subscriptions."

There was a catch, however. "The only thing I didn't count on was that all the guys I had hired were stealing the equipment and they really didn't know how to fix anything. So I had a zillion call-backs and a year or a year-and-a-half afterwards, I went back into the music business." Homeowner's Emergency Services was subsequently closed.

Koppelman, then in his early thirties, returned to the music wars in the early '70s as head of April Blackwood Music, the music publishing arm of CBS. "I did that because I wanted to get into the mainstream of the business. We were in our own business, I sold it and I made a lot of money. We were still a small, not insignificant player, but not really a major player in the industry. I felt if I went to CBS it would immediately give me access to the entire business, which it did." Indeed, one associate of Koppelman's said that his salary—pegged in a 1992 *GQ* magazine article at $35,000—"didn't even pay for his driver."

Koppelman later segued to VP/national director of A&R at Columbia Records, then went back to music publishing at CBS Songs. His official corporate biography claims that he signed Billy Joel, Dave Mason, Janis Ian, Journey, and Phoebe Snow.

In at least one instance he displayed an eye for talent when others did not. Brooks Arthur and his wife, Marilyn, had mortgaged their home and borrowed from friends to back then-unknown singer Janis Ian's *Stars* album. "I went from coast to coast to try to sell the album and nobody would sign it. I'm talking about everyone on the block from the Brill Building to La Brea," Brooks Arthur recalled. "Then one day I ran into Charles and he said, 'Well, do you have anything to listen to?' I said, 'Well, I have this Janis Ian tape we're working on, but you've turned me down before.' He said, 'I have not turned you down.' I said, 'Well, Columbia has.' He said, 'Well, I'm new at Columbia. Let me hear it.' And I left it with him and the next day he called me and said, 'It's a deal.'"

Ian subsequently signed to Columbia Records and made a

major publishing deal with April Blackwood. "As Artie Garfunkel would say, we suddenly went from our final days of poverty," Arthur recalled. The album, which featured the hit "At Seventeen," made Ian a major star.

Koppelman, now VP/general manager of worldwide publishing with the CBS Records Group, used the time with CBS to learn the workings of a major record company. "I learned the good parts and the bad parts," he said later. "I learned that I would never do what they did. It underscored that major companies have no understanding of the music publishing business and no understanding of their value. I mean, CBS treated the music publishing business as not even the stepchild of a distant relative. And I also met an incredible amount of people, artists, managers, lawyers. I held some terrific positions that made everyone come talk to me, so when I went into business for myself the second time, I was really much better prepared to be a major player in the music business."

In 1975, at age thirty-five, Koppelman embarked on his second stab at a music business venture with the Entertainment Company, a business designed to administer and promote song catalogs and serve as the executive producer for artists. The venture marked the beginning of his partnership with Martin Bandier, who would team with Koppelman on most of the biggest deals of their lives.

Bandier, who was working as general counsel for his father-in-law, real estate developer Sam LeFrak, met Koppelman through a mutual friend. Bandier recalled, "He was working at CBS. I think at that time he was either the head of their music publishing company or in A&R—I don't remember exactly what he was. But he had been in business on his own prior to that, and I think he was not ready for corporate life. He really wanted to be in business on his own."

The lure of self-employment also enticed Bandier. "I had tasted a little bit of the music business when I had practiced law and wanted to get into that business. So we were two people moderately unhappy with their position in life and we went into business together."

The LeFrak Organization provided financing for the venture,

which was geared toward investing in copyrights and producing songs in conjunction with artists. Bandier, like Koppelman, was a firm believer in the value of copyrights.

"I was a lawyer at kind of a stuffy firm and this was in the late '60s, so my hair was [long]," Bandier recalled. "One day one of the partners in the firm—without looking at my eyes, he was always looking at my hair—said that they represented a company that was about to acquire a music publishing company and he thought that this might be something that [I] would have a real good feel for. He said, 'You probably listen to the radio, you listen to music. I think you might be one of the few people here that do.'"

The project involved the sale of a music publishing company, which Bandier declines to name. "I think the price of it was about four and a half million dollars. In 1969, four and a half million dollars to someone who was twenty-six years old was like an enormous amount of money. And I couldn't for the life of me figure out during the first two months that I worked on this acquisition what they were paying for, because it wasn't anything that you could touch, or feel, or see. It was just sort of like smoke. When you reached out to grab it, you sort of got nothing in your hand."

The idea behind the Entertainment Company was simple: To make the music publishing operations flourish, the business would have some creative control over what ultimately goes on records. "And the only way you could do that is by being the record producer," Bandier said. "And so we kind of took a page out of the Hollywood studio days. The Hollywood studios used to sign directors by the droves, because the director was responsible for all the creative aspects of making a motion picture. And if you had great directors, you could make great motion pictures, assuming you got the right stars, and the right stars were attracted by great directors. So to us, a record producer was the most analogous to a motion picture director."

The purchase of those catalogs was the first example of Koppelman's vision about what the future would hold. "I think that most people who enter the music business look at the record business as the real deal," he said. "I looked at music publishing as the real deal. I recognized the value of copyrights. I also recognized what I felt was my own ability to take songs and increase their value by understanding the individual songs and by casting them by trying to convince the right artist to sing the right song. And in that endeavor, one can easily increase the value of that group of songs by getting other people to record the songs. So I was always confident that I could accomplish that. Also, by having my own production company, I could effect a change quite easily by just recording a lot of these songs. So it was easy for me to increase the value. Having said all of that, even if I weren't able to do all of the above, I know how to value copyrights. If I could buy them for the right price, I was making a good investment. That's really the way I looked at it."

Having signed numerous producers on an exclusive basis, the Entertainment Company was in position to make its move. As a sideline, Bandier and Koppelman formed a record company, Manhattan Records, distributed through the independent label Island and financed by the head of United Artists records, Artie Mogull. The venture would be less than successful, with artists like Mimi Farina, Ben Vereen, and Tom Saviano suffering because Koppelman and Bandier paid more attention to their production deals than their record company. "I don't think we ever had a record that ever sold a thousand copies," Mogull said. "I think at the time Charles and Marty had publisher's mentalities. They were first getting their feet wet in the record business. This was '77, '78. The label was up and running for about two years." The label was best known for a trait that later would surface at SBK Records: "Their office was a palace," said one employee.

While the production company was originally supposed to be a sideline to the music publishing operation, it soon became much more. Partnered with stars like Dolly Parton, Barbra Streisand, and Glen Campbell in recording ventures, it became one of the hottest production operations on both coasts. Streisand was one of the valuable contacts Koppelman had made while at CBS. "I was actually the only person that dealt with her," Koppelman claimed. "She had very little contact with the people at CBS before I got there. And when I had left, she would ask me to work with her as it pertained to her music on Columbia Records. It wasn't as if I had an eye on Barbra Streisand, but we had a good personal relationship that, in a sense, spilled over to a business relationship."

Bandier recalls the early times at the Entertainment Company as incredibly busy.

"We produced a tremendous amount of records, which Charles acted as the executive producer on, and we had this thriving business where we were producing maybe ten to fifteen albums per year, which is more than the output of a lot of labels," Bandier said. The production team racked up such hit songs as Glen Campbell's "Southern Nights" and Dolly Parton's "Here We Come Again."

Surprisingly, despite the enormous success, there were problems. "The Entertainment Company was always behind in their debts to lots of people, their normal accounts payable," said Stephen Swid, later to partner with Koppelman and Bandier. "They were always living on a shoestring and staying alive through wits as much as anything else. And I'm not denigrating that. I'm just saying [that was the case]."

One clue to the possible source of the cash-flow problems can be traced to Koppelman. As he would do later at SBK Records, Charles was living large. "They would check into the Beverly Hills Hotel and more or less hold court," said Frank DeCaro, who worked as a music supervisor/A&R man for the Entertainment Company. "We'd take our meetings there. We had no offices. There were no faxes. There were no computers. Everything was done with legal pads and shoot from the hip. Strictly all ideas and energy and a creative flow. And I got to say it was tremendously exciting.

"I remember being in the studio with Livingston Taylor," adds DeCaro. "Charles comes in with his entourage, about three or four people, all well-dressed and a big production. And when they leave to get in a limo, Livingston says to me, 'Now, that's management!' Charles was always a father figure to all of us, and he's younger than I am. He was a high achiever at a very young age, a very exciting guy to be around, very positive, very full of tremendous enthusiasm."

One person with whom Koppelman had production dealings was less than enthusiastic about the experience. "I know that on one of my records, we spent about $110,000 making the record and then they tried to recoup over $300,000. And a lot of the money, a big chunk of the money, was for Charlie's bungalow at the Beverly Hills Hotel, and he never showed up once during the recording. He was actually working with Barbra Streisand. He just charged stuff to us. We had to argue all the time. Getting royalty statements was impossible. The artists were always screaming at Columbia, 'Where the hell are our royalty statements?' They'd say, 'Hey, your contract's with Koppelman.'"

The high-flying Entertainment Company was the talk of Los Angeles, according to DeCaro. "The whole concept that Charles wanted to emulate, the whole idea was to be a mini–Atlantic Records. Concentrating on real groove music and developing exciting artists."

Of course, it was all the better that Koppelman had his artists record tunes that he owned as copyrights. And many of the Entertainment Company artists obliged, giving Koppelman two revenue streams—publishing and production—from the same recording.

"I used to call him 'Charles Copyright,' and it became an in-thing," DeCaro said. "He was always selling songs, but this time he was selling songs he owned."

However, the cyclical nature of the business soon kicked in, and the Entertainment Company gradually began to lose force. Dolly Parton moved on to films, while Barbra Streisand also was working in movies, this time with *A Star Is Born*.

During its nine-year history, the Entertainment Company achieved hits with the Four Tops, Eddie Murphy, the Weather Girls, and Cher. The company also had success with two of Streisand's biggest albums, *Guilty* and *Memories*, both multimillion sellers.

One of the last records of the era was the Donna Summer–Barbra Streisand pairing on "No More Tears (Enough Is Enough)." The title proved prophetic.

"Everything was so political with that record, we had problems in the studio," DeCaro said, recalling that "No More Tears (Enough Is Enough)" had to be rerecorded when the tape was accidentally destroyed in the studio during a playback, the actual magnetic strips unspooling onto the floor because everyone involved was so distracted.

However, things were unraveling on another front. Bandier's marriage to LeFrak's daughter was ending. According to *GQ* magazine, "LeFrak went ballistic, accusing Koppelman and Bandier of stealing, and threatened legal action. Koppelman says he gave LeFrak a check for $500,000 just to get the ugly business settled. Bandier dismisses the whole mess as 'really, truly, a minor blip.'

LeFrak, it turned out, was not the only one who had a problem with the way things were run at the Entertainment Company. Paul Jabara was an Oscar-winning songwriter whose works include "Last Dance" from the film *Thank God It's Friday*, "No More Tears (Enough Is Enough)," and "It's Raining Men," a song co-written with Paul Schaffer of the David Letterman show. Jabara sued over royalties.

Jabara was signed to a songwriting contract by the Entertainment Company in 1979, shortly after winning his Oscar. The deal was supposed to be for three years. Soon, however, a dispute arose over Jabara's output. Koppelman claimed it was not commercial enough and suspended Jabara.

The dispute escalated. Jabara claimed to have storyboarded a concept for a Weather Girls TV special that was allegedly taken by Koppelman and given to David Steinberg. Jabara suspected that his songs were generating far more in royalties than he was receiving, a suspicion that only grew when Koppelman and Bandier claimed to have lost the books when asked for a voluntary accounting.

Eventually, the dispute was settled out of court. Bob Cinque, Jabara's attorney, claimed a settlement of $269,912.12 for underpayment of royalties, plus interest. Koppelman and Bandier dispute the amount. Jabara remained bitter, accusing Koppelman and Bandier of ruining his life. "I wish someone would take that cigar out of Charles's mouth and put it where it belongs," he told *GQ*. (Later, Jabara would reconcile with Koppelman. Terminally ill, he received some advance money for future work as a songwriter from Koppelman, money Koppelman likely knew was a charitable donation rather than a business investment.)

*   *   *

With the Entertainment Company played out, it was time for a new venture. In 1984, Koppelman and Bandier formed the Entertainment Music Company, which eventually purchased the Combine Music catalog of 25,000 country titles. They also published Gregory Abbott's No. 1 song "Shake You Down" and signed then-unknown Tracy Chapman, who was discovered by Koppelman's son, Brian, when she performed at an anti-apartheid rally he helped organize.

The company's activity in those areas, though notable, would pale when the pair decided to enter into what would become one of the biggest deals—and steals—in music business history: the purchase of CBS Songs, the publishing arm of CBS Records.

Music publishing is considered by many to be a dull backwater of the record industry, a place to which record companies once banished underachieving executives they couldn't bear to fire. Few understood the enormous profits to be reaped from songs, which is why so many of rock 'n' roll's early stars signed away their songwriting to managers and executives for a pittance and did not benefit from the ongoing, lifelong profits generated by their craft.

In fact, so few understood the publishing end that song exploitation was not a truly proactive business until the mid- to late '70s, when the business slowly became concentrated in the hands of a few major players savvy enough to see the potential.

In 1986, financier Stephen C. Swid joined Koppelman and Bandier to form SBK Entertainment World. His financial background was impressive. A former senior investment officer of the Oppenheimer Fund and a securities analyst for the Dreyfus Fund, he was founder, co-chairman, and co–chief executive officer of Knoll International Holdings Inc., a privately held investment corporation with revenues approximating $2 billion.

Swid had "dabbled" in various entertainment industry deals before being approached on CBS Songs. "That was my first major deal," Swid said, but noted that Koppelman and Bandier had previously contacted him about partnering to purchase ATV Music, the catalog that contained most of the songs authored by John Lennon and Paul McCartney. Swid and a former partner declined to participate. "Those guys lost the deal to Michael Jackson for a variety of reasons," Swid said. "One reason was they're music people. They're not deal people. And to do a deal, you have to have the knowledge and experience. I'm a financier."

CBS Songs was one of the top catalogs in the business, although its presence had more to do with volume than any perception in the outside world that it was vital. The company had long been treated as a dumping ground of the CBS music empire, a place to stick old family retainers and let them work until retirement, out of the way of any important decision making. "They weren't being aggressive," Bandier said. "They weren't being cautious. They treated it as a stepchild. They never looked at it as a major source of revenue. They never looked at it as a major source of creative fertility. It was, 'Maybe the publishing company will find something that they'll give to the record company that will blossom.'"

Bandier and Koppelman, however, looked at the company with the hunger a wolf feels when gazing at a lamb. "This was our main business," Bandier said. "This was something we knew like the back of your hand. And we recognized all of the up sides that this business had. And more importantly, we loved it. I mean, there was nothing more exciting to us than finding a new artist like a Tracy Chapman or signing a new writer who everyone fell in love with."

But there was potentially an even bigger prize at stake, because rumors were floating that the CBS television network needed cash to continue to fund the network's battle against takeover threats by media mogul Ted Turner. To fuel that operation, the record company itself was allegedly in play.

Stephen Swid and Martin Bandier were having lunch in August 1986 when the subject was broached.

"Marty has been a longstanding friend of mine [in fact, Bandier had roomed with Swid's best friend in college] and he was having lunch at my house and he asked me if I knew anybody at CBS," Swid recalled. "And I said no. And oh, it was like a groan. And I said, 'Marty, why, why are you groaning?' And he said, 'Well, we hear that CBS Songs and/or CBS Records is for sale. And we're there every single day but nobody will tell us anything, nobody will give us any material. But we know they're negotiating with people and they just won't tell Koppelman and myself.'"

The resentment at CBS against Bandier and Koppelman evidently extended from their earlier days in the Entertainment Company. The two were apparently viewed as tummlers rather than A-room talent.

Swid did know Lawrence Tisch, the largest CBS shareholder, and agreed to speak to him on behalf of Bandier and Koppelman. But "I didn't think that I was getting into the business," Swid said.

The call to Tisch put Swid in touch with Walter Yetnikoff, possibly the wildest record industry executive in music annals, a man of enormous appetites who conducted business as a three-ring circus of yelling, drinking, and acting out. "Two days later," Swid recalled, "late in the day, my secretary says, 'Walter Yetnikoff is on the phone.' And a guy comes on with a very deep, deep, deep voice and he said, 'Tischberg says you're for real.' I said, 'I don't even know who you're talking about.' I was really taken aback. He said, 'Larry Tisch. I thought he was a friend of yours.' I said he is. I said, 'Why do you call him Tischberg?' He says, 'I'm Yetnikoff. I could be Yates.' And this is how I was introduced to the music industry."

Yetnikoff denied the record company was for sale but was canny as to the music publishing division's availability. He claimed to have already sold the unit but would not tell Swid who the purchaser was.

"I didn't read about it in the paper the next day or the next day. So three days later I call him—I call people like at eight in the morning—and he calls me back at six o'clock at night."

Yetnikoff finally revealed that the company was going to be purchased by its president in a buyout and claimed the deal would happen the next day. It didn't.

Finally, a meeting was set. It was a meeting of two cultures, to be sure. "We're foreign to each other," Swid said. "Where I have a very clean office, he has all these things all over this office, memorabilia and pictures and photographs and monuments—it was like a who's who of his personal history and the House of Wax combined."

A bit of wrangling later, Swid obtained a commitment to get

the financial reports on CBS Songs. "I called Bandier and Koppelman over to my house on Sunday and they brought an accountant. I said, 'It's going to cost you $125 million.'" The deal required $15 million in equity, according to Swid, with $110 million borrowed. Still, he was not sure if the deal was worth it.

"Koppelman and Bandier said it's the greatest catalog in the world, outside of Chappell [another publishing catalog that was on the block at the same time]. They should know. CBS didn't manage it or grow it."

Yetnikoff agreed with that assessment, according to Swid. "He explained to me the things that he had not done that anybody can do [to increase profitability of the publishing company]. Plus it could be managed better because the publishing company—basically you got the Peter Principle—if you couldn't perform in the record company, then you do publishing. But that's the way it was managed. You can always liquidate it to pay down debt and get off the guarantee and do those kind of things. So you're risking your equity."

Finally, Swid joined Koppelman and Bandier in their attempted purchase. "They couldn't do it by themselves. They didn't have the wherewithal. They didn't have the ability to persuade a financial institution to lend to them because of their lack of experience in that area." (Koppelman disputes that claim: "It was my banking relationship which, coincidentally, was the same bank that Stephen uses. I and Marty put up half the money that we needed to buy the company. Obviously, if I was living beyond my means, we wouldn't have been able to put up millions and millions of dollars to buy the company.")

But CBS had some qualms about doing the deal, Swid recalled. "I didn't know this in the beginning, but it reached the point in the middle that Walter didn't want to sell it to Bandier. And I realized that when I was up in Walter's office. I went to the office almost every single night, four nights a week to schmooze him all along. And we became very good friends and we're still very good friends. And I drank with him every night."

Swid added, "I went up one evening and [entertainment industry attorney] Allen Grubman and [then artist manager, now Sony Music chief executive officer] Tommy Mottola were there, and I had no idea why [Mottola] was there. And then while we're just shooting the breeze, Tommy said, 'I don't think you should go into business with Bandier and Koppelman.' I know that's coming out of Walter's mouth. Who the hell is this Tommy? Tommy Mottola was not working for CBS. He had his own management company. And that's when I first realized why they weren't given the numbers. Anyway, I told them I can't do that. I'm halfway through this deal and we're working together and they brought me the deal, and it's something that I wouldn't do. They were trying to detach Koppelman and Bandier from me but I wouldn't permit that to happen.

"Finally, I take out an envelope and I put it in front of Walter and he says, 'What's that?' I said, 'Well, open it.' He said, 'It's for me?' I said, 'Sort of.'"

Inside was a check for $3 million, a good-faith deposit for the $125 million they had floated as the price of the publishing company.

"I said, 'We want to sign an agreement in principle tonight. We can't wait any longer. We've been negotiating with you. We'll pay the highest price. You have some responsibility to the corporation. We'll close and we'll close very fast.'"

CBS internal general counsel Dave Johnson and the trio's attorney, Gary Stiffelman, went off to draft an agreement in principle. "Meanwhile," Swid said, "Koppelman and Bandier were waiting at their office, biting their nails. I'd finally gotten to call them at like nine-thirty at night after we signed the agreement, and we went out for dinner. So I entered the music business."

The new owners, calling their company SBK Entertainment World, had instantly become the world's largest independent publishers, the owners or administrators of over 250,000 copyrights, including such gems as ATV Music, the home of John Lennon and Paul McCartney's catalog; United Artists Music; and April-Blackwood Music. The catalog ran from Tin Pan Alley hits to film themes used in MGM and 20th Century–Fox features to songs by James Taylor, Laura Nyro, Luther Vandross, and Marvin Gaye.

Yet the consensus in the record industry was that the new owners had vastly overpaid. "What do you mean, a lot of people? Everybody," Swid said, laughing.

Bandier agreed that the feedback was mostly negative. "It was by the naysayers who didn't understand the value of intellectual property. I mean, how can you put a value on the score from *The Wizard of Oz*? Is there any doubt in your mind that ten years from now comes some holiday, one of the networks is going to show *The Wizard of Oz* again and every kid is going to be glued to a set and watch it? It's just part of our culture. We recognized from day one that there were things in this catalog that had not been marketed, had not been promoted, had been underexploited. And we also recognized that music was now an integral part of everyone's life and that the market itself just would expand and expand and by sheer expansion of numbers we would be able to increase our business."

Still, Bandier and Koppelman evidently had second thoughts, according to Swid.

"I think the second day after we bought the company Koppelman wanted to sell it," Swid said. "Not because he didn't love it. Not because he didn't think that the copyrights that we bought were not the Hope Diamond of the music industry. But because he was a man who lived above his means. He had assets but needed liquidity."

Bandier, too, had cold feet. "Marty didn't want to do the deal at the last second. When we were signing the papers to close the deal, Marty pulled me aside and said, 'Why are you doing this? Why are you risking so much? Why are you doing this? Are you sure you want to do this?' Marty was against it. Marty's a very conservative man. And Charlie told me that all day long Marty was hammering at him. Charles Koppelman is the only one that I met in the music industry that believed that it was worth more than what we were paying. Everybody else said that we were overpaying. But he wanted money because he lived a certain means. He said afterwards that 'I finally have enough money to live the life that I'm accustomed to.'" (Koppelman disputes Swid's claim that he wanted to sell the company. "I never wanted to sell and still wish that we didn't sell it.")

Bandier also recalls it differently. "I never thought we would sell it. I thought we were there for the long run. My goal was to have the largest music publishing company that there was. We made every attempt to buy any catalog that became available, and because we had done so well in the first year or two, our bankers became real believers with us. They recognized that we knew what we were doing and that this wasn't pie in the sky. We really believed that this was something that was going to be here for ourselves and our families and was going to be sort of a dynasty in this area. Because it's very rare that you find a business that you've been steeped in for twenty years that you can acquire that's enormous."

Had the new owners flipped it, said Swid, CBS Songs would have fetched "five million dollars more." Yet Koppelman had a grander vision of the label's worth at that point. "There was no doubt in my mind," he said, "that the day we bought it, it was worth $75 million more than we paid for it."

Koppelman's alleged quick push to sell eventually led to a falling-out with Swid, an incident about which both declined to reveal specifics but which Swid blamed on money. "Early on something happened which upset Charles," Swid recalled. "He needed money for something. We had just bought the company. We weren't allowed to give a quarter million dollars to shareholders. So I said, 'We can't do that.' And he got very upset and so we had to work through that. Marty Bandier was sort of a referee."

As it turned out, selling CBS Songs quickly would potentially have cost the new owners several hundred million dollars. Market factors were in play that, almost immediately, raised the value of the publishing company, enabling the partners to make a killing when they sold CBS publishing.

"Nineteen-eighty-six was the first year that people started CDs in numbers," Swid said. "Nineteen-eighty-seven was really the year when it broke out, but it started breaking out in the fall of '86. And if you go back, you will find that no American distributors had CD plants because they thought CD was like 8-track and they thought CD would cannibalize the tape business. And vinyl was still a major force at that time—declining, but still major. They were very fearful of that and if it worked, that's what would happen at best. And at worst, it would be like 8-track, and they weren't going to build the plants."

"Anyway, so we had the CD going for us. They would make all these old albums with all our songs on them. That's what a publisher wants, technological change. We came in at the nexus of it happening."

But more good news was on the horizon. Nine months into ownership, the team was paid a visit by one Ed Murphy, the music publishing industry negotiator with the Recording Industry Association of America. "He says, 'You might not know this and because you're the second-largest publisher I wanted to inform you: We're about to reach an agreement with the record industry to resolve the longstanding issue of changing the royalty rate. The royalty rate will be changed every two years by the intervening inflation rate through 1998.' Inflation was, on the average, 5 percent. So we started multiplying by five—we just extrapolated out and it looked like the royalty rate was going to be like eight and a half or nine cents come '98."

Publishers, as owners of the songs, are paid a royalty by licensees every time the song is played on the radio, sold as sheet music, used on a soundtrack, or even played in a restaurant. What Murphy was essentially telling the partners was get ready to run to the bank.

Now the value of CBS Songs became apparent. "It wasn't until Ed Murphy told us that and that agreement was put in place at the end of '87 that [the publishing operation] became valuable," Swid said. "And when that agreement was put in place, the royalty did go up 5 percent, from a nickel to five and a quarter, expected to rise to nine cents." That, combined with the publishing expertise of Koppelman and Bandier, enabled SBK to claim to trade magazines that in its first full year it had revenues 30 percent higher than CBS Songs had had the year before.

SBK Entertainment World now seemed ready to make a great leap forward to become a full-line media company, rivaling entertainment conglomerates like Warner Bros. and MCA. To that end, the company launched an ill-fated foray into the movie business by acquiring nearly 50 percent of Cinecom Entertainment Group, an independent film distributor and producer, in May 1988. The company, a six-year-old art film supplier before its affiliation with SBK, had released the Academy Award–winning *A Room With a View* among its credits but did not provide much income for the new owners.

At the same time, SBK moved even further along the road, expanding into artist management and record production, maintaining offices in twenty-two countries. It was time for bigger ventures.

Artie Mogull, a former owner of United Artists Records who had distributed Koppelman and Bandier's Manhattan Records label, was hired as a consultant by SBK Entertainment. "I think they were kind of being nice to me," Mogull said. "I was out of work, I needed a job, Charles and Marty owed me, so they gave me a job as a consultant. I was a consultant for about six months, and one day I was in New York and Swid cornered me and said, 'I want to buy EMI. I understand you're very close to [chairman Bhaskar] Menon. Why don't you smell him out?'"

Menon said the company was not for sale, but Mogull, perhaps sensing that something else was possible, got Menon to agree to have dinner with Swid, Koppelman, and Bandier when he came to New York. "Well, I made a reservation, and the plane was delayed four, five hours. We didn't meet until almost midnight at the Four Seasons for dinner. Charles, Marty, Steven, Bhaskar, and me. And during the course of the dinner he expressed to them that EMI was not for sale and they were wasting their time."

Swid, however, was intrigued by yet another possibility. Walking back to his hotel with Mogull, he asked if Menon would be interested in buying SBK. "Now, to this day, I don't know whether he ever intended to buy EMI or whether he lured me and Menon in under false pretenses," Mogull said. "I've never quite gotten the hang of that one. I said, 'In a minute I think he'd buy it.' So I called Menon at his hotel. It's 2:00 in the morning, and I said, 'Listen, instead of selling them EMI, how'd you like to buy SBK?' He said, 'I love it.'"

But there was more to the story than met the eye. "They had to sell," Mogull explained. "They had financial problems. Charles and

Marty weren't getting along with Stephen [Swid]. And Charles always had personal financial problems. He's always lived over his head. He had to sell."

The coming increases in the publisher's royalty shares made the deal particularly attractive, even though the rate of inflation had slowed, lowering the increase. Still, the proposition of increased revenues made SBK an enticing acquisition. "It seemed to me that that was the time to sell it because you sell a company when you can get the future," Swid said. "And we were able to get the future."

Menon met with the SBK group the next day and agreed to do the deal. He left the next morning for England to broach the acquisition to the Thorn EMI board.

But there was one lingering question on Menon's mind. He called Mogull in his hotel before he got on the plane and asked him, "Why should I pay more for SBK than Warner paid for Chappell?" Mogul was stumped. "'I don't know about that. By the time you get to London I'll have a fax giving you the answer.' And I sent him a fax. The last thing I said to him in the fax was 'Never again will a publishing company with this kind of catalog be available. How much is a Rembrandt worth?' And subsequently, for six months, in all the secret memos that went around within the EMI organization, the code word for the SBK deal was Rembrandt."

The initial asking price by Koppelman, Bandier & Swid was $375 million, based on what they thought the net publisher's share would be. EMI counter-offered $310 million but intended to go higher. Swid wanted $320 million. Mogull said, laughing, "I remember I got a phone call at midnight London time one night from Marty telling me that Charles was so pissed off at Stephen for holding out for the extra ten that he was threatening to throw him out a window.

"Five minutes later Stephen calls, and he explains to me why he's holding out for the $320 [million] so that obviously I'd repeat it to Menon. And when he's all finished, I said, 'Stephen, are you fucking crazy? You're going to blow a $310 million deal for $10 million? Of the $10 million, only five is yours. And out of the five, after taxes, you'll keep three. So for three million dollars, you're going to blow a $310 million deal?' And he says, 'Artie, three million dollars might not be a lot of money to you…' There was nowhere to go with that conversation."

Finally, both sides concocted a deal based on a multiple of what the net publisher's share (the amount a publisher retains after paying its contractual obligations to songwriters and others) would be after six months of due diligence. It was estimated that it was going to be about $320 million.

The partners had a final meeting to agree on a united front, Mogull recalled. "Swid said to Charles and Marty, 'All right, [EMI CEO Jim] Fifield is coming over here to make us a last and final offer. Now, Charles, you have to sell. I don't want you at the meeting. You let Marty and [me] handle this meeting.'" Charles insisted on being there, and Swid relented. "Okay, you can be there, but don't open your mouth. Let me negotiate this price.

"Fifield walks in and says, 'All right, here's my final offer: $295 million.' Charles says, 'It's a deal!' Marty and Stephen looked at each other!"

The deal was approved by EMI for $295 million, an astonishing increase over the $125 million that many had felt was an overpayment just two years before.

But the most intriguing part of the deal was almost an afterthought. EMI agreed to invest $10 million to establish a record company for Bandier and Koppelman. After the initial $10 million investment, any remaining monies would be split 50/50.

(It should be mentioned that initial published reports indicated a purchase price of $337 million, with the SBK label created with a $30 million stake. Whatever the amount, the price was a record for a publishing acquisition.)

"We were selling out and moving on," Koppelman said. "And I had felt that maybe the time was right to start our own label. And the reason the time was right is I now had all the money I could possibly want. We had just finished launching Tracy Chapman through Elektra Records. We spent a lot of money ourselves in making that happen and felt that we were prepared, emotionally and financially, to take the ups and downs of the record business. And I felt that was kind of like the last challenge that I wanted to throw upon myself."

There was one last unfinished bit of business connnected to their ownership of SBK Entertainment World. As thanks for their efforts, each employee at the company was given a check, the amounts totaling in excess of $3 million.

Swid and the partners agreed to part at that point. Swid took the movie company as his parting gift from the partnership.

For Koppelman, the record company was a crucial factor in the deal. "It was important to Charles's ego," Mogull contends. "He wanted that record company. After years of peddling songs to record companies, he wanted to be the guy who was the buyer instead of the seller."

Koppelman, the record man, newly enriched and with a multinational corporate backer, was about to show the world what he could do from the big stage.

"I never had a year in the music business that I didn't have mega-hits," he said. "A bad year was when I had maybe one. We had a bad year, Marty and I, when we had Eddie Murphy's song 'Party All the Time' and three million of his albums, and Gregory Abbott's [hit] song 'Shake You Down.' That was a bad year. We weren't even concentrating. We were trying to do something in the television business then. I always had hits my entire life in the music business. Lucky? Absolutely. But my mother has a great expression: When luck comes to visit, does it come to stay? My own expression is, the harder you work, the luckier you get. I like contemporary music. I hear artists, I believe in them, and then I try and figure out how to get other people to believe that their music is terrific. How do I get people to play it? How do I get people to work it?

"I was now ready. I had never been ready before because I didn't want to take the financial risk, going way back to the way I got in the business. I knew the financial investment that was required. I was prepared to bet the ranch on the next act I got excited about. Once I had the ranch *and* the apartment house *and* the country house, then I was maybe prepared to bet the ranch."

What was to follow would be one of the wildest rides in record business history.

FOUR

SMOKE AND MUSIC

For one of the few times in his life, Chris Blackwell was being yelled at by a boss.

The founder of Island Records had sold his holdings in the label to PolyGram in 1989 for the outrageous sum of $300 million. Insiders at his company had postulated that Island Records, the home of Bob Marley, was worth somewhere around $125 million. But in the frenzied, market-share–hungry world of multinational music corporations, Blackwell was able to make a killing. The sale was a huge reward to Blackwell, and an unexpected one as well. In the bargain, he agreed to an employment contract and remained on deck to play a managerial role.

Just under a year later, though, he was not experiencing one of the joys of selling for a huge number. Blackwell was absently scribbling on a tablet of yellow lined paper and silently listening to a harangue by Alain Levy, the brusque French attorney who was the company's worldwide chief executive officer.

"What kind of a company did you sell me?" Levy screamed, a sea of red-ink–stained accounting sheets in front of him. In truth, it was not a good time for the business. Island was in one of those periodic record industry cycles where established artists are between albums, new acts are failing to prove themselves, and the bills are still coming due every month.

Blackwell listened to Levy's tirade, but he was savoring every moment. Shortly after selling the company, he was forced into accepting a candidate for Island president who was not his personal choice. At first, Blackwell balked, but perhaps reminded himself of the opportunity for revenge that comes to those who bide their time, particularly when he realized that Island was in for a dry spell.

After listening to the corporate moans, Blackwell continued doodling on his yellow legal pad. Speaking softly without looking up, he said, "We were generating eight million dollars a year. Then you bought it and it turned to shit."

But PolyGram was not the only company to watch helplessly as a record label they purchased turned sour. EMI also had that sad experience with SBK, hookwinked into buying a label that proved not nearly worth its price.

To understand the circumstances that allowed Swid, Koppelman, and Bandier to pull off some of the most astonishing record and publishing deals in music business history, it's worth examining the age-old question of what a record company is worth. The argument hasn't been resolved in over thirty years of buying and selling, which reached its peak in the past ten years as three of the industry's traditional runners-up engaged in a feeding frenzy of acquisition, all in the name of boosting market share and becoming players.

PolyGram jumped on A&M, Island, and Motown Records; MCA purchased Geffen and GRP Records; and the distributor with the largest appetite, EMI Music, acquired IRS, SBK, Chrysalis, Enigma, and the kingfish of them all, Virgin Records.

Each deal was marked by controversy at its inception. To this day, debate rages in record company corridors as to whether any of them were worth the sums paid for them. And surprisingly, some of those still questioning the deals are the people who made the deals in the first place.

As Island sank slowly into the sunset following its 1989 sale to PolyGram, its staff cut and ancillary functions placed within other PolyGram labels, it began to seem like less of a record label than a logo with much past glory and little current success. That lead to the confrontation with Levy.

Blackwell, perhaps suffering from the ennui that afflicts all entrepreneurs who no longer call the shots, seemed to fade from the picture for a time, concentrating on outside ventures that had nothing to do with music. However, at the three-quarter mark of his five-year contract, he suddenly emerged from hibernation just as albums by U2 and the Cranberries made Island red-hot.

Faced with the prospect of losing a man who appeared to have the magic touch, PolyGram quickly offered Blackwell another employment contract and restored Island's status as a self-functioning entity within the PolyGram system just a few years after slashing the label's work force to the bone.

That chain of events underlines how record company acquisitions are among the shakiest of investments. Aside from the company's catalog of past hits, which may be of negligible value, the only tangible asset of the firm is its management expertise. As is often the case with ecosystems, removing anything from the balance may cause the whole food chain to suffer, and the assumption that the man who is the biggest fish is the true genius behind various ventures has been proven wrong time and again.

What record companies are really gambling on is that the catalog of the acquired company will continue to sell, and that the management it retains will continue to sign enough fresh talent to keep the company's momentum going. Unfortunately for the purchasers, hungry record entrepreneurs often turn lazy upon reaping millions of dollars or lose contact with the street sense that made them successful.

As a result, some companies have been bought because of their past revenues, not their future returns. Which means, at first glance, that many deals do not look promising.

Island Records is one such example of a company that many thought had been purchased for a price far above its value. A confidant of owner Chris Blackwell recalls the initial discussions about a sale.

"We were on the boat in Nassau in the Bahamas, and [Blackwell] said to me, 'What do you think my company is worth?' In my opinion, it's worth between $125 million and $150 million. That was my honest opinion because we just had a new U2 contract, six records left, and our distribution deal was coming available."

Blackwell was hesitant. The record company had been his entire life, fortune, and fame. "So I said 'Look, here's what I would do. Why don't we shop it around a little bit, see what type of offers we get. If we get offers in the range of what we think the company is worth, let's go for it. If we get offers that are lower, let's not even consider it.'"

The contenders for the prize included Atlantic Records and the Walt Disney Company. Disney "wasn't really interested," according to Blackwell's confidant. "Atlantic made an offer of about $175 million." EMI music head Jim Fifield also took a look and passed, claiming the price was too high. Because EMI once distributed Island overseas, Fifield perhaps had the best angle on what the company was actually worth.

"At the time, I thought the price was a bit high," Fifield said later. "They had a long-term distribution agreement with BMG in Europe, so I couldn't get access to that for several years. And he was asking for a good price. There was a bit of a feeding frenzy going on, and I just didn't think it was the right thing for EMI."

Then PolyGram arrived on the scene. The company, a money-loser for most of its tenure in the American market, was desperate to turn itself around. Rather than trying to sign new bands and wait for them to develop, PolyGram opted to purchase other record companies, instantly gaining an increased market share.

"They came in and said they want to be the first one, they want to strike first, don't talk to anybody else," said Blackwell's confidant.

PolyGram weighed in to the tune of $331 million, approximately double what Blackwell and his aides thought they would receive. "They paid a substantial premium above book value. Substantial," says the source. "On the other hand, look what they did."

The deal was made palatable to the corporate bean counters when PolyGram used a stock offering to recoup the huge financial outlay for Island and then A&M Records, the latter purchased shortly after Island for an estimated $500 million in a cash deal that promised continued autonomy under co-founders Jerry Moss and Herb Alpert. Besides the record company, PolyGram obtained real estate holdings that included the A&M Studios, the landmark Charlie Chaplin Studio lot in Hollywood, and the label's headquarters.

Although those were the official figures, they resemble the bustline of movie starlets and the height of NBA centers in relation to reality. The official stock offering pegged Island's price at a still-hefty $272 million, with A&M allegedly at $460 million.

In mid-December 1989, PolyGram NV offered 20 percent of its outstanding shares on the New York and Amsterdam stock exchanges, an action that was expected to raise $512 million. Of that sum, Philips would receive $334 million and Polygram $152 million, after broker commissions.

The immediate effect was to bolster PolyGram's lagging North America market share, which a prospectus for the stock offering claimed was around 19 percent in the United States and Canada. Internationally, the company fared better, claiming to be No. 3 in the world, with 15 percent of the market. A good deal of that share was in classical music.

"So they didn't use any of their cash," said the Island source. "To an extent, if you looked at it as a pure asset purchase, a company purchase, they grossly overpaid. But I think [PolyGram CEO Alain] Levy was very bright and floated a stock issue that basically didn't dilute his company at all. He still controls it, and the share price has been very, very strong. So what seemed a very high price really turned out to be a stroke of genius for them."

The multinational world of the music industry in the 1990s can essentially be broken into three categories: the titans of the industry (Time Warner and Sony), the acquirers (Polygram, Thorn EMI, and MCA), and the outsider who thinks it knows best (Bertelsmann).

Record companies can grow in one of three ways: They can develop their own acts, license labels for distribution, or acquire A&R expertise by purchasing an outside source of talent—for example, an established record label. In the late '80s, Warner and Sony, as the two far-and-away market leaders, expanded through solid internal growth buttressed by key acquisitions.

In the case of Warner Bros., a few select labels headed by proven key executives like Tom Silverman, Rick Rubin, and Irving Azoff were augmented by internal talent growth; at Sony, internal growth was augmented by a few startup labels for key Sony executives (WTG, by Jerry Greenberg, is one example), some of which were more successful than others.

However, in both cases, the enormous reserves provided by choice catalog titles from such industry superstars as Eric Clapton, Madonna, and Neil Young (all Time Warner) and Bob Dylan, Bruce Springsteen, and Billy Joel (all Sony) cushioned any short-term costs of internal growth.

Bertelsmann, a German company grounded on the principle of guaranteed returns to shareholders (a concept known in German as *Betriebsergebnis*, or roughly, "return on assets"), did little in the way of acquisitions and in the process made some bad choices in some startups (the money-losing Imago Records, a joint venture with Chrysalis Records cofounder Terry Ellis that generated little beyond one minor hit album by Henry Rollins) and gaining some decent market share (Private Music, the label that spawned Yanni) via purchase.

However, most of the key action in the decade came from the so-called "third world" labels, those that perpetually were jockeying to join the upper stratum of Warner and Sony. To this day, their race is almost interchangeable. When one label gets hot, it temporarily becomes number three; when it is not, it could slip down to the bottom of the charts. None of them, however, appears capable of dislodging Sony or Warner Music from atop the market-share charts for more than a month or two.

The solution to changing the fortunes of BMG, MCA, EMI, and PolyGram, at least in the minds of the executives in charge, was to build volume and increase market share worldwide, but particularly in the key U.S. and British markets, which provide most of the exportable pop music for the world. Volume growth would bolster stock prices, keeping shareholders happy. The fact that most of that growth has apparently been fueled by high compact disc prices is a subject scarcely acknowledged among executives.

Jim Fifield, the leading acquirer among the Big Six executives, explained that purchasing a record company is a matter of "what it's worth to you."

"It's kind of like if you had four Rolls Royces," Fifield said. "What's the fifth one worth? Whereas if you have none, what's the first one worth? It's kind of a question of value."

The past is an indication of the future for record companies, according to Fifield. "You look at the strength of [a label's] catalog, you look at their existing artist roster, you look obviously at how many albums those artists have on their contract. You look at the management of the company and whether they're making good contribution to the business going forward. You look at what synergies you can put into the deal. So hopefully two and two equal more than four."

But even Fifield admits that many in the record industry didn't understand what he was doing when he rolled the dice for the biggest stakes in the history of the record industry: Virgin Records.

At first glance, Jim Fifield would seem an unlikely choice to lead an entertainment company. A graduate of Southern Methodist University, the fifty-year-old Fifield could be mistaken for a church deacon—tall, thin, conservative in dress, with a quiet but direct approach.

Fifield had spent some twenty years at General Mills before that company decided to spin off its nonfood businesses, which included specialty retailing and toys, leaving Fifield without a job. "I really wanted to stay at General Mills, but there really wasn't a position, so at that point it was a midlife crisis. I really didn't want to go off and be the president of the toy group."

Fifield had a hidden passion for R&B music, but his background in consumer goods proved to be his entree to the glamorous life. "Fortunately, Barry Diller and Tom Wyman and Jon Dolgen at the time thought that somone with consumer marketing experience would actually be a better hire to run CBS-Fox Video than someone who was from a studio world who thought about production and distribution. They wanted someone who would treat the videos as after-market, using package goods marketing skills. And I had that international experience."

Named president/CEO of CBS-Fox Video in 1985, Fifield learned the mechanics of the entertainment business—recoupability, unrecoupability, royalities, cross-collateralization, production deals, and other esoterica—all of it very transferrable to the music industry. An added bonus was a chance to be associated with people like Chris Blackwell, Walter Yetnikoff, artist manager Shep Gordon, and others whose music videos and films were distributed through CBS-Fox.

But in 1988, things were about to take a turn beyond Fifield's wildest dreams. The Thorn board had long been after chairman Bhaskar Menon to appoint a successor. Now, the pressure had been stepped up, and Menon enlisted an executive search firm that discovered Fifield. "So over the course of about three years, I went from, 'Gee, wouldn't that be nice' to actually being in the job," Fifield said.

Fifield was appointed April 7, 1988, as president and chief operating officer of EMI Music Worldwide, and he assumed command of day-to-day operations May 2. It was a nomination that was termed the culmination of eighteen months of executive changes at the company that included new faces at virtually every unit of the empire. Menon continued as chairman but clearly had been shunted to an emeritus position.

Thorn EMI told Fifield it believed it had a sleeping giant on its hands, an organization that was better known for selling off its media assets than growing them, leading to frequent and anxious inquiries from hungry conglomerates. Colin Southgate, the Thorn EMI chairman/CEO, had apparently decided that it was time to build the business and gave Fifield definitive marching orders.

"It was one of those meetings where he said, 'We think it's under-performing,'" Fifield recalled. "'We think it's got a lot of potential. We'd like you to come and aggressively manage it.' So I went in with the understanding that my job was to turn it around and to try to bring it back to the preeminence that it had in the '60s. All our meetings were very aggressive. It was, 'We're not selling. We want to build.'"

Fifield was eager, but cautious enough to warn the newly eager entertainment architects that their plan was not without risk. "I said at the time, 'Well, if I make mistakes, which we all do, I'm going to make mistakes from trying to push it too hard, too fast.'"

Thorn EMI could have used a good push. The organization, embroiled in yet another round of Beatles/Apple lawsuits, had not even put out the Beatles on CD when Fifield arrived in 1988. The company had long paid lip service to the idea of growing its own artists and judiciously acquiring choice companies that became available. Unfortunately, the internal work needed to attract great artists and make the company the place to be was not done. A succession of presidents marked Capitol and EMI during the '80s, as one regime after another was brought in and phased out. But the company was willing to spend money to acquire talent, no matter how much it took.

"When they bought Virgin, they paid more than anyone else," said an executive familiar with the tactics. "Capitol had to offer more money than two or three or four of the leading companies just to get the same artists. The biggest problem with Capitol-EMI was that they did not allow their own management teams to grow and make mistakes. When you look at any successful record company, any one of them have had major droughts. It's management understanding that and understanding the music business.

If Fifield did not understand the alchemy that goes into developing talent, he did understand how to keep expenses under wraps to pay for his acquisitions. He instituted the first system of cost controls in EMI's A&R and other departments.

"It was just a company that had become, from a management standpoint, an obsolete organization," Fifield said. "More importantly, it was a company that was not an international company. It was only international because it was in a lot of countries. But it was really, operationally, a multiterritorial company with a lot of individual fiefdoms that had grown up without much integration and coordination. There wasn't any planning. There wasn't any moving as a unit. It was all moving as individual operations."

Fifield was determined to move the company from its No. 5 position in the Big Six upon his arrival to a place in the top three record distributors. As a result of his observations, a plan of action took place. Efficiency was the watchword, as the old family retainers who populated the EMI corporate world were gradually shunted aside. Vinyl factories were closed and cassette manufacturers were consolidated. Milestones for market share, manufacturing and distribution, return on sales, and inventory management were established.

Some resistance to and suspicion of the perceived outsider was encountered. "Yeah, there was some resistance because I hadn't grown up in the music business, so I wouldn't be successful," Fifield said. "And, of course, there were a lot of typical press things about how could someone who's worked at a straight-arrow company like General Mills know anything about the music business. But that didn't bother me, because I happen to know a lot about how to run a business, and how to run a global business, and that's what this is. It's not my job, obviously, to sign bands or to call on radio or develop marketing plans. But my job is to ensure that those things get done and provide leadership and strategic focus and direction. That's what I do."

Despite being perceived as the epitome of the corporate suit, Fifield feels that any lamentations about corporate practices and rigidity versus the good old days are misguided.

"It's just more sophisticated," he said. "But so is the automotive industry. So is the computer industry. The world is more sophisticated, more complicated. We have more resources. We have more information. Things were seat-of-the-pants because that was all that was available. This business, in my opinion, has been slow in responding to the more professional management techniques that exist in other industries which are equally as creative. It's hard to imagine that SoundScan [a computerized method to track chart sales] has just come to this industry three years ago, when it's a $10 billion industry. Now [companies] look at their inventories, they

EMI Music president and CEO Jim Fifield was one of the new breed of record executives, a man whose business background was not primarily in music. (EMI Music)

Songwriter, publisher, record executive, cigar connoisseur— no one understood the game better than Charles Koppelman. (EMI Music)

Wilson Phillips celebrating gold status for their debut album. Four years later, the group dissolved. *Left to right:* Wendy Wilson, Carnie Wilson, Charles Koppelman, Chynna Phillips. (EMI Music)

U2's Bono catches up with his boss, PolyGram CEO Alain Levy. U2 was the act that kept Levy's financial house of cards afloat in the first years after PolyGram's purchase of Island Records. (Polygram Music)

The highlight of the Milgrim-Smith era at EMI: Bonnie Raitt takes home four Grammys. *Left to right:* Capitol-EMI president and CEO Joe Smith; Hale Milgrim, president of Capitol Records; artists BeBe Winans, Bonnie Raitt, and CeCe Winans; Russ Back, CEMA Distribution president; and Jim Fifield, EMI Music president and CEO. (EMI Music)

Vanilla Ice, missing the point once again. *Left to right:* Vanilla Ice, SBK president Charles Koppelman, sales head Bob Cahill, promotion man Ken Lane, and head of promotion Daniel Glass. (EMI Music)

The man who signed Nirvana when he was a Geffen Records A&R man, Capitol Records president and CEO Gary Gersh had the unenviable task of following one of the music industry's most beloved executives, Hale Milgrim. (EMI Music)

One of the high points of Bertelsmann's U.S. tenure, as the senior executives celebrate the chart success of Clint Black. Country music would be the bright spot on Bertelsmann's horizon for years to come, eclipsing its lackluster pop side. *Left to right:* Bertelsmann Music Group chairman Michael Dornemann, RCA Nashville president Joe Galante, artist Clint Black, and RCA Records president Bob Buziak. (Bertelsmann Music Group)

The senior brain trust of Warner Music before politics took precedence over music. *Left to right:* Warner U.S. CEO Doug Morris; Time Warner chairman Gerald Levin; Warner Music chairman Robert Morgado; Atlantic Records chairman Ahmet Ertegun; artist Laura Branigan. (Warner Music Group)

aniel Glass was the promotion man behind SBK Records' initial success nd later graduated to president and CEO of EMI Records Group North America. He and his staff were known for their sharp suits. (EMI Music)

Florida attorney Jack Thompson threatened to bring racketeering lawsuits against the record industry for selling The 2 Live Crew, whose lyrics Thompson deemed harmful to minors. (Courtesy Jack Thompson)

Madonna's business instincts made her one of the few artists to successfully start a record company in the 1990s. Her Maverick Records produced hits by Candelbox and Alanis Morrisette. *Left to right:* Warner Music chairman Robert Morgado, Madonna, Warner Bros. Records chairman Mo Ostin. (Warner Music Group)

rrested Development's intellectual and compelling music lifted it to heights few
roups ever attain. The group's leader, Speech, is shown with South African president
elson Mandela. (EMI Music)

Artist George Michael
mpares hair with Sony
Music CEO and Mariah
Carey husband Tommy
Mottola before the big
fallout over an alleged
sexual slur by another
Sony executive.
(Sony Music)

EMI Records president Sal Licata with Richard Marx, before Marx's manager, Allen Kovac, pulled his artist from the EMI roster in a dispute. Marx and oth Kovac-controlled artists generated an estimated $60 million for EMI Record (EMI Music)

Atlantic's big push for avant garde singer Tori Amos raised eyebrows throughout the industry. *Left to right:* Jason Flom, senior vice president A&R; Doug Morris, Warner Music CEO; artist Tori Amos; Robert Morgado, Warner Music chairman. (Warner Music Group)

know exactly where they sit. It's no longer done with mirrors and B.S. But they were resistant. It was insane."

Fifield was also appalled at the artistic state of the company he had inherited. "Obviously what's been wrong with EMI Music for let's say twenty years has been weak—relatively weak—Anglo-American and British music [signings]. If you looked at the percent of the market that English accounts for globally and if you compared it to how much it accounts for the music that EMI had in 1988, you would have found that there's a weakness there."

In essence, Fifield admitted, the entire company was being carried by the back catalog generated by the Beatles, Beach Boys, and other relics. "All we had in North America at the time was Capitol Records. Capitol Records hadn't had a hit of major substance for the last decade."

The mission was clear: beef up Capitol Records and EMI U.K. while looking for acquisitions or joint ventures to put through the distribution machine, which, according to Fifield, was running at 70 percent capacity. "The same was true in the publishing business. I thought, wow, here's a tremendous equity, highly profitable, a totally fragmented industry—nobody has more than a 10 percent share— and I said we should be really aggressively pursuing acquisitions in the publishing field."

Thus was born the idea to acquire SBK Music Publishing. "I made a smart move there," Fifield crows. But as part of the deal, he did a joint venture to create the SBK Records label. "They felt that they wanted to continue to be in the recorded music side. So I made a joint venture with them, which at the time no one had ever done. No one had ever put down a line of credit against a few entrepreneurs to go out and sign bands and run them through the system. I did that."

SBK was only the start. Deals with Enigma, IRS Records, and Chrysalis followed, while expansion in Nashville came with the hiring of legendary country music executive Jimmy Bowen, who brought the roster of his Universal Records label to what was then called Capitol/Nashville.

"I passed on a few opportunities, such as Island," Fifield continued, "but I was thinking all the time, just get a number of feeders into the system. Mainly pop music. And then later on in this whole process, we started doing production deals in the black music area, and then I got involved just lately here in the Christian music business with the acquisition of Sparrow. At the same time, I was closing cassette plants, consolidating, getting out of the vinyl business and beefing up substantially my CD capacity. We probably went from 50 percent in-house [EMI manufactured] to about 100 percent in-house today." Fifield was also opening in new markets like eastern Europe and Asia.

While Fifield was dealing in those new markets, he was battling prejudice against the American way of business within his own company. "Everybody, of course, was afraid to death in EMI that I was going to totally Anglicize it. They think here's an American who doesn't come from this great EMI buracracy and he's making all these U.S. deals. He's going to just tell us to do nothing but sell Paul McCartney and Iron Maiden and won't understand our local needs."

But the grand prize awaited. As Ahab had his great white whale, so Fifield had Virgin Records.

Virgin Records founder Richard Branson was born on July 18, 1950. He quit his academic career at age sixteen and proceeded to make his first million one year later by publishing a national magazine, *Student*, that sold 50,000 copies in its first issue on the strength of its stable of prominent authors, all of whom had been cajoled by Branson's brashness into contributing.

Ever the entrepreneur, Branson founded Virgin in 1970 as a mail-order discount record operation, which soon mushroomed into a retail chain. The logical next step was a record label, leading to Virgin Records' 1973 debut with the signing of its first artist, Mike Oldfield.

Like Branson's magazine, the recording company became an immediate hit. Oldfield's "Tubular Bells" was the theme song for that year's hottest movie, *The Exorcist*, and went on sell over 5 million copies, laying a nice foundation for Branson's other ventures, which included the 1982 purchase of Necker Island, a seventy-four-acre land mass in the British Virgin Islands, and the 1984 launch of Virgin Atlantic Airways.

As might be expected, Virgin Records was, by all accounts, a fun and rebellious place to work in its early years. The company was on the cutting edge for most of the pop trends of the moment, particularly when it signed the Queen-hating Sex Pistols in 1977 after both EMI and A&M decided the act was too controversial.

Virgin Records originally tried to enter the U.S. market in the early '80s, but the underfunded effort didn't succeed. Returning exclusively to the overseas market, Branson briefly took his Virgin Group public in 1986. However, the fluctuations of the record market perhaps scared investors, leading the company stock to drop as low as £1.45 in pound sterling from its original price of £1.70.

The October 1987 stock market crash led the Virgin Group to return to private hands, with Branson and his management buying the outstanding 37 percent held by institutions and small investors for an estimated $150 million in U.S. funds in January 1989, a price that pegged the overall company's worth at around $414 million. Company employees and Virgin artists Peter Gabriel, Steve Winwood, and Phil Collins were among the beneficiaries. Branson later that year raised some cash when he sold a 25 percent stake in the record company to Japan's Fujisankei for $150 million.

Had the stock market not crashed in 1987, record industry history might have taken a different turn. Branson and several unnamed partners had gathered cash and began buying Thorn EMI shares, "with the idea of making a bid for Thorn EMI and then selling everything else off except for their record division," Branson said. "And then the October 1987 crash took place, which sent the shares plummeting and we backed off it."

Virgin began its new U.S. operation in 1987 with a staff of thirty-five, a number that doubled in a year, and established its first Japanese subsidiary, giving Virgin true worldwide coverage for the first time.

The Virgin Records U.S. division was serious about spending money, as the company quickly established its own black music division; Virgin Classics, a classical music arm; Virgin Movie Music for soundtracks; Earthworks, a Third World/ethnic music label; and Virgin Video Music, a home video division. The new U.S. operation was distributed through the industry leader, WEA.

Jordan Harris and Jeff Ayeroff, who worked at A&M Records, were tapped to be managing directors at the new label. Cutting Crew's "I Just Died In Your Arms" was Virgin's first No. 1 record stateside, although the massive amounts of promotion used to pump up Virgin's domestic profile and its habit of outbidding the competition for available talent left the company's U.S. division mostly in the red. However, from outside appearances, the company looked solid, boasting a roster that ran from veterans Steve Winwood, Keith Richards, Roy Orbison, and Warren Zevon through such relative unknowns as Danny Wilson, Deja, Pretty Poison, and Camper Van Beethoven.

Through it all, purchase offers for the label continued, at least one or two a year, according to Branson. "We get courted occasionally and are pleased by the attention and fuss," said one typically cheeky Branson press release on the topic. "However, we find it far more fun to be flirting with new boyfriends than actually getting married." A standard line issued by spokesmen indicated that the company had received a number of unsolicited offers during its lifespan, but all had been rejected.

When Branson started shopping the label, the stated reason in the press was that he wanted money for the airline, which was involved in an acrimonious legal battle with British Airways, which was, in Branson's words, "doing everything they could to try to put our airline out of business. There was an element of me that just wanted to flick a V sign at the enemy and say, 'Look, you don't realize it, but we've got a billion dollars there which we can use. So why don't you just give up, because with that billion dollars in the bank, it's unlikely that you're going to succeed.'"

Branson admits, however, that he had some disenchantment with what the record industry had become.

"I mean, it had changed in the twenty years since we started," he said. "It had become sort of a more lawyer-oriented industry and had begun to become a bit more like big business, whereas when we started twenty years before, I think there was a little more fun."

Branson, interviewed during a whirlwind visit to New York City in May, 1994 to open his second U.S. Virgin Megastore, had the perfect example of what he meant. "Today I was at a record company [referring to Bertelsmann Music Group, whose headquarters housed his store] which was just like being in a mausoleum, you know, massive marble corridors and it just felt very cold. And obviously, I think, in one sense, it was sad that Chrysalis and Virgin and Island and A&M and Geffen and other independent record labels sold. On the other hand, nothing is forever, and we'd all reached our forties, and I think the best record companies are the ones which are run by hungry eighteen-, nineteen-, twenty-, twenty-one-, twenty-two-year-olds."

Bertelsmann Music Group, EMI, and MCA were the Virgin suitors. All were deep-pocket corporations, but Branson was interested in more than cash.

"The most important thing from my point of view is that Virgin stay independent, that Ken Berry, who'd worked with me since we were eighteen years old, become the chairman," said Branson. "And obviously, that the name of course be protected and the logo be protected and so on. Thorn has honored that."

The key for Thorn was market share. But, as Branson notes, "Virgin is a name which attracts artists, which perhaps even more so than Thorn, they have a track record of attracting artists and then breaking artists."

Branson retained a Goldman-Sachs representative to front the negotiations. First to drop out of the picture was Bertelsmann, "because they thought the price was too high," Branson said.

Actually, Bertelsmann claimed, it was never really in the game.

"Officially we were never in, in a way, because we were not represented by an investment banker," said BMG chairman Michael Dornemann. "We didn't talk to their investment bankers. Unofficially, we were informed, of course, and the point was that we were always clear about what we wanted to pay for it. We were always there for Richard Branson as a backup system. But he was in negotiations only with EMI because it was probably very clear to him that this was a company that was willing to pay more." Branson estimated BMG's offer at about $700 million.

Whatever the case, the stakes were down to MCA and Thorn EMI. "David Geffen [who had sold Geffen Records to MCA a few years previous] went to Japan to try to persuade the Japanese to put the money up to do the acquisition and failed to persuade them," Branson said. He accused Geffen of attempting to undermine his sale. "Instead of ringing me up and saying it failed, he woke up somebody from Thorn EMI at two in the morning and told them that he'd pulled out. If you are negotiating to sell the company for a billion dollars and the only other people bidding have pulled out, there's quite a strong possibility the price would collapse.

"As it was," Branson continued, "Thorn EMI did not trust David Geffen and thought that he was just trying to pull the wool over their eyes. They'd had dealings with David before where, for some reason or another, they didn't feel they could trust him, I think over the sale of his own record company." (In fact, Geffen had been set to sell his company to Thorn before MCA and was so close that Thorn EMI employees were readying welcome banners. The *Wall Street Journal* had in fact, written that Geffen was going there before MCA announced the deal.)

"So all it did was make them all the more determined to do the deal quickly," Branson said, "because they assumed that Geffen was trying to put them off the scent. And so as far as getting the right price, we were obviously very relieved that Geffen's reputation went against him."

A published report suggests a last-minute approach by BMG to Virgin's 25 percent owner, Fujisankei, for a joint venture to acquire Virgin. Fujisankei passed, the Japanese firm nervous that Thorn EMI might walk—or possibly run—away.

Thus, at two-thirty in the morning on March 6, lawyers at the Virgin attorneys offices in London concluded the deal. Later that morning, Branson told the press and his employees.

The $872 million price was shocking. The big independent record companies that had already gone on the block—Geffen,

Island, A&M—sold for much lower prices than did Virgin. The figure was additionally surprising because, as Branson admitted, Virgin had never made a profit in the United States, the world's largest market, and had lost money overall in the year it was sold to Thorn.

"But it was very much heading in the right direction," Branson said. "People like Lenny Kravitz and Janet Jackson and others were on the verge of turning it around, and it's now very much turned around and very profitable. I think the commentators got it wrong. As often happens, at the time they didn't fully understand the real value of copyrights and the kinds of bands we had, and the fact that some of our bands have lasted for twenty years and they're likely to carry on lasting for another ten, fifteen years."

Branson received roughly 60 percent of the purchase price, with executive officers Ken Berry (later to become a key player at EMI as its first official head of international) and Simon Draper garnering 5 percent and 10 percent, respectively. Fujisankei went home happy with $205 million for its 25.01 percent stake in Virgin, a nice increase over its $150 million investment.

For its money, EMI got five core labels of the Virgin Music Group: Virgin, Charisma, Cardiac, Virgin Classics, and 10 Circa. The music publishing operation and three U.K. recording studios were included. The roster boasted the Rolling Stones (who had signed a somewhat pricey deal months before, rumored at $35 million to $40 million, but which included catalog), Janet Jackson, Paula Abdul, Right Said Fred, Maxi Priest, UB40, Lenny Kravitz, Cracker, Simple Minds, and, in certain territories, Phil Collins and Genesis.

Despite the difference in their wagers, Fifield was as confident as a two-dollar punter at the racetrack. "When I did it, everyone kind of looked at it, like, what is he doing? But I knew exactly what I was doing. I mean, to me, it made total sense. And I explained to anyone who wanted to know how I could pay what I paid because of what I thought I could earn. Not just through Virgin, but through EMI owning Virgin, which is a different combination."

There are two bets being placed when purchasing such a company. One involves predicting that the record company will keep returning somewhat near the same sales as it did for a benchmark year and taking a derivative to figure your earnings, and then seeing if that sum provides you with a fair return on investment. Then comes the hard, cold business facts: What assets do you already have in your system, and how many of those functions can be eliminated in the new company, producing a cost savings with, you hope, the same returns?

Fifield estimated that Virgin's costs could be met by a 40 percent savings from internal synergies, with 60 percent met by sales from Virgin Records. "The way that I came up with that estimate was looking at what they were paying for distribution, what they were paying for the manufacture of CDs and cassettes, what they were paying for outside services and packaging, labeling, what we could consolidate to our warehouses and things like that. I knew what Virgin was paying for a CD and I knew what I could charge them for a CD, which was lower, and I also knew what my margin would be on that CD itself."

The early returns on Fifield's investment made him look like a genius. Virgin Music Group had its best year ever, turning revenues of $390 million and operating profits of $82 million for ten months of EMI's 1992–1993 fiscal year. The boost lifted EMI worldwide sales and earnings to $2.3 billion, up 34 percent. Fifield, of course, as a senior executive, has stock options and profit incentives built into his contract. As for his Virgin acquisition, he said, "I got all the benefits I was hoping for," a comment that can be taken two ways, given his financial interests.

About 155 Virgin employees at Virgin's U.S. operations found that their positions were being eliminated as a result of the synergies. Charisma and Cardiac Records were shuttered, as the company admitted that Virgin had lost more than $20 million in fiscal 1991.

The brilliance of Thorn's acquisition was a strategy similar to PolyGram's deal to snare Island. A stock issue was scheduled to raise the $872 million, offering 81.3 million units of convertible unsecured stock, payable in two installments. When fully paid, the stock was convertible to ordinary Thorn EMI shares.

But, as Fifield himself admits, "It takes ten years for a deal to prove itself."

* * *

The fact that BMG passed on Virgin came as no surprise to the record community. The German company had made a habit of sniffing at bait and then declining to bite.

In 1959, Bertelsmann founded a music company in Germany called Ariola. The establishment "was part of a general diversification," acccording to Michael Dornemann, chairman of Bertelsmann Music Group. "Our club business, which is our core business, wanted to go into the music business, and we had trouble getting licenses from the other music companies. That was the original idea. And it grew quite fast."

In the 1970s, Bertelsmann joined the U.S. market by establishing Arista Records with Clive Davis. The results were not an immediate smash. "It was the right strategic move, but it came at a very difficult time, the recession at the beginning of the '80s, and all the businesses went down."

At that point, Bertelsmann decided that it had to make a commitment to enter the U.S. market in a bigger way.

"That was a difficult decision," Dornemann said. "The options we had were either to buy something—it was impossible to buy into a major—or to joint venture. The company that was available at that time was RCA Records. And we were very happy to have at least a platform now to be a major player, a weak one at that point, quite a weak one, because RCA was not so strong. But together with us we improved that platform and so we were at least a player with a good starting position, but not a very strong competitive position at that time."

Owning only 25 percent of the company, Bertelsmann was a minority shareholder in RCA. A contractual provision allowed it the right of first refusal if the remaining shares changed hands. Two years after Bertelsmann bought in, General Electric became the owners of RCA Corp. The contract kicked in, and Bertelsmann bought the other 75 percent of the label plus the club business, which they had no previous stake in, for $330 million.

"From that point forward, we as a company wanted the music area to develop as the top of our entertainment strategy," Dornemann said. "The company was growing very fast. We were in the magazine business, in the club business, in book publishing, and so we said we want to be in the record business and we want to be in the United States."

Within a year to a year and a half after buying RCA, according to Dornemann's estimate, the company was in profits. "The growth is still going on," Dornemann claimed in 1994. "We are now, for the first time, in a market share situation around 14 percent in the United States and 15 percent worldwide, compared with 8 percent when we started."

Currently, Bertelsmann is looking to further expand its reach into entertainment, possibly into film, and definitely into multimedia. "In the movie business," Dornemann said, "we are more or less still in the research approach, because it's very difficult to enter except to decide to spend big, which we think is not the right way, because the returns are not very good on that."

Dornemann seemed almost nostalgic as he explained the company's reluctance to deal.

"I would have liked to acquire," Dornemann said. "When you look worldwide at our distribution, we usually had most of the labels, because we're very good in our infrastructure and distribution. We had [the international distribution rights to] Chrysalis, Island, A&M, Virgin."

However, the Bertelsmann insistence on adequate return on investment was in the way. Moreover, Dornemann questioned how anyone could pay the prices they were paying for record labels.

"We calculate in a way that when you pay a price for a company, that you have to do it compared to what you would get if you put your money in the bank. I mean, this is a normal way of looking at attractive opportunities. So it has to pay interest, it has to be amortized, and it has to bring profits. And I don't see on these high prices how this could work out."

Time Warner also did not see the wisdom in rolling the dice for one of the available independent record labels during the 1980s, Dornemann pointed out. "It was other companies that bought it, who probably needed it for their strategic reasons. People say we needed them; that might be true, but I don't see it that way. I saw the option and chose to use our money for inside growth."

To that end, Dornemann established Zoo Entertainment in Los Angeles and Imago in New York and bought Jive Records. He also purchased smaller labels like Private Music and Windham Hill, companies best known for new age music by artists like Yanni and George Winston. Dornemann said that the core labels—in this case, Zoo, Imago, and Jive—"should be really big labels, full-service labels, inside the company, hopefully, or ones you have a very long-term relationship with, that generate product for the whole world."

"Everybody looks for market share," Dornemann said. "It's true for us as well. Buying is a very safe way to gain market share. But because it's so safe, you pay so much. We, as a private company, have a simple approach to pay for [potential market share]: Buy it and pay for it. We made our decision from our point of view and our calculation. Whatever other people say about it, conservative or not, I have seen nothing that would cause us to make the decision differently at the point in time where it had to be made."

One record company looks at a purchase and sees a smart business move, another sees folly. Yet one manages to pull the trigger and the other stands pat.

A veteran record industry accountant, asking for anonymity, said he is perplexed about how EMI will pay for its purchases.

"EMI seems to have paid any price, but they have methods of accommodating that. I have a feeling I'm about to say something that could get me killed, but EMI's method is to pay the top price and then pay for it out of other people's royalties that they are then slow or reluctant to pay out at all, and I just make that comment out of what I've seen in dealing with Capitol and EMI over the years from a royalty auditing point of view. They seem to be everybody's first choice as the biggest culprits in not paying royalties.

The accountant compared EMI's management of its royalty system to passive-aggressive behavior brought on by understaffing. "They [claim] they just don't have the manpower to handle all the details involved in putting together a complete and correct royalty statement, so a lot of money ends up being left off the statement and therefore not paid out."

Thorn EMI also came in for its lumps when its claims of financial success were examined by the veteran industry accountant. "Paying these big prices and then at the same time reporting record profit—I could go out and buy a billion dollar company with debt and make a hundred million dollars and say, 'I just made $100 million.' But I'm still $900 million in the hole."

Virgin Records, in particular, looks like a Trojan horse. "Virgin was [rumored] to be throwing off about 24 million dollars a year in cash flow," said the accountant, "and the interest on the debt [incurred by EMI in its purchase] was something like $65 million. The objective is to have this stuff pay for itself—I think."

Fifield explained that his strategy to obtain a certain return on investment is based on forecasts of what that company's going to be doing going forward, say, for the next ten years. The forecast compares projections of how the market will grow with the company's performance, factoring in costs of operation and manufacturing. "You see what the sales potential could be if you achieve a certain market share against a market assumption."

Fifield correctly points out that certain functions that are duplicative or more costly for an independent label have to be factored into the equation, using a favorite corporate-speak term, "synergies." The synergies are not to be factored into what you will pay the company.

The earnings strength that comes from an acquisition over a long period of time is factored next. "You then present-value it," Fifield said. "You bring it all back to today and then you see what kind of return that will give you against the money you're putting out."

Bertelsmann did the same equation that Fifield did, presumably. "We do not pay prices where we do not believe we can get the return," Bertelsmann's Dornemann said.

Fifield admitted that it's a gamble, one that may show him to be the record industry's most prescient investor, or its most reckless.

"So the truth is that the jury's still out on every acquisition that's made," Fifield said. "The jury's out on Virgin, the jury's out on

Motown with PolyGram, the jury's still out on the acquisition of SBK Publishing. Because I made assumptions that ran out ten years. It just happens to be that the first couple years have been pretty good. But they could have been pretty bad. But the only time you really know is after a long period of time, because that's what all these acquisitions are made against."

Of course, as Fifield acknowledges, the assumptions are made against the most volatile of indicators—the fickle taste of the music-consuming public.

"In the short term, you look at the artists that are under contract, how many albums they have to go, so that you have some base in which to make a projection for the near term. The near term could be, let's say, five years. Besides, a company has a superstar with three albums firm, well, you know, three albums means you have seven years. You can go out with some assumptions."

Management is also factored in. "Because the management has to continue to sign new acts that make years five through ten work out." New earnings presents new problems, Fifield indicated. "You have to make sure they won't go off to the horse track or second homes, or whatever. That's why some deals are done with earnings, where you pay so much up front and then if you hit certain sales threshholds and profit threshholds, there would actually be bonuses paid for performance."

The biggest bet of all, though, is that the CEO will be around to collect on his bet, Fifield allowed. "I, too, have a banker. My board of directors [before approving a purchase], they're saying, "What's our confidence in Fifield? He says he wants to do it. What's his track record. Do we want to bet on what Jim wants to do?"

"But it always comes down in the end to how much are you paying and how much you're going to earn. What's your guess? And it's a guess. And, of course, the responsibility's on the CEO, in this case, Jim Fifield, because I'm making the bets. So now I have to make my bet pay off. Because I, too, have a banker, my board of directors. So when they say go ahead, I'm almost on an earn-out, because my credibility's at stake. I'm the one trying to make it work. And that's why there's no real one way to do anything."

While Fifield is adept at explaining the art of the deal, many of the industry's biggest deals perplex even its biggest dealers. Even David Geffen, who became one of the richest music industry entrepreneurs of all time when he sold Geffen Records to MCA for company stock, which soared upon its acquisition by Matsushita, takes issue with the prices being paid. Geffen was asked in a September 1994 interview by *Playboy* magazine about the film studios that have been sold; his reply could just as easily fit recording companies.

"They cannot be run in the same manner as manufacturing businesses," he said. "And often the prices are ridiculous. When Sony bought Columbia and Matsushita bought MCA, both overpaid tremendously. But the prices in the Paramount deal [which Viacom purchased for over $10 billion in 1994] now make those prices seem like bargains. It's all madness. And the chickens may come home to roost one day."

(Indeed. Matsushita, upon selling 80 percent of its stake in MCA to Canadian liquor magnate Edgar Bronfman in 1995, said it expected to write off $1.9 billion in foreign exchange losses, leading to a net loss for the entire company of $719 million for fiscal 1996. However, it's difficult to assess whether Matsushita made or lost money on its original $6.1 billion purchase in 1990 investment, because the company did not disclose how much additional investment was paid in or dividends taken out of the company. On its face, the $5.7 billion sale of 80 percent to Bronfman values MCA at $1 billion more than Matsushita originally paid.)

Geffen continued, "You don't have to buy companies to have access to software. Software is and always has been available. And the truth is, if Sony sold its software companies, Matsushita would probably sell its software companies, because the return on the investment in the movie and television business hasn't been great. They all talk about the synergy of owning it all, but the only synergy that has come out of these deals is a huge amount of debt and elephantine companies that are hard to manage."

Even the companies that make the purchases often aren't sure just what they've bought.

"I remember being in a meeting after Bertelsmann had owned the company for about two years," says a former executive at the German record giant. "I'm in a business meeting and talking about building the catalog, and [Bertelsmann Music Group] chairman Michael Dornemann says, 'I bought one of the biggest, best catalogs in the record business.' And I said, 'What, a lot of old Harry Belafonte records and Elvis? But you didn't buy any Billy Joel or Bruce Springsteen, the Rolling Stones or Pink Floyd records. You bought an old catalog. The catalog's not worth anything. The catalog does $25 million a year.' He was flabbergasted. He didn't know what he bought. That's a true story."

Even if the company does not understand what it bought, and even if it is not doing as well as it should, there are ways to disguise the matter.

"So what they do now is they run out these figures that they're doing $3 billion worldwide," says the former BMG executive. "But then if you read the Bertelsmann figures released by Bertelsmann in Europe to the financial papers, it says that the record division worldwide did 4.42 billion Deutschemarks, which is $2.5 billion. So they're selling one figure to the trades, and the real numbers Bertelsmann's reporting are lost in that."

The executive notes that EMI also raises questions with its financial statements to the trade press.

"Listen, I think that EMI calls it 'operating profits.' Which means what? Operating profit? Then what do you deduct? But EMI's got English bookkeeping. They do their whole system of issuing stock and writing off the goodwill and it's all razzle-dazzle stuff."

Another veteran record executive who worked for two major distributors calls the public financial face that record companies put on "smoke and mirrors," financial statements that do not break out results by division or highlight the contributions of catalog to the bottom line versus the contributions of new artists.

"MCA is a good example," says the veteran executive, noting that record-industry trade magazine Radio & Records had just named the company No. 1 for 1994. The assumption that MCA was the No. 1 record company of the year rang false to knowledgeable observers, who note that the company has been lagging in rock and pop music.

However, because the Radio & Records survey covered a large number of country music stations, a division that carries MCA, the label appeared to be stronger than it is.

"So MCA (reports) all these record-breaking years and everything, and the truth is, it's with country music and kind of with black music even with the black it's smoke and mirrors, because MCA's black music division hasn't broken a black act in eight to ten years. They had a "record-breaking" year by issuing tons of Chess reissues and Decca reissues and Jimi Hendrix reissues, a banner year in country and some success from Uptown Records (a joint venture with MCA, but separately operated) and one or two soundtracks." Thus, the trumpeted "success" is built on a foundation that is, by music industry standards, rather shaky, filled with records that have short-term impact.

The point of using the smoke-and-mirrors tactics for financial reporting, according to the executive, is to attract up-and-coming artists, who look for hot labels to sign with. "And it's a crime for that talent," said the executive, "because there's no chance [for success within an unsuccessful management umbrella]."

One expert, a record company executive with experience ranging from chairman to branch salesman, outlined the real bottom line in determining what a record company is worth.

"Let's say that PolyGram had a three-year deal with A&M. They'd probably have to advance them $25 million a year. You're trying to build a distribution system, so what you need is clout in the market. You need a constant flow of product to be a real player. You need the kind of product flow that an A&M has. Okay? And for every record they sell, you get a 14 percent distribution fee for your distribution company. So that's a contribution to that distribution company over a buck a record, average. So it's $1.25 or something a record."

Once the distribution system is accounted for, the company can also feed its manufacturing system, which also needs to be constantly running, according to the executive. CD manufacturing companies, which churn out discs that cost 50 cents to manufacture and can be sold for much more, are extremely profitable.

"And if you have one, you can start making CD-ROM, and that becomes profitable," adds the executive. "So you've got a contribution there. Then you've got your overseas businesses that you're putting product into, and not having to pay the advance. You are corraling this product as well for your international business, which makes it stronger."

The debt service on the $500 million purchase of an A&M Records is "about $50 million a year" by the executive's estimate. "And that's high end. Maybe for a European company it's 8 percent. What do we have to do to justify that $50 million for the debt service? Not a lot. And as we grow and the asset value grows, somehow the $500 million—maybe the profits from an A&M, where they had a good year, maybe the profits start to reduce down that debt, the asset value of the company continues to go up.

"All of a sudden, you say, if you have the $500 million, or you can get it easily, it's a good deal."

Even if the company has a bad year with its new artists, the catalog, use of the master recordings in various ways, and the potential contributions from new technology must be factored into the financial picture. "You're talking about a finite number of record companies that are available to buy," the executive concludes. "If you're aggressive and you're a player and you're looking to build your business bigger and bigger, I don't know what other choice you have."

But if there's no catalog, no long-term artist development, you spend more on marketing to create hits than the sales generate, and you have a company that is owned by a parent corporation better known for divesting its media properties than building on its synergies, thus obviating the potential contributions from new technology—then you have SBK Records, one of the most incredible stories of the modern record age.

FIVE

INSTANT HEAT

Chynna Phillips, one of three members of Wilson Phillips, was running down the hall of the hotel. The high-strung songstress was in the middle of her first tour and was having a bit of trouble handling the pressure.

"This is not reality! This is not reality!" she shrieked.

It was not reality. But it was a good reflection on the wild and woolly way SBK Records took unknown acts with little credibility and blew them up to astronomical heights.

A small but significant part of the sale of SBK Publishing's acquisition by Thorn EMI was the startup in June 1989 of SBK Records, a record label deal that would be financed jointly through EMI Music and the partners.

At the time, it looked as if EMI were buying genius. After all, who but Koppelman and Bandier would have predicted that an obscure black folksinger like Tracy Chapman would go on to platinum status, as she did when her Elektra Records debut was released via in a production deal with SBK? And after all, Koppelman was the man behind the Lovin' Spoonful, Barbra Streisand, Dolly Parton...the names kept tripping off the tongue, and what better way to exploit that executive talent than to set it up in its own deal?

Stephen Swid, who had acted as a governor on the funds spent during SBK's days as a production company, was out of the label by midyear, having had a falling out with his partners over some undisclosed financial matter. (The joke at the time was that SBK now stood for "Simply Bandier and Koppelman.) But already Swid had seen signs of the free-spending days to come when he oversaw the production budgets before the official SBK label was up and running.

"I mean, my chief financial officer said, 'You know, promotions in dollars are extraordinary.' I mean, we were lucky because Tracy Chapman was covering all the ills. That's what happens in a record company. You make ten bad decisions and one extraordinary decision. Her first album sold two and a half million by the time I left the company. Extraordinary. And so it covered all the other ills."

Swid noted, however, that a strong financial guide is needed to ensure profitability. "Warner always had a strong financial hand and when they don't—they let a guy like [Elektra chairman] Bob Krasnow get caught up in the milieu of spending the money and so on and so forth—you see what happens. The expenses outrun the revenues. And Koppelman doesn't know how to control those expenses. 'Put another $250,000 behind Tracy Chapman because it's on the move.' You know what I mean? That's not his strength. He has other strengths. And if EMI lets him do whatever he does, it's possible—without putting the controls in that I was able to put in—it's possible for someone like him to do $80 million and not earn any money."

Marty Bandier put it succinctly: "Our philosophy was to have a small number of artists that we believed in quite heavily and to spend whatever we could in terms of development money, marketing money, and promotion money to let the world decide whether this was something that was a hit or not."

At its birth, SBK Records was structured as a joint venture. The partners would put up 50 percent, and EMI would fund the rest. At a later date, EMI would have the option to purchase the remaining half, based on a multiple of sales and profits, according to Fifield and Koppelman. "We knew at the end of the day they were going to end up buying," Koppelman said.

In any event, little did EMI know that it had signed a deal that would be looked upon later by many in the industry as a monumental mistake.

In many ways, SBK Records became the record industry equivalent of a Ponzi scheme, ironically also invented by a man named Charles. In that case, Charles Ponzi paid off early investors in his investment plan with monies put up by later ones in order to encourage a bigger investment by the latecomers.

SBK, in a sense, used the same approach: build up the company to enormous heights, give the impression of success, however fleeting, pump up the sales volume, and damn the costs. So what if long-term value isn't there? The name of the game in the modern record industry was the impression of success, and with six multinational corporate machines hungry for software that would increase market share, you'll be elsewhere long before the truth is discovered.

"When you build a record company from scratch, it would take at least ten years before you could really say that you built something that will, each year, earn a lot of money," Koppelman said. "When we started SBK Records, the whole point was to build assets and build the value of the company, albeit maybe not making a lot of money, because you can't. You're building infrastructure with new acts. So I didn't believe I was going to continue running SBK Records for ten years. My attention span is too short."

The circumstances for SBK's success were exactly right. The Top 40 radio world was perhaps at its peak, with several genres of music moving in and out of the spotlight. Artists as diverse as Guns N' Roses, Paula Abdul, and Milli Vanilli all had one thing in common: a strong song that fit neatly with radio and particularly with MTV.

After a lull in the mid-'80s, when government investigations into independent record promotion's possible ties to organized crime had curtailed major label use of their services, the industry habit of using indie promoters had returned. The independent promoters, an assortment of contracted salesmen adept at pushing product at radio, had again become such a force that they could virtually guarantee a decent amount of airplay at certain stations.

Both circumstances played neatly into the executive talents of Charles Koppelman. Who better than a veteran song man to take advantage of this situation? Koppelman, who had the instincts of P. T. Barnum when it came to promotion, had to know that the public hunger for pop music at that moment could be combined with huge promotion, resulting in (hopefully) at least one or two hits. If Koppelman created a buzz at the beginning of a recording's cycle, then projects would inevitably take on a life of their own, making SBK appear to be a giant whose momentum could not be stopped, at least in the minds of potential multinational purchasers for the label.

The Koppelman habit of extravagance was immediately apparent in the SBK office suites, among the most lavish in the industry. The luxury may not have been planned: Koppelman calls the decoration scheme "Swid's folly."

After the sale of SBK Entertainment World to EMI, Swid allegedly demanded the company move into upscale offices. Koppelman claims Swid told him, "I don't want to come to work in a place that doesn't look like an art gallery." But Swid, according to Koppelman, wildly overspent on the office, exceeding his $2.5 million budget by almost four times that amount.

"It all looked to me like the music equivalent of the Museum of Modern Art," said one veteran record industry executive who frequently visited the offices, located at 1290 Avenue of the Americas. "Black scissors with matching staplers, the whole thing. They were absolutely throwing money around insanely. They also had the most amazing screening room, rivaling anything the studios would have, a giant screen and probably seating as many thirty people."

Senior executives had massive offices with their own bathrooms and kitchens—perks unusual for established record companies, let alone startups.

The SBK offices, which took up a whole floor of EMI's Manhattan skyscraper headquarters, were also decorated with walls and walls of gold and platinum records from Koppelman's career.

But the design of the offices was not the only thing that looked sharp. Certain SBK executives were also required to look the part. "They were paying promotion men outrageous salaries, and I heard they were taken to stores and bought up to eight really expensive

Italian suits that the company paid for," said the veteran record executive. "They wanted all their executives and everything about the company to look like class."

Class was needed, because the early going of SBK wasn't full of artistic greatness. The roster included such forgettables as Darryl Tookes, Katrina & the Waves, Scotland's Shine, Boogie Box High, Spunk-A-Delic, Wendy Wall, Will & the Bushmen, Gordon Grody, Everyday People, Icii Blue, and Herbert Groenemeyer, moving on to equally past tense Riff, Loud Sugar, Russ Irwin, and Red House in its later years.

The first "hit" was "Pump Up the Jam," a dance record by the group Technotronic, a quickie that took advantage of a public taste for dance music that was peaking at the time with hits by such phenomena as Milli Vanilli and Paula Abdul. Koppelman also struck gold, as he had so many times before, by riding the instant trend of the Teen-Age Mutant Ninja Turtles movie, managing to push that soundtrack to platinum status.

But his real genius was the discovery of a streetwise suburban white kid who soon would be dubbed "The Elvis of Rap" by the cognoscenti. Robert Van Winkle, a.k.a. Vanilla Ice, was about to emerge on the scene.

How Vanilla Ice was discovered is a matter of several different stories. A 1992 article in *GQ* has Koppelman listening to "Ice Ice Baby" over the telephone as it is being pitched by entertainment attorney Peter Lopez. "And then when I saw him [Ice, not Lopez], I said, 'Holy smokes. It was like the Russian from *Rocky IV* walked in. Maybe he is the hula hoop. We'll find out.'"

In a different version of events, Koppelman claims to have discovered the act while lounging around his pool at his estate in Rosalind Harbor on Long Island. "I was sitting there with a couple of my daughter's friends," he recalled. "I listened to 'Ice Ice Baby' twenty times at the pool that morning. Everyone there was saying, 'Stop listening to it already!' They were getting bored by it. And that afternoon I made a deal and committed $300,000 to it. Walked in the next morning and told our troops, get ready, this is going to be a landslide."

A third story has Koppelman contacted by Lopez, who was

disgruntled about a potential deal with Atlantic. Koppelman sent one of his field promotion men to a radio station that had a copy of the song and had the DJ play it for him over the phone. "The guy told me that as soon as it went on the radio, he got all kinds of phones," Koppelman told *Rolling Stone*. Asked later about the signing, Koppelman claims all three stories are correct and all refer to the same event.

Ice was not exactly an unknown performer at that point. An independently released album on manager Tommy Quon's own Ultrax label had moved 40,000 units, and Georgia radio, prompted by prominent independent record distributor Ichiban, had picked up on "Ice Ice Baby," leading other radio stations to leap onto the wagon. Ice was also the opening act at Quon's 2,000-seat club in Dallas, warming up for such national attractions as Tone Loc, Public Enemy, and Paula Abdul.

In any case, SBK leaped to sign Vanilla Ice, ordering remixes of all the tracks on his independent album. The label inserted a concert scene into the sequel to the *Teen-Age Mutant Ninja Turtles* movie to build some fan base for Ice among prepubescents, but the real momentum began when the throbbing bass line of "Ice Ice Baby," lifted from the David Bowie-penned, Queen-covered "Under Pressure," hit the radio waves.

Bandier was among those surprised by the almost instant success of "Ice Ice Baby." "It was one of those records that I don't know what it was. Everyone looked at it like, 'Wow! This is where rap ultimately takes us.' I think that was wrong, but ten million people had to buy the record to find out whether [the notion] was right or wrong."

Vanilla Ice's debut album, *To the Extreme*, released on September 10, 1990, was the fastest-selling album since Michael Jackson's *Thriller*. With momentum building as Ice toured as the opening act for M.C. Hammer, the year's other hot rapper, the disc sold 5 million units in the United States in its first 12 weeks, according to the Recording Industry Association of America, which awards sales certifications. "Ice Ice Baby" became the first rap single to reach No. 1 on the Billboard Hot 100 singles chart.

The album sold 4 million copies before the November 19 launch of its second single, "Play That Funky Music," an adaptation of Wild Cherry's 1976 hit.

SBK had played some smart business angles on the album as well, withdrawing "Ice Ice Baby" as a single shortly after it hit No. 1, forcing fans who wanted the song to buy the album.

However, all was not well within the Ice man's camp. Word circulated that he was not the street kid he made himself out to be. Ice claimed to have been stabbed five times one night and nearly died. "Lost half the blood in my body," he told *People* magazine, a medical miracle worthy of attention by itself if true. He also claimed to be a poor street kid who had won three pro motorcross titles and had attended the same Miami high school as 2 Live Crew leader Luther Campbell.

The other—and true—story is that Robert Van Winkle was an upper-middle-class kid from Texas who had won motorcross trophies on the amateur circuit. His mother, a music teacher and classical pianist, claimed in a *People* magazine interview that the lies were an attempt to protect his family.

An SBK executive said the company decided to put on a straight face and carry on with the campaign. "We were proceeding as if the claims were really true. It was, 'Yeah, he really did come from the streets.' But, to me, he seemed perfectly capable of behaving that way. He seemed like he came from the streets. I didn't think he was some genteel individual that an image had been created for. He seemed exactly what his bio presented him to be, and then some."

One thing they couldn't exaggerate was Vanilla Ice's very real arrogance. Recalled one publicist, "I was sent over to the house he was renting in the Hollywood Hills and there was a big photo shoot and an interview that was going to be happening with *People* magazine. I had never met this Vanilla Ice person before, and he had kept the journalists and the photographer waiting and waiting for a really long time. His flunkies would be going back and forth from his bedroom to me and saying, 'He'll be down in a minute,' and the photographer especially was getting very nervous, because he was losing daylight and he wanted to do the shoot outdoors."

The newly wealthy Ice was proud of his toys. "I remember in the middle of the interview process, Vanilla Ice came out and took me into his garage and showed me the new Ford Mustang 5.0 convertible he had and all of these other very expensive toys, a pair of jet skis and he had another car in there that was something very exotic. I was thinking to myself that he was going to spend it all. His next record was absolutely going to bomb. He was going to fade into oblivion. At the time he had it he acted like it was owed to him. He was very arrogant. Not too smart at all. But hey, who needs intelligence when you have just barrels of money."

Vanilla Ice's wild ride to glory ended rather quickly. Plagued by a backlash from the black community, who resented the new "Elvis" co-opting their style, a total lack of street credibility, and the growing perception that his primary appeal was to know-nothing pubescents, ice began to melt from public affection. The final dagger to his chances for hanging on as a children's entertainer came when Vanilla Ice was arrested after a report that he brandished a pistol in a North Hollywood supermarket parking lot.

SBK, perhaps sensing the end was near, rush-released *Extremely Live* in June 1991, notable for terrible studio and concert remakes of the Stones classic "Satisfaction," and four new cuts to go with live material that was extremely underwhelming. Trade reports indicated that SBK opened with a $500,000 promotional push, shipping 800,000 units. It undoubtedly received most of that allotment in returns.

A tried-and-true record industry formula to get people excited about a certain song is to get that song played incessantly on the radio. SBK relentlessly used the peculiar institution known as independent promotion to achieve that end.

Independent promotion is a system usually used to augment a record company's regular staff. It resembles an old-school fraternity in its buddy-boy backslapping and dealmaking, not to mention its trading of favors.

For a brief period in the 1980s, the practice was under severe scrutiny by the federal government, which believed several of its major players had ties to organized crime and were possibly part of a web of conspiracy that included money laundering and drug trafficking. The government's major thrust to invade the cloistered world came when it indicted independent promoter Joe Isgro, former Epic Records executive Ray Anderson, and Isgro associate Jeffrey Monka on over fifty counts, including payola allegations. The charges were later dismissed by a federal judge because the government allegedly withheld information from the defense, a flaw termed "extreme misconduct" in the dismissal.

Even with the shadow of a federal investigation and massive press scrutiny of their practices, independent promoters were just too valuable to record companies to allow them to forever fade from the scene. Thus, they returned in time to greet the emergence of SBK, a company that would do anything it took to break a song.

Radio wasn't the only target, of course. Many stations relied on retail sales in their markets as barometers of interest in a particular act. In the pre-SoundScan days, when record industry charts relied on retail clerks' estimates of what was selling, the system was easily compromised.

SBK took full advantage of the loopholes in the retail system, purchasing items on its own acts in key stores that would then report tremendous activity to *Billboard*'s charts and local radio stations, according to several former executives, although it should be added that SBK was not the only label in the industry using the practice. But it was spending money in a fashion that was, in the words of a former EMI executive, "legendary" in the music industry:

"The old system, you call the guy at one of the reporting stores and say 'How is Michael Jackson doing? How is Wilson Phillips doing this week?' And by going in and buying CDs, you could make the difference between it being reported Top 20 versus Top 10. You bring in the Top 10, it would have that impression of being a Top 10 album and then it would get more publicity and more attention and therefore more people would buy it because it was such a hot album. They wanted to see what they were missing."

The idea behind such wild spending was apparent to anyone, according to the executive. "It was hits at all costs. It was spend whatever it takes, make these acts big. They're not going to be so concerned with net profits as much as if they're able to capture market share out of the box. Significant market share, you can fix the rest of the company later. You can tone down the spending, whatever. You have already established a foothold. Hopefully, on the second Wilson Phillips or Vanilla Ice album, you won't have to spend as much as you did on the first one. You'll start seeing more return on your investment."

The goal, according to the executive, was equally apparent. "But for Charles, whose end goal seems to always be how much money can I make, it did really pay for him to pump up the profile of SBK and to have hits so he would look hot so that when he did eventually sell the rest of it to EMI, he would reap that much more money than if he had done the slow building sort of thing that could take years and years to really find long-term artists. He had no long-term artists in that plan. I mean, it was Technotronic, Wilson Phillips, Vanilla Ice, and the Ninja Turtles, with Wilson Phillips being the only one you could see maybe three albums down the line."

Koppelman denies that money was a factor in his incredible run of success out of the box. "One of the things that people said about SBK Records, we spent a fortune marketing and promoting our acts. Totally untrue. First, we spent very little money on Vanilla Ice. It just exploded. I mean, we couldn't get out of the way of it, quite honestly. On Wilson Phillips, we spent considerably less than any launching of any new artists during that period of time. What we were able to do at SBK is be very highly focused. We were working just one or two projects at a time. We would make a great news story and get a lot of free press. We hired independent promotion people when it was applicable. We paid the same thing as everybody else did. We'd send our people to visit radio the same way everybody else did. We just focused harder."

Former United Artists Records owner Artie Mogull was working as a consultant for SBK in its production company days when he had a lunch meeting one day with veteran record producer Richard Perry.

"He was trying to sell me Thelma Houston, and he casually

mentioned that he had made some demos with the Wilson Phillips girls. And I was very friendly with Marilyn Wilson, the mother of the two girls. I said, 'Let me hear it.' He sent the tape over and I went crazy."

Wilson Phillips had a great story behind it. The daughters of Beach Boys legend Brian Wilson had been teenage friends with Chynna Phillips, daughter of John Phillips of the Mamas and the Papas. Actually, the group had originally included another famous offspring, Owen Vanessa Elliot, daughter of late Mamas and the Papas vocalist Cass Elliott, who had hooked up with her cousin Chynna and developed the high-concept idea of a vocal group of '60s showbiz kids. Elliot was given the boot a few nights into the first session with Perry, ostensibly because her fourth vocal was akin to a fifth wheel when combined with those of the other three singers.

The group seemed a natural to Koppelman, so Mogull began to shop it around town. Capitol and Columbia were both interested. One notable mogul was not.

In the middle of the Wilson Phillips shopping spree, Perry went to work at Warner Bros. and took the act to legendary record man Mo Ostin. "The girls didn't like Mo," said Mogull. "They didn't hit it off. Mo didn't believe in this. Warner's has a reputation for having very hip artists. And I think he probably thought they were too square." Perry was fired as manager after that. He didn't walk away empty-handed, claiming a share of the song publishing that reportedly amounted to $210,000.

To Koppelman, however, the fresh, airy pop sound of three harmonizing females was something that a former songwriter could relate to, even though it flew in the face of most of the trends of the late '80s. Armed with a pet project—and half the publishing rights, acccording to Mogull—Koppelman set his promotion machine in motion.

"When Charles makes up his mind that something's going to be a hit, he'll spend anything," Mogull said. "All right? I mean, I get the credit for being the one who discovered Wilson Phillips. But in the hands of somebody else, I don't know that it would have happened. He made it happen."

A promotional video touting Wilson Phillips to radio and retail was the first volley of the campaign.

"It was unbelieveable," said a publicist who worked closely with the group. "It was like a little documentary. I have never seen anything like it."

Another campaign worker agrees. "The spending was extraordinary by any measure. When you have a new artist like that, first-class travel is something you don't do, and they were first class all the way. They spent more money on the setup of that record than anything I can remember. Expense was not an issue."

Pricey photography sessions, elaborate road trips to radio stations and trade conventions, and expensive videos for MTV were all part of the setup. Exhaustive and expensive promotion to radio's most powerful stations were made in several key markets, augmented with the usual retail purchases, then broadened throughout the country by heavy use of independent promotion. Daniel Glass later claimed that he modeled the radio station tour after one he had conducted for Huey Lewis at Chrysalis Records, the latter hugely successful.

"Originally with Wilson Phillips when it first came out, I think it peaked at 43 on the Billboard chart," said an SBK employee familiar with the strategy used in the early stages. "They figured out, 'We got a hit on our hands. We got to do something.' They took a few key cities like Miami and Chicago and they went out and they just promoted the hell out of radio. And then they went in and bought a couple hundred units in each city and said, 'Hey, look at the sales on this thing. You're playing it!' And it just kind of built out, and the next thing you know, they have three million copies sold."

The seamier side of the record business was in evidence during the project, at least according to one source at the company. "I really saw some unbelieveable things there. I mean, payola is a common accepted thing there. They paid off a music director's mortgage in Miami at some big station in exchange for making a record number one at the station. I mean, everyone does it, but they were just really blatant about it. I was surprised that they just didn't try to make it discreet. They were really open about it. You walk by someone's office and you hear like, 'Well, what's it going to cost me to get it on your station?'"

Wilson Phillips's eponymously titled debut, released April 14, 1990, sold five million copies, spawning the hit singles "Hold On," "Release Me," "Impulsive," and "You're in Love."

SBK was, according to several sources, spending an enormous amount of money per unit to break the act. However, with publishing rights and the girls signed to SBK Management, there were ancillary revenue streams to bolster the marketing attack.

Video shoots were a particular fountain of cash spending, according to the executive. "In terms of lavishness, it was incredible, with incredibly large quantities of very expensive clothes, vast makeup people, excellent directors, and big, big spreads of food."

"I always came away from those experiences with them feeling so depressed that I would end up going on $5,000 shopping sprees and redlining my checkbook and maxing out my credit cards," said one executive who worked with the group on the sets.

Despite their show business pedigrees, the Wilsons and Chynna Phillips were not taking all of it in stride. "I think they had a lot of problems handling fame," said one tour publicist. "They would just blow off major interviews because they couldn't deal with it." The girls soon gained a reputation as notoriously difficult, although Carnie was considered the best of the bunch, with Wendy the introvert and Chynna the Hollywood diva.

The first overseas tour was, by one executive's description, "in several ways disastrous. They were in Japan and they had some big falling out and the tour was basically unraveling and they were not selling shows very well in spite of the popularity of the record. They had to cancel shows and there was lots of backbiting. So much was going wrong that they cut the tour short."

The sugary, All-American girl image was something that was being carefully constructed for Wilson Phillips as well, in keeping with the wholesome sound and mainstream audience. Writers interviewing the group were instructed not to dig for information on Carnie and Wendy's father, Brian Wilson, the Beach Boy, whose bouts with drugs and dissolution had led him to abandon life for a sandbox in his bedroom until psychiatric care raised him again to a functioning level.

Wilson Phillips was also experiencing problems among themselves, and were known to throw fits at the slightest provocation. The pressures of the road were apparently not being assuaged by the boyfriends each of them took on the road, another fact that was kept discreet from the press, the better to preserve their wholesome image.

The initial press and performance tour was so stressful, according to a road publicist, that Carnie Wilson, already less than svelte at the beginning of the campaign, "gained forty to fifty pounds from the start of the project to the end of it."

Perhaps Wilson knew that she should enjoy the good times while they lasted. Five years after they were a smash, Wilson Phillips dissolved, its second album falling far short of its first.

While SBK could point to significant success on its four big artists—all of who had little credibility and a short shelf life—it also had its share of very expensive flops that sharply lowered the company bottom line. Most of the roster shows Koppelman's taste for pop singer songwriters.

Smokey Robinson stunned many in the industry when he departed his longtime home at Motown for SBK for a reported $1 million signing bonus. Perhaps SBK envisoned that Robinson would have a renaissance of his respected singing/songwriting career, casting off the staleness of the Las Vegas/Atlantic City/summer shed circuit in which he had been mired for years. Perhaps the public would embrace him as an elder statesman and rediscover his magic.

The public didn't

Francesca Beghe, a New York singer described as "the poor man's Tori Amos" by one executive who worked with her, was another major Koppelman pet. The strategy was to service her record to hair salons and clothing stores so that the captive audience would be subjected to her music and feel the need to play it in the comfort of their homes and automobiles.

They didn't.

Russ Irwin was another failed attempt. "They did lots and lots of cross-country promotion," said one publicist. "It went to radio, to radio, to radio, to retail, getting him out there in everybody's face because he was so incredibly visually appealing and the attitude at SBK was that when someone would meet him and fall under the spell of his charm—and he was charming—then it would stand to reason that they would be more inclined to give preferential treatment to his record."

They didn't.

"The attitude was these were career artists," said an SBK executive. "The party line was always that Charles was 10,000 percent behind the artist, and everyone else was expected to make it happen, no matter what."

Many of the artists were hand-picked by Koppelman, perhaps fulfilling his A&R fantasies. "On some level or another, they really captured the attention of Charles Koppelman, or of someone who was close to him whom he listened to. He was very much out and about on the New York music scene. He knew what was out there, and when he found an artist that he believed in, then it was an all-or-nothing proposition for him, for upper management at SBK, for middle management, and even for the assistants. Everyone right down to the guy in the mailroom."

At least, that was the surface appearance.

"Everybody, no matter what their real feelings were, it was 'Charles wants this to happen and it's going to happen.' But underneath it all, they really didn't have that much faith in what they were working. But nobody dared to speak up. It was the 'emperor's new clothes' syndrome."

Abbo (no last name, like Snoopy, Popeye, and Cher), owner of Big Cat Records and an artist manager for EMI acts EMF and Carter the Unstoppable Sex Machine, described the situation at EMI at the time as resembling "the ultimate corporate" label.

"They had no other interest in music other than what was shipped in units. That's what it seemed like from the outside." Abbo had started life in an English punk band and made no secret of his distaste for the suits at SBK. "We were at a point of our life where we were working with Pavement and Cop Shoot Cop—bands that all have such a great idea about what they want to do, and then to go and try to work with a company that had no belief in that sort of artistic involvement or integrity—they wanted to be involved in what type of venues you were playing. I remember sitting down with them here and having a conversation about the type of venues they wanted the band to be playing."

The venues suggested for Abbo's underground acts were ludicrous. "You wouldn't be playing these if you were a cabaret act," he said. "But they were the type of venues where you could pull up with a limo and take your chick out for the night and do that whole thing."

Worse, the music experts on the staff apparently hadn't a clue as to where the business was heading.

Abbo added, "I really can't name this person because I'd end up in a lawsuit, but there was one person there that we went in to with the Nirvana record *Nevermind* as it was just about to come out. Everywhere you went you were hearing that record, for the right reasons. And everybody knew this record and everybody's getting off on it. No one foresaw how big it was going to be. And we sat down the A&R guy and we said, 'All right. You've got to hear this.' And we played this record and the guy said, 'Well, it's tuneless. They've got no songs.' And they just had no idea, they couldn't make that type of musical judgment. It was sort of like playing someone [the seminal Beatles hit] 'Love Me Do,' and saying, 'This has a lot of pop potential.'"

Abbo's take is corroborated by an inside source.

"Their internal philosophy was it was quantity, not quality," says a former employee now running his own label. "I made a joke that they would put out a record of fart sounds if they knew they could sell eight million copies of it. They don't care. I mean, everything there is based on marketing and strategy. I mean, there were records that they put out that literally they had a market plan before they had the bands. 'This is how we're going to market it. Let's go find the band to fit this marketing plan.'

A band ironically called Mr. Reality was the prime example of that "instant band" plan. It was signed to SBK in the wake of Extreme's hit "More Than Words," which brought the concept of the power ballad to new commercial heights.

"So their idea was, 'Well, here's a [heavy metal-looking] band that does a ballad,'" says the former SBK employee. "'Every metal band seems to do really well commercially with a ballad. Let's find a band that looks like a heavy metal band but all they do is ballads. Figure we'll make ten times the amount of money.' And that was their philosophy. And they went out and found a band to fit that, long hair and tight jeans and cowboy boots, and they played ballads."

Although Mr. Reality was not a sensation, the executive insists that the pattern is mirrored in such SBK CD tie-ins as Barney the Dinosaur and the Teen-age Mutant Ninja Turtles, both marketing-driven rather than music-driven sensations.

No one knows why EMI Music decided to step in and purchase SBK when it did, which was earlier than contractually required. In retrospect, EMI may have been afraid to lose a company that appeared to be hot, with Fifield's inexperience in the record business blinding him to the reality that the long-term career potential of most of the roster was seriously in question.

Under the terms of its deal, EMI agreed to acquire the remaining 50 percent of the company from Koppelman and Bandier. The deal also included contractual ties that would keep Koppelman and Bandier working for EMI through 1995. Cash payments were tendered to SBK Record Productions Inc.

The first payment under the deal was $26 million, plus the return of Koppelman and Bandier's initial $5 million investment. But the big return still lay on the horizon: deferred considerations, or payments that could be made later, to be calculated on multiples of sales and profits achieved by SBK over the calendar years 1991–1993. Calculated on 1991 sales, the deal would eventually be worth $100 million, with a cap of $400 million.

Considering that Geffen Records sold for a multiple of 3.7 in sales, it's likely that Bandier and Koppelman easily saw their $100 million from the deal, and likely much more.

More amazing than that was EMI's confirmation in its purchase announcement of a longtime rumor: SBK, despite its mega-success and four platinum albums, had managed to spend more than it earned. According to EMI, SBK gross revenues exceeded $85 million during its first full financial year ended December 31, 1990. But EMI claimed "startup costs" led to a loss of $7.4 million.

The fig leaf offered stockholders: Services performed by EMI Music Worldwide under the 50/50 partnership provided net contributions in parent Thorn EMI's financial year to March 31, 1991, that "more than" offset Thorn EMI's share of the startup losses, according to a company statement. In other words, the profits to Thorn EMI's worldwide distribution and its manufacturing charges, plus unspecified "marketing margins" from representing the label worldwide, had made the balance sheet come clean.

Former partner Stephen Swid was among the skeptical. "It was unbelievable to do $85 million. What people said in the record business was, 'How can you do $85 million in your first year and lose money?' Record companies for decades don't do $85 million a year when you start a record company. But that's Charlie's way, to promote, promote, promote."

Swid, a financier who had made millions in deals, assessed the purchase of SBK. He found fault with Thorn EMI's acquisition strategy.

"[EMI chairman] Colin Southgate and Jim Fifield have made lots of mistakes. And what they do is they pay multiples of revenues and so you build up the revenues with Vanilla Ice and Wilson Phillips and Tracy Chapman, and then they disappear. But they're in the revenues that [EMI] had to count for, on average, five years. So was that a smart deal that [Fifield] negotiated to buy out? The answer is no. It was stupid. Plain stupid. The SBK Records deal was a ridiculous deal."

"I'll never undertand why [Fifield] bought it early," added Artie Mogull. "He had the option to wait until it came due. And he bought it when they were hot as a pistol."

One prominent music attorney agreed. "SBK might have just been good timing for Charles and maybe a mistake for Jim Fifield in terms of the timing. Because it looked like to Jim that they had developed some artists. They really didn't develop them. You know, [they were] one-hit wonders."

The real reason for the purchase boils down to a horse race, according to the attorney.

"No one wants to be sixth or fifth in the race, and there's a very fine margin between being second and being fifth or sixth. Certainly not much of a margin between third and sixth. So they're all competing for market share and they're having trouble developing their own A&R capacity, so the easy way to go ahead is buy labels and good executives. The hardest thing in business other than knowing which is a good artist is to find a good executive."

The attorney, who has done innumerable deals uniting labels with prospective buyers, was asked what ultimately could be the $400 million question, if SBK sales were strong enough to produce that payoff to Koppelman and Bandier: Was Koppelman smart enough to figure out that if he inflated the value of this company, nothing else mattered?

"Yeah."

But that was not the end of Koppelman's relationship with his rich uncle, Thorn EMI. He was about to assume an even larger role in the company's future direction.

EVERY MISTAKE IMAGINABLE

"Just after I had left SBK, they laid off like forty people," recalls one former employee who now runs his own independent record label. "But the next week, they could [install] a new antique Wurlitzer jukebox for the new conference room that they were building. And that's the kind of philosophy they had. It's really ridiculous. It's very much appearance oriented."

By early 1991, the bloom was off the SBK rose. Vanilla Ice was starting to feel the backlash and allegedly was trying to convince any streetwise producer who would talk to him that he indeed had a career, and would they please work with him.

Other outposts in the EMI Music empire were also troubled. Chrysalis Records was struggling, and EMI Records, although doing well financially, was not perceived as a serious contender by many in the music industry. More to the point, a noted bottom-line man like Fifield undoubtedly looked at the redundancies present in separate staffs for all three labels, an overhead that was not nearly justified by the volume of music sales. All of which led to rumors that the deck was going to be shuffled at some point, with SBK, Chrysalis, and EMI combined under one roof.

After months of rumors, things came to a head in mid-November. EMI Records chief Sal Licata was fired on November 15.

Shortly thereafter, a prepared statement issued on November 19 announced what the various staffs had anticipated: "I regret that the consolidation will mean reducing the number of people currently employed by the three labels."

Thorn EMI's profits had shown a 12 percent increase in the first half of the company's 1991–1992 fiscal year, which ends March 31, so the memo cited "duplication'" as the reason for the restructuring.

At the same time it was consolidating, EMI bought for $30 million plus assumption of debt the 50 percent of Chrysalis that it did not own. Under terms of the deal that label co-founder Chris Wright signed in 1989, he had the option of retaining his 50 percent share of Chrysalis for another seven and a half years. However, a few dry years had caught up with Wright, leaving him financially unable to continue.

EMI bought its original 50 percent share in Chrysalis for $79 million and could have paid out up to $25 million more to the label through 1993, depending on profit and volume growth. According to EMI, Chrysalis had, over the years 1990–1991, averaged annual worldwide revenues of $170 million. It was not enough, however, to keep the label functioning as it had been. As Koppelman liked to note, "It's not the money—it's the money." Thus, Chrysalis as the world had known it ceased to exist.

Wright remained head of Chrysalis Group and was expected to be given the title of non–executive chairman of Chrysalis Records, a lofty badge that meant little. He still had charge of television, music publishing, and other interests. But he refused to go quietly. "I'm a record man and will always be a record man," he said, almost defiantly. Two years later, he was forming his own independent record label, unhappy that he had become a small cog in the large machine of EMI.

"Chris Wright didn't really want to sell his company," Fifield said later. "He had to sell his company because it was basically insolvent. That wasn't my fault. He would have been worse off if he didn't have EMI as his partner. But yeah, he was disappointed because he didn't get what he wanted. I was disappointed because he wasn't as successful as I assumed he would be, so I had to take over Chrysalis Records because they ran out of money."

The consolidation of EMI Records was harder to explain. It was having a spectacular sales year. Acts like Queensryche and Richard Marx were booming on the rock side, while the O'Jays had their first gold album in twelve years and newcomer Karen Wheeler had a No. 1 record on the R&B chart. As for new acts, EMF was hot with the world-wide hit "Unbelievable," and Roxette's debut album was breaking out.

"We felt really good," said one senior executive at the company, who now works in a similar capacity at another label. "Sal was a warm, wonderful guy, not like what I'd call an intellectual genius, but a very, very good guy. And so we all had very high hopes. And at the time of the merger, it seemed like not a merger at all, but very much a hostile takeover and a dismantling to fit into Koppelman's plan."

EMI Records, despite its success, could not fend off the winds of change because of several key missteps by president Sal Licata over the previous two years, errors that cost him potentially the hottest roster in music.

Natalie Cole had approached Licata about doing an album of her father's music and was rebuffed. "I need hits," Licata allegedly informed management. "I don't want that Nat King Cole. Do that next. Give me an album with hits now." Cole, in the middle of a creative dry spell, owed EMI over a million dollars in unrecouped costs at that time.

Cole, however, was adamant about doing her father's music. In a compromise, Licata negotiated a deal with his old friend, Elektra chairman Bob Krasnow, receiving cash and interests in Cole's catalog in return for allowing Cole to move to that label. The error in judgment by Licata would prove to be one of the biggest in music history; Cole went on to make *Unforgettable*, which sold millions of copies and won a slew of Grammy awards.

The Red Hot Chili Peppers were another big fish that got away from EMI. "The head of promotion at the time, Jack Satter, did not want to work the Chili Peppers at Top 40 radio," according to the same former EMI executive who discussed Cole. "This is in the early days of alternative, we're talking 1988–89, there wasn't a big crossover pipeline like Weezer, Green Day, Offspring, where shit would slam out to alternative and cross right over."

The Peppers' album *Mother's Milk* was the object of the problem. The most commercially oriented album by the band to date, it featured a cover of Stevie Wonder's "Higher Ground" as its show piece. However, not only did EMI not take it to Top 40, "We never even tried," said the record executive. "Sal, instead of going to the head of promotion and saying I want you to take this record out even if you get five stations, get the record on where you can, allowed it to be swept under the rug."

Citing the California law which states that performing contracts cannot be longer than seven years, the band walked out the door and into a lucrative bidding war that eventually saw them land at Warner Bros. Records, where they succeeded in their quest for Top 40 success with their next album, *Blood Sugar Sex Magik*. EMI retained the catalog rights, but it was small consolation. A band that could have attracted other talent to EMI Records was gone, leaving the lingering perception that the label was just not interested in working with alternative acts.

But the biggest mistake was yet to come. Artist manager Allen Kovac, whose clients include the Bee Gees, Meat Loaf, and Richard Marx, got into a dispute with Licata over Marx, an artist whose best-selling albums were providing approximately 50 percent of EMI Records' sales volume.

Kovac had called for an audit of Marx's finances. What he discovered was appalling. "In examining the books and records, we found a very substantial amount of money had been withheld from [Marx]," said attorney Don Engel, who supervised the audit.

It was also discovered during the audit that the contract Marx had renegotiated with EMI Records after the big sales success of his self-titled debut album and follow-up disc, *Repeat Offender*, was a lot less wonderful than it first had appeared.

According to Engel, who had not been the contract's negotiator, "When he thought he was getting a very, very sizeable advance, he was actually getting what we in the record industry call 'pipeline' money, money that was already collected by the company that he was already entitled to."

Pipeline money, as described by Engle, resembles a shell game. Marx's renegotiated contract called for him to receive an advance (we will use $10 million for the example, although Engel declined to name the actual figure) in return for certain concessions on the number of albums to be delivered under the contract terms and other considerations.

However, in Marx's case, already "in the pipeline" was a check for $10 million due for royalties on his debut album and *Repeat Offender*. This "pipeline" money was given to Marx, who assumed that it had been "advanced" to him. Marx was being paid an advance with his own money.

Asked to characterize the financial shenanigans, Engel said he found the conduct "improper, incorrect, and at least one of them (the withholding of money) was clearly illegal."

Kovac was more blunt about EMI Music's procedures. "They have no conscience. They do it to the Beatles, Richard Marx, Duran Duran." In Marx's case, Kovac said, "Sal Licata told me to walk away. He'd said he'd pay him sooner or later. I said, 'Richard Marx is my client, not you.'"

Faced with losing an artist that was contributing millions to its bottom line, EMI Music's chief executives stepped into the battle. Marx's finances were settled, and he was transferred away from Licata to the roster of Capitol Records, along with four other Kovac clients, including the then-hot band Vixen. The end result was that Marx, whose work included several No. 1 hits and over six million albums sold, would now contribute to the bottom line of a different record label within the EMI family.

Needless to say, Licata's stock plummeted in the corporate hierarchy after that fiasco. "Those three situations were really, really bad for Sal, and we started hearing, 'He's out, he's out, he's out,'" said a former EMI Records executive. "We heard the jungle drums beating and [saw] the smoke signals in the distance. And ultimately, one day, quite suddenly, Charles Koppelman entered our life and summarily fired Sal and took over the company and announced the merger of Chrysalis, EMI, and SBK."

The employees at EMI Records—at least at the senior level—did not quite believe that the day would come when their operation would be disbanded.

"We honestly believed all the way—down the aisle—that they would leave us alone, that we were the company that was making money, that was on its way and that there would be no business sense in merging it, which turned out to be true," said the executive. "Because the entire merger was a financial fiasco and it created nothing. You know, SBK was in tatters, Chrysalis is history for the most part, and EMI is like gone."

Koppelman, who was serving as chairman and CEO of SBK, became chairman and CEO of the merged units. Joe Smith, CEO of Capitol-EMI, ran the de facto West Coast division.

About 150 employees were thrown out of work from the three labels, which had a total combined staff of about 350. Artists were also cast aside. Promotion, marketing, sales, publicity, and administrative departments were merged into one centralized group, although the A&R departments were maintained—at least at first—to give the illusion that the labels retained a distinct flavor.

The merger came at a time when the company apparently was doing extremely well financially. EMI Music's six months results to September 30, 1991, saw sales increase 1.5 percent to $837.4 million, producing a profit of $88.9 million, up 12 percent. The record and music publishing results were termed by a corporate release as the company's "best ever," albeit with the publishing results slightly skewed by the acquisition of the huge Filmtrax catalog.

Overall, thanks to Fifield's claims of improved efficiency, profitabliity was now at around 11 percent, up from 5 percent when he took over. But it was still not enough to prevent the ax from falling on 140 jobs.

Koppelman, who wielded the hatchet for the combined companies, defended the merger. "Chrysalis had no hits, a roster and history, EMI had no hits, no roster, no history; and SBK records...I knew as soon as we didn't have a couple of mega-hits, we'd lose a lot of money."

Koppelman, looking at the three companies with similar

problems, said it was inevitable that they be combined. "Then we'd have a company with a history, with a roster—a company with hits."

Whatever the case, the announced results looked extremely profitable. The synergies produced by reducing the staff created a financial swing from $20 million in losses to over $40 million in gross profits. However, one year after the consolidation, the artistic impact became more apparent: The new EMI Records Group North America was trimming its roster by at least a third, with plans to release 50 percent fewer albums than it had in 1991, and many of the acts that did remain were unhappy that they would have to adjust to working with a new executive team.

It was hard not to consider the merger an insider corporate takeover by SBK. The new executive team's key people were all SBK veterans. SBK senior VP/general manager Daniel Glass was now an executive VP/general manager. Terri Santisi joined him at that rank, a rise from her slot as chief financial officer for SBK/EMI Music publishing.

Despite assurances that each of the merged labels would have a separate A&R head, Koppelman brought in Fred Davis, an attorney with little A&R experience, and appointed him the head of the talent acquisition department, granting Davis the title of senior VP of A&R. The son of industry legend Clive Davis, Fred was not considered his father's equal in recognizing talent.

Other employees in marketing and in the international department also came from SBK.

Koppelman says the consolidation was tough for him.

"That's always difficult. For my first thirty years in this business, I never fired anybody. I had people that worked for me their entire lifetime. Some of them deserved to do that. Some of them probably didn't deserve to do that. But they always had a job. And I was fortunate enough to have a business that could deal with that. [At EMI] in my numerous responsibilities, I had to look at it in a different light. What was my goal? My goal was to have the most efficient, well-run company, with one person doing one job. I found out pretty early, when I had to do this the first time, that when you have two people doing one job, neither one of them does the job. So then maybe you find a third person to try and do the job [while retaining the first two]. I found that when you had two and three people doing one job there was no real pride of authorship."

Employees fired from EMI were left to a somewhat sorry fate. "It was a human resources debacle," recalled one of the victims, "where they had a building across town where all the displaced employees were supposed to go. 'Oh, yeah, we're providing you with office space and phones,' and we had this weird outplacement firm that would say we're going to help you find another job—totally irrelevant to the music business. They didn't even know what the fucking *Billboard* chart was. If you were in the mining business or something, it might be helpful. And they came and said, 'Well, we'll give you your own letterhead. This has been provided to you by your employer.' They called it the Black Hole. And it was just awful."

There was no shortage of Koppelman's cronies in the newly restructured EMI Records Group North America. Some called it nepotism, and not just because Koppelman's son, Brian Koppelman, worked as an A&R man, or that Larry Katz, head of business affairs, was a Koppelman nephew.

"When I worked in the A&R department, every single person in the A&R department—that's all seven people—got their jobs through some sort of nepotism," says one former employee now working elsewhere in the record industry. "Brian Koppelman, son of the head of the company; Pete Ganbarg, director of A&R, was Brian Koppelman's buddy; Don Rubin, the senior VP of A&R, he's known Charles Koppelman for thirty years; Fred Davis, son of Clive, a friend of Charles Koppelman."

However they got their jobs, the A&R team had some successes. Brian Koppelman claims to have discovered Tracy Chapman, Joshua Kadison, and Eddie Murphy; while Ganbarg signed the group Blessid Union of Souls, which achieved a measure of success in 1995. Rubin was a long-standing and respected industry veteran.

The family atmosphere at SBK extended to other employees' relatives and relationships, with unpaid summer internships granted to their children.

Charles Koppelman defended his choices. "A couple of those

sons and daughters of friends are now vice presidents at different record companies because we started them at SBK."

Although EMI Records Group North America was now almost an entirely new company standing in the place where Chrysalis, SBK, and EMI Records had stood before, the dust had not completely settled within the overall company. Capitol Records and its operations on the West Coast, particularly Capitol president Hale Milgrim, still maintained autonomy.

Hale Milgrim was named president of Capitol Records on October 24, 1989, replacing David Berman. He came to the company from Elektra Records, where he was a senior VP of marketing and creative services.

Milgrim inherited a company that listed the Doobie Brothers, Bonnie Raitt, Paul McCartney, Tina Turner, Donnie Osmond, and Queen on its roster. Like everyone at EMI, he stressed the need for Capitol to grow its own new music, but Milgrim seemed to be capable of carrying it out.

Milgrim was an anomaly in the increasingly corporate world of the music industry, a stone-cold music fan whose personal warmth and enthusiasm for new sounds made him one of the business's most beloved characters, an admitted old-school hippie known for his hugs and for hanging out at various music events. "Hale would have loved to have Charles go down with him to Tower Records in a T-shirt and shorts and look at records," said one ex-employee.

Milgrim grew up in Palm Springs, the son of toy store owners. After working in the store creating displays, he convinced his father to lend him $3,000 to go to Cal-Racks, a record distributor, and purchase some singles and albums. At age fifteen, Milgrim was in the record business.

A year and a half later, record racking was 50 percent of the store's business, where it remained until Milgrim went off to the University of California at Santa Barbara. Milgrim kept up his record store contacts in college, working at Discount Records, then moved postschool to Discount's Berkeley outlet in San Francisco. From there, it was on to WEA, Warner Bros., and, finally, in 1984, Elektra Records, where he became head of creative services in New York.

It was an exciting time at the label. Elektra was working several acts that couldn't buy radio time yet were selling to a select, cultivated audience of music fans. Such acts as 10,000 Maniacs, Simply Red, the Cure, the Gipsy Kings, and Anita Baker were marketing-driven, their music placed in select retail and service establishments, immersing potential customers in a sound they couldn't get on the radio.

Joe Smith took notice of the activity and contacted Milgrim about replacing David Berman, who was having problems with the new business methodologies imposed by Jim Fifield. Elektra chairman Krasnow, who didn't have Milgrim under contract, initially balked at the negotiations, but he could not stop Milgrim from leaving.

Milgrim was up front about what he wanted to do at Capitol: eschew the quick fix and go for long-term artist development. It was a familiar song for executives at the label, who were constantly trying to build their own sources of repertoire.

Milgrim had a lovely parting gift from Berman waiting in the form of Bonnie Raitt, whose *Nick of Time* was bursting out of the stores thanks to her four Grammy Awards. But the aging Capitol roster was not a hotbed of fresh, new talent, leaving Milgrim with a formidable task.

As Capitol's fiftieth anniversary approached, Milgrim held a three-year contract and the resources of an international corporation that seemed to agree with his plans to build its business. It looked like the beginning of a long-term relationship, with Capitol ready to move forward and seriously pursue a roster of hot new artists.

But the changes that were going on elsewhere in the company—specifically with Charles Koppelman's ascension—did not augur well for Milgrim's long-term future.

At two years into his deal, Milgrim was boosted to CEO as well as president, signing a lucrative five-year extension. In the release trumpeting the new pact, Fifield said Milgrim "has considerably bolstered EMI Music's North American operations." Smith echoed Fifield: "Capitol Records' extraordinary success over the last few years aptly reflects the tremendous job Hale has done."

Indeed, Milgrim could point to Raitt's *Luck of the Draw*, a five-million seller; Hammer's *Too Legit to Quit* certified triple platinum for sales exceeding three million units; the Beastie Boys' *Check Your Head*, certified gold for surpassing the 500,000 unit mark; and Megadeth's *Countdown to Extinction* and Tom Cochrane's *Mad Mad World*, both successful beyond expectations. Add in good reviews for albums by Graham Parker, Charles & Eddie, Blind Melon, Television, and Thelonious Monster, and Capitol had the makings of something special.

But Koppelman felt that Capitol had a weak A&R staff. Coming from a world of pop hits and radio-driven product, he might also have looked askance at some of the acts on the roster, many of them alternative-music projects that would likely take several albums to build into massive sellers. The long-term potential was there, but the short term would require biting the financial bullet, investing in artists whose future was uncertain.

A restructuring in the fall of 1992 of Capitol's A&R department and other executive positions on Koppelman's order was viewed in some music-industry quarters as planting the seeds of doubt about Milgrim's job status, something denied all around at the time. "Other than more rumors that I hear from time to time, it's just another rumor," Milgrim told *Billboard*. "I don't think that has anything to do with what I'm trying to put together. I have been given a free hand by Jim Fifield and Joe Smith from day one."

Despite the public happy face, Milgrim was said to be not at all happy at the changes Koppelman wanted, which included dropping some of his favorite artists from the Capitol roster. But the sales of some of Milgrim's new artists were not great, and EMI had a tradition of impatience.

One sign that the mood of the corporate office was shifting was when Capitol-EMI president and CEO Joe Smith was shown the door and his powers were given to Koppelman. Smith had wanted a contract extension for a few years and claimed to have been offered one. But the general consensus from those close to the situation was that he was invited to leave by Fifield and really didn't need much coaxing to escape the increasingly corporate environment at EMI.

"In reality, Joe Smith was not Jim's guy," says someone familiar with the situation. "He just wasn't. That became more and more apparent as time went on."

Smith had adopted a somewhat laissez-faire approach to the business, letting Milgrim have almost total control of the record operation. Fifield, according to insiders, wanted Smith to take a strong hand in directing the somewhat inexperienced Milgrim. However, "Joe was being the ambassador," said a source in the record company. "The good part is that Joe would be there if we were trying to woo somebody and use his great stories and expertise. It wasn't like he was out drinking or golfing. He was there, but he was sort of toward the end of what he once was."

The operations of Capitol-EMI became consolidated under Koppelman's control in the fall of 1992. But it was clear that more changes were to come.

Koppelman explained the need for the consolidation by stressing the need for streamlining a previously unwieldy operation. "I looked at a company that had no synergies whatsoever," he said. "It had a West Coast group and an East Coast group and nobody had ever really communicated. There was no coordination. If someone called up and said that we need five million Garth Brooks CDs pressed and that was the first call in the morning, they were pressing five million CDs. If, an hour later, someone called and said, 'We need Arrested Development,' they might be told, 'We gotta wait until we get these five million done.' Where's somebody there as a traffic cop? We didn't have that. We have that now."

Koppelman even admitted that he was starting to sound a bit more like Fifield than he cared to. "It's scary for me to say that because it's so alien to what I'm about. But I'll tell you what I'm about. I'm about having hits. And if we ain't putting records out there, they ain't gonna have hits."

With Smith gone, Koppelman's first order of business upon assuming command of EMI's North American operations was a house cleaning at Capitol, ordering Milgrim to trim thirty artists and fifty employeees. "He wanted to show Jim that Joe Smith wasn't capable of doing it," said one executive at the company. "Jim had been hammering the shit out of us from July or August. He saw we weren't having the sales, and the best thing to do is cut your losses."

Some artists who were dropped from Capitol were painful for Milgrim to part with, particularly The Cages, once the object of a super bidding war. Others were kept mainly for contractual reasons. Billy Squier, whose career seemed to have collapsed since he embarrassed himself in an MTV video that portrayed him crawling around his bedroom, a sissy image that struck down his macho metal persona, was kept. Squier had a five-album deal that would have cost the company more to buy out than retain.

Milgrim's eventual fate was most likely sealed at a press dinner for music industry reporters held at the Los Angeles restaurant Patina in March 1993. Earlier that day, Milgrim had met with Koppelman to check on whether Capitol was performing to his satisfaction. Milgrim confidants at Capitol familar with the meeting insist that Koppelman told Milgrim there were absolutely no problems. Milgrim left on a high note, assured that he could ignore the rumors that his job was at risk.

At the dinner—an informal event held several times during Milgrim's tenure—Milgrim, the ardent music fan, waxed rhapsodic about the upcoming acts on Capitol's release schedule. The question then was put to Milgrim about his relationship with Koppelman. While admitting that the two had competed before, Milgrim assured the gathering of reporters that things had never been better between himself and Koppelman and that he was looking forward to a good working relationship—"a partnership," in Milgrim's words.

Koppelman allegedly went nuclear when *Daily Variety* reported Milgrim's upbeat prognosis the following morning. Koppelman was on a golf outing in Florida and phoned to voice his displeasure at the fact that he had not been invited to the dinner. It was a theme Koppelman would sound later when he fired Milgrim: "He was about exclusion."

Some of Milgrim's closest lieutenants tried to warn him that there was trouble brewing. But Milgrim, an honest man to a fault, believed that no one was capable of lying to his face. He was wrong.

"There were rumors afoot that Hale and Art were going to be

gone," says a former Capitol executive, "and [Milgrim] came in to a VP meeting one day and he goes, 'I just talked with Charles. We're doing great. If we continue to keep on progressing like we're progressing, we're here for a long time.' He believed it. Hale believed he was not out until five days before he was out."

Milgrim's fate was all but confirmed in a very cold way on May 29. Geffen executive Gary Gersh, the man who signed Nirvana to that label and pushed alternative music into the mainstream, had re-signed from his A&R job at Geffen and was believed to be heading to Capitol to take Milgrim's job. Jim Fifield responded in *Billboard* to the rumors about Gersh and Milgrim, basically confirming Milgrim's fate with his oblique comments.

"There are going to be changes," Fifield said. "I can't really comment on what Milgrim will be doing or will not be doing. I can just say that we want this record company to be the No. 1 record company on the West Coast. Koppelman has got the mandate to do whatever it takes, and he's looking at a lot of things, getting a lot of phone calls, and talking to a lot of people. Unfortunately, the Milgrim rumor has been in play. I'm going to tell him to keep his head down and keep doing his job and if there are any changes he will be the first guy to know."

A few weeks later, Milgrim flew to Washington, D.C., for the signing of the so-called motor-voter bill, which allowed citizens to register to vote when applying for driver's licenses. Rock the Vote, an organization founded and supported by the music industry, had been instrumental in pushing through the measure. Milgrim was accom-panied by several of his employees, plus Megadeth's Dave Mustaine, Virgin Records co-chairmen Jeff Ayeroff and Jordan Harris, and Charisma Records president Phil Quartararo. He was assured by all that he had nothing to worry about, that the scuttlebutt about his demise was typical in an industry that feeds on gossip.

But when Milgrim told Koppelman he would be on the East Coast, Koppelman urged him to stop by his New York office for a little chat. It was then that Milgrim was informed that he and his No. 2 man, Art Jaeger, were being dismissed. Nine months had passed since Milgrim had signed a new employment contract.

In truth, the Milgrim regime had made some bad choices. The creation of Bust It Productions with Hammer, coming on the heels of his multiplatinum *Please Hammer Don't Hurt 'Em*, was a particularly costly failure, running up losses rumored as high as $10 million. The marketing plan for Hammer's follow-up album was also a failure, loudly trumpeted as a record-setting budget for a Capitol artist, but one that proved way too high in light of the album's sales. "Frankly, a number of key executives thought there's no way he would sell another twenty million," admitted one senior Capitol executive. "If he could have sold half that, it would have been good. But he sold a quarter. It became one of those things that at every big company happens from time to time. It was as poor a situation as could be."

Capitol's plans for *Too Legit to Quit* included videos for twelve of the album's seventeen cuts, a $500,000 prerelease TV ad campaign, cross-promos with Paramount on the *Addams Family* movie, two longform home videos, and more than $1 million on account advertising. Hammer also saw fit to drop the M.C. from his name. "That's what happens when you sell more than ten million units in the U.S. and are No. 1 for twenty-one weeks," said a senior executive, explaining how the sales of the first album influenced the second.

"I mean, we spent a lot of money to market that second Hammer—technically the third Hammer, but the second big, big Hammer album, but those were big spending days," said one former executive. "If you remember, all the superstar acts that came out at that time—it was scary. The entire record business was spending, we were all doing events, and the whole industry was a little crazy spending-wise at the time. So, God, it looks stupid now to have thrown money into that guy, but at the time, probably a lot of other labels would have done the same thing, and how embarrassing it would have been to say no to your number one artist and the No. 1 artist in the business—'No, I'm not going to give you a label deal. No you're not going to get a production deal. No, we don't believe in you. You're not going to get any money.' And then if you let it go somewhere else and it explodes, how horrible do you look? So you almost had to have done it."

Despite the Hammer debacle, many executives in the record

business remain dumbfounded to this day that EMI made the change at Capitol, given the company's longstanding lament that it had to grow its own talent, a path on which Milgrim had firmly set the company. In the end, Milgrim's dismissal was simply a matter of Koppelman's being in charge and desiring to name his own executive.

So why did Koppelman go through the song and dance of lukewarm denials? Gary Gersh, the man who would become the new king of Capitol, was under contract as an A&R man at Geffen until November. "They weren't sure if they could get him out of it, so it's like, 'I'm not going to have an interim president between Hale and Gersh,'" said an executive familiar with the situation. "'I'm eventually going to get Gersh. I'll keep Hale going for six months and eventually say it's not working out.' It was a risky move for Charles because we were about to break through. Charles & Eddie was breaking big internationally, Blind Melon had just delivered that video [the huge hit "No Rain" featuring the dancing "Bee Girl"] and we all knew that [would break them big]. So suddenly in six months you're in danger of firing a guy who's pretty hot and you're going to have to search harder to find something. So he needed to get Hale out of there before things broke so he could say, 'Look, he wasn't breaking anything.'"

The senior executive knew only too well the scenario being drawn about Milgrim.

"You can paint that kind of negative picture about anyone if you want to. And I'm sure that's what Charles did. And if Charles wants Hale out, Jim Fifield's going to say, 'Well, it's going to cost me X millions of dollars to get rid of all these people, but if you believe in Gersh, I gotta believe in you, and you've got a track record, Charles. So, yeah, let's do what you have to do.'"

Ironically, at the time of the purge, EMI was again trumpeting record sales and profits. However, as one executive notes, "The worldwide business is expanding so much. I mean there are territories that were untapped before, southeast Asia, Singapore, Malaysia, Indonesia. But if you saw it broken down into frontline product, American operation, yeah, you'd see there's no way [business is looking that good]. All you got to do is look at the charts."

One former Capitol executive remembers Milgrim's farewell speech to his assembled troops at the Capitol Tower and the arrival of the new regime the next morning. "We hugged Hale goodbye, and the next day the VPs had a meeting with [new president] Gary Gersh and Koppelman. And all [Koppelman] kept saying was, 'Everyone else wanted to include me. Hale was exclusive. He wasn't inclusive.' Well, Hale Milgrim is the warmest, nicest guy in the world. Did he invite Charles to cigar-smoking poker nights? I mean, Hale doesn't do that. Hale goes to concerts and listens to music and goes to record stores. Hale's not an industry schmoozer kind of guy. But to say Hale was not being inclusive—I know he probably didn't want Charles coming to every Capitol event or whatever. But Hale would never deliberately exclude a guy. I mean, even if he didn't like a person. I mean, this is a guy who will hug anybody. He'll see the good in anybody."

The rancor among those left behind was boiling, and not all of it was because a beloved executive had been let go in unseemly fashion. There were other things about Koppelman's style that rankled the rank and file. For one, his habit of driving around in a beloved Bentley when he was visiting the West Coast. (Many employees believed Koppelman flew the car out from the East Coast. Koppelman maintains the car is housed in Los Angeles.) One former employee claimed that the venerable Capitol Tower itself was violated, a wall knocked out so that a special desk could be placed in an office that would be rarely used by Koppelman.

"There were a lot of things going on at the time," the former Capitol executive continues. "The layoffs, Hale and Art being gone, Charles and his fucking Bentley with Havana cigars just reeking of wealth and ostentation. There was a guy who came down from corporate to be the business affairs guy—his name escapes me—but he had his marble floor installed on the ninth floor, a beautiful Italian marble floor installed at a time when—not that we had to watch every pencil we used, but certainly at a time of belt-tightening and layoffs and so on. The severance packages for people who were laid off were apparently very small because [Koppelman] had given such big severances to the people laid off when SBK, Chrysalis and EMI Records merged."

The efforts to put a bandage on the situation didn't seem to help either, according to one executive. Focus groups organized by outside counselors generated more anticompany sentiment than healing. "The company was getting trashed by its own employees," the executive recalled. "They couldn't even absorb all the data coming in. They hated Charles and everything he stands for. Not as a guy; he's a totally charming guy to be around. But they hate what he stands for, they hate what he's done. They came in talking really bad about Hale. They really did. It was just handled really, really poorly."

Another move that raised eyebrows both within the company and throughout the business was the formal embrace of independent promotion men who had been shunned in the industry since being caught up in the record promotion scandals of the mid-1980s.

Koppelman personally brought in Fred DiSipio, who was mentioned in news accounts of the government's mid-'80s probe into payola but was never charged with a crime. However, controversial indie Joe Isgro, who was indicted by the federal government for counts that included payola (the practice of bribing radio stations to obtain airplay for certain records) but had his charges dismissed by a federal judge for extreme government misconduct in its prosecution, was reported to have billed the company for at least one R&B record he promoted to obtain radio airplay for Capitol Records. (The government later refiled its case against Isgro; by September 1995, no resolution or plea agreement had been reached.)

DiSipio, who was on the EMI payroll as of 1991, according to the *Los Angeles Times*, had allegedly come out of retirement to help the company. Koppelman said, "Joe Isgro, on the other hand, is just another guy passing through the revolving door, no different from hundreds of other businessmen each week who request a meeting one time with me. I gave the guy ten minutes. He does not work for Capitol or EMI."

Despite those controversies, Koppelman claims it was the firings at Capitol that made him seem like a bad guy. "My image in the industry was changed by an asshole at the *L.A. Times* who had a personal vendetta because I fired Hale Milgrim. And this guy wrote one line in a newspaper that was totally inaccurate about who I am."

[The line referred to Koppelman as "the most disliked mogul in the record business."] By the way, Hale Milgrim got millions of dollars. He'll never have to work again a day in his life and I fired him the best way possible. Was he a nice guy? The nicest guy. But that's business."

Koppelman admitted that Giant Records co-owner Irving Azoff, whose reputation as the meanest man in the business was, according to the *Los Angeles Times*, usurped temporarily by Koppelman's ascension, called to commiserate.

"It's such a joke. I mean, if you ever followed me around for like a day...of course Irving called. I've known Irving for a long time." Did he want his title back? "Totally—no, he didn't want his title back."

Finally, with Milgrim gone, Koppelman clearly had all of his ducks in a row. It was time to show what the new regime could do.

Koppelman had brought in Fred Davis to oversee A&R at the new EMI Records Group North America. But it was clear that Davis had a big learning curve ahead, according to one source familiar with the situation. "Fred was truly a gentlemen's gentleman and a great guy but virtually lost in the process of signing artists and making records, particularly the record-making side, from the viewpoint of being inside the company." Koppelman had tried to assure the remaining A&R people after the consolidation that creative decisions would remain in their hands. The source recalls that when Davis was hired, Koppelman waved off complaints, saying, "I don't want to make three phone calls. I want to make one phone call. You guys all feed into Fred. Fred's the guy I'll be in touch with. Fred will be hanging with me. He'll tell me what you're doing and this is how we'll run it."

A grand plan. But Charles Koppelman had long been his own A&R man. He needed to put his personal imprint on the releases.

What followed were some successes achieved using the old-fashioned SBK standard of spending large amounts on marketing and promotion—as was the case with debut albums from Jon Secada and Joshua Kadison—but more often, the result from EMI Records Group North America was a string of costly and high-profile failures.

Down the hatch went Slaughter and Jesus Jones, to be followed by albums by Sinead O'Connor, Queensryche, Billy Idol, and Pat Benatar.

Even the old SBK magic acts couldn't be revived. On June 6, 1992, Wilson Phillips released *Shadows and Light*, its second album. The first single, "You Won't See Me Cry," tried to paint them as grown up. The album's title, however, proved prophetic. Advance ticket sales for the group's tour were so bad that the road trip was canceled. Despite worldwide sales of eight million albums and three No. 1 singles on the group's debut album, there was no enduring fan base.

A costly longform home video, "Shadows and Light From a Different View," and an expensive publicity campaign highlighted by a documentary-style film trailer shown in Cineplex Odeon theaters both failed to ignite sales for Wilson Phillips. The album eventually was certified platinum for sales of one million units by the Recording Industry Association of America; however, certifications reflect the number of albums shipped to retail over a three-month period following the album's release. It's likely that hundreds of thousands of Wilson Phillips albums were sent back by retail following the end of the certification period.

The last, dying gasp of Wilson Phillips could be heard on a Christmas album that went nowhere. The group that had had the highest-selling debut album in history could also claim the honor of the biggest fall from grace following a debut album.

"Historically, I've always had the feeling that the industry regurgitates an overhype," Artie Mogull, the man who helped discover the group, told *Rolling Stone*. "That's an aspect of the business that I don't think Charles has ever learned."

Why were things going so badly at EMI Records Group North America? "Because you took three thriving little cultures where people's lives were at stake about an act and you removed those people, and the acts get transferred to underlings or different people and the emotional connection's not there," says one former EMI executive. "Chrysalis was a very cool, seminal independent label at one time with a tremendous success ratio. In its first incarnation with Jethro Tull and Ten Years After and all that, and then later on in life with Pat Benatar, Huey Lewis, Billy Idol. That history is critical to a label's drawing power, and the lineage is exactly what was wiped out when they merged those three labels."

One executive ousted during the consolidation agreed. "They spent millions of dollars on contractual payouts just to get rid of people, good people, people who ended up being vice presidents and senior vice presidents at other major labels within weeks and months of being let go out of there, and paid a high price to do it. They accomplished nothing business-wise except the loss of millions of dollars and a lot of pain. Musically, it was a failure because the idea of three separate banners under one roof failed. That entire venture, the merger of those three labels, is a debacle that will be infamous in the record business forever, I think. They took three cultures and they wiped it out and achieved nothing."

Of all the labels affected by the consolidation, Chrysalis Records proved to be the most tragic death. The downsizing of the company—once one of the most vibrant independent labels in the music business—into a larger corporate entity may have also led to the subsequent failure of one of the most culturally significant acts of the 1990s.

By the time Chrysalis sold a half interest to EMI in 1989, it was a label rich in heritage, but short on acts. Chris Wright, who cofounded the label with Terry Ellis, was running the company from the U.K. Underneath him, there was two-headed leadership, with MTV and label veteran John Sykes as the president and former Adidas executive Joe Kiener as CEO.

The atmosphere was still collegiate at the label following the EMI half-purchase. There were frequent A&R retreats where the U.K. and American staffs would go to a countryside mansion and discuss the merits of particular artists. Travel budgets were generous, and autonomy was freely given, according to several executives.

Chrysalis in the late '80s was a somewhat stolid label, more known for Jethro Tull, Billy Idol, and Pat Benatar than its cutting-edge artists. But hope was on the horizon, as several A&R executives sought to inject new life into the label. One example of that thinking was Arrested Development, signed to Chrysalis in 1990, a group that celebrated the mingling of rural South and African roots, a combination that would prove commercially irresistible.

Arrested Development's *3 Years, 5 Months and 2 Days in the Life Of...* album was titled after the amount of time it took to create and release its first record from the group's inception to its final production.

Group members Speech and DJ Headliner (Tim Barnwell) were the creators of Arrested Development, having met at the Art Institute of Atlanta. After a false start as gangsta rappers, they fused "southern-folk-ethnic rap," termed "life music," and joined with singer-designer Aerle "Early Ta-Ree" Taree, choreographer Montsho "Ee-She" Eshe, drummer-vocalist Rasa Don, dancer-counselor Baba "O.J." Oje, and singer Dionne Farris.

The group touched a public nerve with its sparkling single "Tennessee" and later became so hot it didn't even need to promote the single "Mr. Wendal," which competed with the group's *Malcolm X* soundtrack single "Revolution" for airplay.

Arrested Development was just hitting its stride in 1992, having survived the company chaos of consolidation, but faced with an executive team different than the corporate structure that had signed them. The changes were initially a blessing. Arrested Development was, at that time, on its way to selling four million albums using the SBK methodology. But the long-term prospects for the group were also affected by the tactics of the new team.

"There was about an initial period of maybe six months of total confusion, and actually the effect on my job was really just to try to keep my acts afloat and not lose them in the face of having a company going through this transition," recalled one executive who worked closely with the group. He noted that many promising bands that should have been worked during the transition were lost because of the change in executives and tactics.

"What happens is that an act gets worked in the wrong way," the executive said. "I mean, it's not so much they get ignored." But "the players that are supposed to make this act a hit are not always motivated purely by 'I love this song.'" Fear of losing your job, corporate game-playing and incompetent handling are often the reason an act fails. "I've seen assignments given to people that shouldn't have have been given [the assignment]."

Arrested Development was a case in point.

"When EMI took over, of all the three labels, Arrested Development was perhaps the biggest, newest, most successful act they had," the executive continued. "I think what happened was the hierarchy in the new EMI Records Group North America structure really grabbed it and wanted it and wanted that success and wanted to have a piece of that success. Here's the new company. Here are the toys that are in their sandbox. This is the prettiest one. I'm going to have it. And I think during the time that that happened, a lot of people got the wrong acts. They got them because of they were able to make certain power moves."

Because of the changes during the consolidation, a lot of executives working acts were shuffled, a decision that ruffled many management feathers. "This was a brand new company, all new personalities you're dealing with, and maybe you do have some Chrysalis people there, but their job is changing because their relationship with the new person is going to be different," said the executive. "And I think each company works better when everybody who's doing their jobs has personal relationships and is familiar with the way that that person works. And really, everybody does every job differently, so you can't slide a new person into the head of publicity and have, you know, all the systems operate the same way."

The SBK influence was immediate. SBK holdovers turned EMI Records Group North America executives Daniel Glass (president), head of marketing Ken Baumstein, and Koppelman-approved import Fred Davis (head of A&R) were the people whose word was law in the new company.

"I was pressured to bring instant hits," said one A&R executive. "They wanted stuff that's going to sell right away. 'Bring me home a hit.' That's right from Fred's mouth. 'I need a hit.' I was often told that 'We need an instant hip-hop hit like Snoop Doggy Dogg. Find it.'"

The reason for the pressure was the massive losses being piled up as act after act failed for the new EMI Records Group North America, which was using SBK's formula of spend, spend, spend, but without the success of Wilson Phillips and Vanilla Ice to keep plowing money into the Ponzi scheme. "They saw it going down the toilet," the executive said. "They saw returns, the acts not delivering, and they really wanted to make some numbers, and I think their numbers were looking more and more dismal and I think that reflected directly on them. I think they were really worried about the bottom-line numbers, because that's all that Charles and Fifield really looked at was the bottom line."

That mentality led Davis to take over Arrested Development, which was pushed, in much the same way Vanilla Ice was used, to make a live album. Although, in this case, it was the group's appearance on *MTV Unplugged* that became its Waterloo.

In order to appear on *MTV Unplugged*, the group wanted some good terms, including a huge advance and one of their production companies, Gumbo, to be issued through Chrysalis Records. They got what they wanted.

Unfortunately, at that point the public was burned out on Arrested Development and, perhaps, on *MTV Unplugged* albums as well. The disc did not sell well. Moreover, the production deal with Gumbo faltered.

Normally, a company would have realized that it had pushed too hard, too fast, and let the band go into hibernation. But the consolidated EMI Records Group North America was drowning, and to make its numbers, it wanted another Arrested Development studio album.

"They demanded it from the group and they got it from the group," the executive recalled. "And the group wasn't ready to make the record at all. What would have been best for them would have been to chill out and have some members do solo records and then come back with Arrested Development when they're ready. But they were pressured, and maybe it's destroyed Arrested Development. It probably could have been a much longer-lived experience. But I mean, the title of their album—*3 Years, 5 Months, 2 Days*. That's how long it took them to make that record. So that's how plain it is. They're looking at a gold record that says *3 Years* on the cover and yet they think in six months they can bring another album of that quality from the group. It's not going to happen."

The result of the rush release was a follow-up album, *Zingalamaduni*, that the *Village Voice* called "possibly the biggest bomb in music industry history." The album sold fewer than 100,000 units. That poor showing, combined with the virtual across-the-board failures of other major artists, led to the firing of almost every top gun at the EMI Records Group North America, including Glass, Davis, and Baumstein.

Ironically, upon taking over after the consolidation, Koppelman had told the surviving A&R executives that it would be an A&R-driven company. The reality, as proven by Arrested Development, was far different.

With a new administration in place at EMI post-Glass, the label entered a period of belt tightening. At least for certain employees. "Like, for instance, EMI cut back the cream for the coffee," said one executive at the company. "They're cutting back office expenses. So there must be some resentment because they can't have cream in their coffee and you can reach Charles at the Bel Air Hotel."

So far, the effect of the slippage has not touched Charles Koppelman, who has developed his own Teflon presidency. "I thought Charlie was a little like Gertrude Ederle, the first woman to swim the English Channel," former CBS president Irwin Segelstein once told *Hit Men* author Fredric Dannen. "She greased her body every day. I always felt like Charlie did that."

Some song men are slippery enough to survive the changing tides of the corporate world. Some resist and wind up getting drowned. Such was the case at Time Warner, where Mo Ostin, whom many considered the greatest record man ever to grace the business, went down swinging against the corporate machine.

SEVEN

WAR AT WARNER BROS.

At the dawn of the 1990s, Warner Bros. Records was the model of what most other record companies wanted to be—enormously profitable, an artist roster of established hitmakers, stable management with a reputation as nurturing and artist-oriented, and a vision for the future that included affiliation with some of the leading record industry entrepreneurs and leaders of the 1980s, including Rick Rubin, Irving Azoff, and Tom Silverman.

Four years later, the situation was starting to unravel. Remarkably, it was all being dismantled by the head of the company.

Bob Morgado, fifty-one, with a personality stiffer than a beefeater's, was the man responsible for the turmoil. An old-line political player, Morgado was a prototypical 1990s CEO, from his polished black dress shoes to his boardroom demeanor. The *Wall Street Journal* called him "the ultimate suit," and Morgado would not argue with that sobriquet, although, like many senior music industry executives, he took umbrage at the notion that he was out of step with his artists.

The evidence showed otherwise. In one example, when Metallica filed suit to sever its association with Elektra Entertainment, it blamed Morgado. Drummer Lars Ulrich said that Morgado reneged on a promise to restructure their deal.

Morgado was the antithesis of the management style of Steve

Ross, the legendary Warner Communications head who bought his underlings' allegiance with lavish gifts and total autonomy. Although Ross had passed away in 1992, his legacy lived on in the relatively loose management style of Warner Bros. Records chairman Mo Ostin, who shunned the spotlight but had developed a well-earned reputation as the man behind the wheel of the Cadillac of record labels.

Despite a bottom line at Warner Bros. firmly lodged in the black, there was a long-simmering feud between Morgado and Ostin. The issue was control, based mostly on Ostin's desire to totally avoid Morgado, whom he regarded as a bean-counting know-nothing who didn't understand what made the Warner Music Group the industry leader.

Ostin, who had always reported to Ross and now answered to Time Warner chairman Gerald Levin, could get away with bypassing the chain of command represented by Morgado while Ross was alive. However, at age sixty-seven, his contract was expiring, and he was presented with a new deal by Morgado: Designate Warner Bros. Records president Lenny Waronker as his successor, a transition that would take place in 1996, and be prepared to report directly to Morgado instead of Levin.

There were other, informal considerations to the new pact. Ostin would be asked to bend a bit on his levels of executive staffing and on the large artist roster. Simple choices, on the surface. But ones that Ostin would have nothing to do with. As a company elder statesman and head of the most venerated label in one of Time Warner's most profitable divisions, Ostin perhaps thought he was entitled to special treatment as a reward.

But Warner Bros. had experienced a rare poor first half in 1993, leading to music industry gossip about whether Ostin and his team still had what it takes to keep a record company vital. Chatter circulated about a Warner Bros. roster heavy with aging superstars and a management system of entrenched bureaucrats that had resisted the corporate streamlining in vogue elsewhere in the industry.

Morgado, sensing the mood, decided the time was right to settle the score with Ostin once and for all. The strategy to undermine Ostin was simple: Put a proud man in a position that clearly indicated that Ostin would not be allowed to operate in the manner he saw fit. Morgado did that by naming Doug Morris, the co-chairman of Atlantic Records, to a new position as president of the U.S. operations of Warner Music Group. As a result of that move, Ostin, Elektra chairman Bob Krasnow, and Danny Goldberg, then president of Atlantic Records, would report to Morris, who in turn would report to Morgado.

Morgado explained his decision to the *Wall Street Journal*: "I saw the need for a new generation of managers, but I wanted to make those transitions smoothly."

Morris and Ahmet Ertegun, the co-chairmen of the Atlantic Records Group, had faced a similar situation with Morgado several years before and had managed to come up with a solution that worked for both.

Ertegun, one of the early legends of the record industry, was in his seventies when approached by Morgado to name a successor. Instead of battling, Ertegun elevated his close lieutenant, Morris, to head of Atlantic's day-to-day operations but continued to maintain an active role in the company's creative direction. While not embracing Morgado, Morris and Ertegun adopted the pragmatic approach of recognizing who was in charge of Time Warner's music division, something Ostin seemingly refused to do by neglecting his relationship with Morgado.

When Morris was promoted by Morgado, record industry people wondered whether Ostin and Krasnow, two old-line record men, would buy into the new world order. Goldberg, a Morris protegé, was presumed to be in full agreement.

Observers didn't have to wait long for their answer. A day after the Morris announcement, Krasnow was said to have resigned. The announcement was a cover for a grimmer leave-taking: Elektra was perceived to be "spiraling out of control," according to one senior Warner executive, as Krasnow's illness with cancer coincided with a particularly cold spell on the charts, and Morgado decided to fire Krasnow in order to move up Sylvia Rhone, a favorite of Time Warner executives for her ability to bring projects in on time and within budget.

Ostin didn't react immediately to the news that he would now have to report to Morris, but there was little doubt in the music community on his eventual decision. It came as no surprise when Ostin announced in the fall that he would step down at the end of 1994. However, he made it clear that he was not retiring.

"It was the toughest thing I've ever been through in the business—and it shook me to the core," Ostin said, remembering his mood in a rare interview with the *Los Angeles Times* shortly before his exit. "It made me doubt myself. It made me wonder whether I was just living on my laurels like my critics were saying, or what? I even went to a shrink. But it just wasn't true. The company was doing terrific. The idea of leaving Warner's really troubled me, but I decided I just could not continue working here under those conditions."

Lenny Waronker, Warner Bros.' longtime president and Ostin's right-hand man, agreed to assume the chairmanship of the company. But weeks later, Waronker, perhaps sensing the kind of company he was going to lead, decided to back out of his commitment. The result was executive turmoil that even Morgado admitted, in a speech at the *Billboard* Video Music Conference, "makes the situation in Bosnia look tame."

While the issues between Morgado and Ostin were undoubtedly personal, they also point to the fundamental differences between running a company like a corporation and running it as a haven for artists. Morgado thought that his duty was to the shareholders, to squeeze the rock for hidden profits. Ostin, on the other hand, kept the company profitable for twenty years not by a laissez-faire approach to spending money—he was, after all, a former chief financial officer at Verve Records—but by realizing that musicians don't necessarily produce results on the first single or the first album. That was something that cannot be explained in dollars and cents.

The record industry of the late 1990s had evolved to the point where artist development, the process by which new acts are nurtured, had become a concept every label saluted but few actually practiced on a broad scale. According to *Hits* magazine, of the forty most competitive bidding wars for artists in the early 1990s, the results produced six unquestionable smashes, nine instances where the result was still undetermined, and twenty-five signings that did not make back their initial investment and were financial disasters. Whether any of those musicians who have yet to succeed will be allowed the proper growth period is dubious.

In the end, despite all the lip service paid to nurturing new artists and allowing new independent labels to find their own way with minimal financial backing from the major labels, the big corporate machine that is the music industry has become a monster that swallows up art and spits out product, creating fewer and fewer artists that have a lifespan beyond two albums.

The 1990 New Music Seminar in New York addressed one of the reasons why artists were being given short shrift. The answer, culled from an A&R panel, was fundamental: too many records in the marketplace.

Ed Eckstine, at the time a VP of talent and later Mercury Records president, blamed the "limited amount of [available radio] airspace" for the lack of new successful artists. He said PolyGram would seek to cut down its release schedule to afford proper treatment. "We're trying not to produce twenty records a month, so that the fewer records that do come out get a shot." It's worth noting that Mercury's release schedule did not seem to diminish in any significant way once Eckstine took control of the company.

While music industry veterans will argue that one-hit wonders have always existed in the business, the ultimate proof of the half-life of today's artists is the way alternative music has so quickly become the mainstream. Since Nirvana's *Nevermind* unexpectedly exploded in 1991, the Big Six distributors have engaged in a feeding frenzy of signings, throwing money at new bands and independent labels with the idea of building up market share.

But instead of building a healthy and expanding base that nurtures the qualities that made alternative music thrive, the result of that influx of major label money has been a bastardization of the alternative-music market, with former left-of-center artists promoted in much the same manner pop musicians are, with videos and one big song the key to breaking out of the pack. Needless to say, that mentality, which relies on instant impact in the marketplace, has squashed many promising careers before they could blossom.

Many reasons are given by experts in the music industry as to why the business seems to be eating its own.

"The notion that you're going to find one individual who can pass creative judgment on every style of music is impossible," said one senior A&R executive at a major label, who asked not to be named. "I mean, even in the metal area, there's speed metal, funk metal, death metal, rap metal—there's like nine kinds of metal that these guys over here who like this kind don't even know what that kind is. If you can cover a few styles, you're an all-arounder. So the notion that one pinnacle guy is going to pass judgment on all the music is a business plan for disaster."

Even in the early '80s, when the corporatization of the record industry was just starting to happen, an artist's success was often based on an old Columbia Records formula—that is, "It takes three albums for an act to break out."

That concept "eroded as alternative got more and more legs to where it is today," said the senior executive, "where alternative music is now a singles business, where you have a hit with Juliana Hatfield and then you have a hit with Belly and then a hit with this one and that one. The alternative format is basically songs and singles. You spend a ton of money and get MTV and make expensive videos, get them on the road,—it's a whole different thing now. They still offer lip service about building [careers], but everybody's trying to sign the next Weezer, the next Green Day and the next Offspring and the next alternative band that's going to grab MTV and be the heroes of the kids. Nobody's trying to sign the next Mariah [Carey], the next Michael Bolton, all that pop shit. Nobody wanted to sign Ace of Base. It was kicked around BMG before Clive Davis said 'This is good,' and then they scrapped the album and cut five new songs real quick and remixed the rest and put it out.

"So the pressure on A&R right now is to have credible, groovy hits," he continued. "It's like nobody wants to sign the Bee Gees and sell twenty-two million records. Everybody wants to sign Offspring and sell two million, because it's cool. That coolness thing is really,

really important. So there's a lot of other types of music that aren't as popular or maybe not as cool, and they're being ignored. They're not being developed."

The U.S. market, once the home of artist development, has been speeded up to the point where it resembles England, according to the A&R executive. "I lived there for two years, man. These fucking groups were coming by like clouds on a windy day. And the music community would latch on to them. It was like, 'Man, Transvision Vamp. No, Zodiac Mindwarp. No, man. Deacon Blue.' And they were touring arenas and selling records and people were absorbing them and chucking them out just like that, because it's a real small place. But I'm finding that it's getting like that here. It's hard to build loyal followings that stick with you. I mean, we'll see how many Juliana Hatfield fans there are going to be after Liz Phair has taken them all away. What about the Spin Doctors? They're dead in the water. I mean, this was a big, big band a year ago."

As a result of this hyperdrive, the A&R executive is constantly on the move, seeking the next big thing—or something like it.

"What happens is when something like a Green Day pops, the president of the label calls downstairs and says, 'Where were we? Show me the fucking paper trail on Green Day,'" said another major label A&R executive, whose job security requires that his name not be revealed. "And they want to see we went to this gig on such and such a date, and then we went to San Diego, and then we had lunch with them, but then [A&R executive superstar] John Kalodner and [Geffen chairman] David Geffen came in and then Mo Ostin came in and they want to know how we lost it. They want to see blood. They want to know why didn't we have a shot at it? And they go fucking nuclear. What happens is it creates a lemming thing where if one talent scout jumps in, they all jump in because they don't want to get in trouble with the boss. And as a result, you're constantly behind the curve, because once Green Day breaks, you're looking for the next Green Day. By the time it gets there, the ship has passed."

A veteran marketing man sees it another way. "There's no synergy between the A&R guys who sign the acts and the marketing guys and the promotion guys. I can't tell you how many marketing meetings I've been to where the marketing team will say, 'Why did you sign this act? They've got nothin'. We don't like the music. We don't like the image. We don't like this. We don't like that.' Unfortunately, certain music-industry executives have got this attitude of, 'If I like the act, I'll work it.' The analogy I use is in the shoe store. If you're a shoe salesman and there's a tremendously ugly pair of orange and purple shoes, if it's the music industry it'd say, 'I don't like those shoes. I'm not gonna sell them.' In the real world, however, if you really want to prove how good you are as an executive, you could say, 'I can sell those shoes. Those are the ugliest shoes in the world, but I can sell them.'"

Band manager–label owner Abbo, who runs independent label Big Cat Records and manages Cop Shoot Cop, EMF, and Pavement, says big distributors are not using their independent label deals to grow new sources of talent. Rather, they're merely using the labels as a farm system, taking the cream of available talent off the rosters and doing little to nurture the creative vision of the label's executives or artists, both likely to end up discarded after a short shelf life.

"I've seen most of these deals on paper, the actual contracts, like the Matador deal and the Mammoth deal and numerous deals in Europe," Abbo said, "[Big distributors] are buying these labels, but the way the deals work is [not conducive] to the type of acts the labels work with. None of [the deals] are going to work for the actual guys that run the label. It's always going to work for the corporation because they can cherry-pick stuff. And sure, two of their ten bands have gotten to jump into a bigger pond. But the other eight are totally discarded."

Abbo added, "What I'm trying to say is the people that do these deals on the corporate side don't understand that discovering the talent is 50 percent of the effort. The development system that that talent goes through is the other 50 percent. And because they don't control the other 50 percent or have someone that can articulate it into their system, then more and more bands are going to fall by the wayside."

One major label veteran, in charge of a division devoted to developing acts, agrees. "Artist development today is a lot harder than it was a couple years ago, because of the cost of marketing records, the cost of competing in the market place, the sheer size of the competition's product flow, and the amount of resources available. If a major record company breaks the average of one act a year to multiplatinum, they're doing great. They're the hottest record company around. In ten years, at that pace, you would have ten multiplatinum acts—if you stay on course for ten years with that."

There is still a fair amount of instant product at work. Never was it so apparent than with Veruca Salt, a band that had played a mere handful of dates before appearing at the 1994 South by Southwest Convention in Austin, Texas, a major industry talent festival. The feeding frenzy after the band's set was so intense that Veruca Salt wound up with one of the largest new-artist deals in record industry history, rumored to include a nonrecoupable half-million-dollar signing bonus.

Chicago-based Minty Fresh Records was the label that birthed Veruca Salt. Run by Jim Powers, that label had issued a Liz Phair single before signing Veruca Salt for an album. "And then people are ready to pay Jim Powers a million dollars," says one veteran label executive.

One prominent music industry attorney saw the A&R game as a conspiracy by the multinational corporations. "I think there's definitely been a period of a little arrogance by the labels," he said. "I think that the six major labels get together under the guise of Recording Industry Association of America meetings and they talk to each other about things like, 'Well, we're not going to sign any of your artists if they try to leave and, in return, we expect you not to do the same.' So that stuff goes on. It's sort of a ganging up of the labels against the artists and the people that represent artists. Labels use long-term, seven-, eight-album contracts to hold their artists in check, which gives them maybe an unequal amount of bargaining power when you're dealing with the artists."

Once Doug Morris was firmly in control of the U.S. division of Warner Music, he did not have long to enjoy his position. There was more trouble ahead.

Morris had earned his new position through a strong string of successes since being named Atlantic co-chairman in 1989. He had cut deals with Matador, Mammoth, Delicious Vinyl, Rhino, Beggars Banquet, and Interscope Records. He nurtured the startups of EastWest Records and A*Vision Entertainment, a fitness and children's home video division, and had hired such executives as Jimmy Iovine, Danny Goldberg, Sylvia Rhone, Stuart Hersch, and Rick Blackburn, none of them considered front-line executives when recruited.

Overall, revenues at the firm had risen from approximately $300 million—a sizeable amount of that number in older releases rather than new artists—to close to a billion dollars. Perhaps more important, the spin control on Morris was being stepped up as well; just two years after he assumed control, Morris's triumph at Atlantic was loudly proclaimed in a front-page article in *Billboard* that told of the label's passing the $700 million mark in revenues for 1992. In fact, the 1992 revenue represented just $1 million more than 1991's revenue.

But the good press had clearly been earned. Morris instituted a thriving management culture at the Atlantic Group, and although his ascension to U.S. division head was surprising in its timing—insiders had foreseen it happening at least a year or two later—the appointment had been anticipated for some time.

While Morris looked good, it put a burr under Morgado's saddle, as the notoriously sensitive corporate gamesman took umbrage at an employee who did not share the credit. Worse, several press articles on Morris even suggested that Morgado would be given new duties higher in Time Warner's ranks—possibly positioning him as chairman Gerald Levin's No. 2—with Morris assuming his duties. If Morgado desired such a move, he went out of his way to deny it, noting in one rare interview, "I'm not going anywhere."

It soon became clear to Morris that as president of Warner Music U.S. he did not have the power or duties his title implied. As a result, he did not sign an employment contract for his new job, even though he had formally assumed the position. In two particularly galling examples of Morgado usurping Morris's implied authority,

Morgado left his imprint on the issue of re-signing of Metallica to a deal at Elektra and renegotiating a deal with executive Seymour Stein, both of them seemingly part of Morris's new job. Morris remained outwardly calm but was wondering where it was all leading.

He got his answer when *Entertainment Weekly*'s annual list of the one hundred most powerful executives in the business came out.

Morris had been nominated to the lower portion of the list the year before, thanks to his status at the time as co-chairman of the Atlantic Group. Initial word from the editorial team at the magazine indicated that Morris would be moving way up, thanks to his promotion. But when *Entertainment Weekly* staffers called to do a fact check on Atlantic president Danny Goldberg, the truth was revealed: Morris was not on the list.

One Warner Music executive familiar with the story said that back-room intrigue had kept Morris out of contention. "Doug Morris was so successful that the editors at *Entertainment Weekly* believed that Doug Morris was the only significant senior player at the Warner Music Group and they put Doug Morris at No. 16, up from 97, and Bob Morgado, who was 17, 18, or 19, they just took off the list. And when Bob Morgado's people found out about it, they went beyond berserk."

At that point, the deadline for the issue was looming. Tired of dealing with the situation, managing editor Jim Seymour chose the simplest solution: remove Morris from the list.

Morris was in Los Angeles at the time the news was delivered. "He was supposed to be here for a few days," said an inside executive. "He marched out of the office, got in a car, went to the airport and flew to New York."

And that's when the real war at Time Warner started.

"Doug Morris is a good man," said one friend. "After his entire career being devoted to Ahmet Ertegun and being treated well by Ahmet, looking at what his new boss just did to him, he couldn't believe it. And he basically decided 'I'm not going to be publicly humiliated and publicly disrespected.' He said, 'I've been treated too well my whole career, I've worked too hard, I've treated my people too well, and I don't need the money or the aggravation.'"

However, more was at stake than an affront in a national magazine. Morgado had again taken a task that logically should have been Morris's province, deigning to name Warner U.K. head Rob Dickins as the replacement for Mo Ostin.

Morris, according to one senior executive, was not budging from one concrete demand: that he be given the duties implied by his new job or he would resign. The nomination of Dickins as Warner Bros. Records chairman was a particular sticking point. According to a source at Warner Bros., there had been enmity between Dickins and Morris dating back to the early '90s, when Morris dropped an artist named Enya from the Atlantic roster. Atlantic was, at the time, distributed by Warner Bros. International, run by Dickins. Warner Bros. International decided not to follow Morris's lead and eliminate Enya from the international roster. Shortly thereafter, Enya had a huge worldwide hit.

Morris allegedly took Dickins's refusal to follow his lead as a personal affront, feeling that his talent-hunting abilities had been disparaged within his own company. The professional slight was something Morris did not forget, making it unlikely that he would nominate Dickins for so venerated a position as Warner Bros. chairman, replacing an industry legend like Mo Ostin.

When Morgado told Morris that he would have to accept Dickins as head of Warner Bros., Morris threatened to quit and take his invaluable cabal of record label heads with him. However, what he didn't anticipate was that Morgado was not threatened when told that Rhone, Azzoli, and Goldberg would support Morris by quitting. The discussion escalated beyond words—outside the Warner Music offices, Morris and Morgado briefly engaged in a shoving match that was broken up by A&R executive Jason Flom.

With the situation escalating out of control, there entered a hidden player in the Time Warner battle, one whose influence over the whole affair was the key to solving the puzzle, yet whose name never surfaced in press accounts.

Joe Flom, father of Atlantic senior VP of A&R Jason Flom, is an influential attorney who introduced Doug Morris to the Time Warner board when he was just starting to ascend in the Time Warner turnover. Flom called Time Warner chairman Levin on Morris's behalf, asking Levin to involve himself personally in the dispute.

Levin was close to Morgado but was made to realize by Flom what was at stake: a devastating walkout by the top executives at one of Time Warner's most profitable divisions at a time when the company was burdened by debt and had a stock price that was not rising swiftly enough.

"I understand that the number of complaints about Morgado had gotten to the point where Levin and the board didn't want to hear about it," said one executive at Time Warner, explaining the reasons for the inaction amidst the infighting. "They basically didn't understand the music business. They thought that the music business was 65 percent international and 35 percent American and this was a small problem. What they didn't realize is that a large part of that 65 percent international is product fed from America, and that [the situation at Warner Music U.S.] was much more important than they thought. If Doug Morris and his entire team walked, that the whole global music operation—with Mo leaving and Bob Krasnow already gone—could have some serious problems."

Morris called a meeting of his top lieutenants at the apartment of Stuart Hersch, the head of A*Vision Entertainment. Present were Atlantic founder Ahmet Ertegun; Atlantic president Danny Goldberg; Mel Lewinter, the executive vice president of Warner Music U.S.; Sylvia Rhone, the head of EastWest Records; Val Azzoli, then the general manager of Atlantic; Jason Flom, the senior VP of A&R at Atlantic; Tony O'Brien, the Atlantic Group's chief financial officer; and Ina Meibach, executive vice president of the Atlantic Group.

But Morgado, prompted by an edict from Levin to settle his differences with his rebel executives, called Morris for yet another meeting, and Morris missed most of the conversation at the apartment, arriving as the meeting was breaking up. According to one senior executive, Morris knew that his team was willing to follow him if he decided to resign, but he would not have asked for a mass resignation.

"Doug was going to say to them that '[The Morgado situation] is unacceptable and I need to go,'" said a Morris confidant. "'Any of you that will come with me, I would appreciate; but I don't have to work another day in my life, and a lot of you do. You have young families and I don't anymore.' And from what I understand, every single one of them was willing to never go back to their job again."

Dickins, meanwhile, had been asked by Morgado to fly to New York for his coronation as the new chairman of Warner Bros. Records. Dickins checked into the Carlyle Hotel in Manhattan and waited for a phone call from Morgado's office. It was to be a long wait.

Faced with pressure from Levin and the board and the executives below him, Morgado succumbed. Morris was put in control of the American record operation, albeit with some checks and balances.

A somewhat absurd four-paragraph statement issued by Morgado's office argued unpersuasively that rumors of trouble between him and his comrades were "merely speculation" and "without merit." In the last paragraph, Morris was mentioned as Warner Music U.S. chairman and CEO. Morris was formerly president. The between-the-lines message: Morris had won.

Dickins learned late that night that he was not to be the new chairman at Warner Bros. Records. He flew back to London the next day, angry at his corporate humiliation.

Morris's first duty in his new job was to name the successor to Ostin and Waronker at Warner Bros. Records. He tapped protegé Danny Goldberg to become chairman of Warner Bros., a move which clearly indicated that Morris had consolidated his power. Val Azzoli, the general manager at Atlantic, was later elevated to president of the label.

Morris now had his people in place, with Sylvia Rhone helming a newly combined EastWest/Elektra label and Iovine negotiating with Time Warner to sell the remainder of his Interscope Records to the company.

Morgado was "defanged but not declawed," in the words of the *Los Angeles Times*. A few months after the war with Morris, a *Wall Street Journal* story broke concerning several executives who had profited dealing in so-called "cleans," albums that are used by record companies for promotional purposes at retail. The records, which are not marked "for promotion only," as is the case with radio and press promotion materials, are usually used as an incentive for retailers to grant shelf space, or given in exchange for advertising at retail. The retail store is allowed to sell the record without having paid for it, in effect receiving a cash award.

However, the *Journal* article said, it was believed that Atlantic executives had sold the records to wholesalers and pocketed the profits.

The article was widely viewed in many quarters as a plant by Morgado to subtly undermine Morris's regime, since the alleged practice of selling the "cleans" happened on Morris's watch at Atlantic.

Ron Shapiro, who had been responsible for the positive press Morris had enjoyed in the two years before the Time Warner war, had been promoted to general manager of the West Coast offices at Atlantic, a big reward for his efforts. Now, Morris promoted Shapiro to general manager of the overall label, moving him to New York. Not only was the promotion a reward for Shapiro's competence, but it was also viewed as Morris's attempt to have a rear guard in the home office to counterspin against Morgado.

Ultimately, Morgado's efforts at undermining Morris proved to be his undoing. Faced with bitterness within the label leaders and the perception among managers and artists that the Warner Music Group was fighting within its ranks—a spin other labels were using to gain an advantage in signing acts—Time Warner chairman Levin made a decision. Morgado was out, albeit with a golden parachute estimated at $50 million.

Michael Fuchs, chairman and CEO of Time Warner's Home Box Office cable television outlet, was named to replace Morgado. Fuchs, who had no music business experience, was widely believed to be a caretaker who would make sure things were under control at the music division before yielding power to Morris.

Morgado's firing set off a round of unusually candid press quotes. But former Warner Bros. chairman Mo Ostin had the final word on Morgado.

"In this business, the company should never underestimate the power of its artists," Ostin said to the *Los Angeles Times*. "But look, at Warner's we've seen Frank Sinatra retire. We've seen Jimi Hendrix die. We've seen The Who break up and James Taylor leave the label. And yet the company continues to grow and prosper. So what is the common thread? It's management. And while artists are what a music company is made up of, management has some real value—and it should never be underestimated."

The jubilation at Morgado's demise was undisguised among the Warner Music executives. In the *New York Times*, Danny Goldberg noted the difference in managerial style between Fuchs and Morgado: "It's the difference between painting and painting by numbers."

Goldberg would soon learn how wrong he was.

Fuchs had spent eleven years as chairman of HBO and appeared to be growing bored with the job. The opportunity to be the only Time Warner executive holding responsibility for two divisions seemed to be the chance he was waiting for.

In statements made at the time of his appointment, Fuchs said he had a "good reputation for being able to relate to talent, and I consider music executives themselves to be talent." Fuchs indicated that he did not want to run the day-to-day business of the record division.

Morris was allegedly given in mid-May a letter that indicated he would soon be promoted to the head of worldwide operations of the music group, Morgado's former position.

However, some six weeks after Fuchs assumed command, he stunned the world by firing Morris. In a meeting that was expected to cover the terms of Morris's ascension to Warner Music worldwide CEO, Morris was instead given a five-paragraph press release that detailed the reasons for his firing. "I have made a careful but difficult decision which I strongly believe is in the best interest of the growth and stability of the entire Warner Music Group," read Fuchs's statement.

Backing Fuchs in the same release, a statement from Gerry Levin noted, "Michael's decision has my full and complete support." Payback for having to fire Morgado, a Levin loyalist.

The meeting between Fuchs and Morris lasted two minutes, after which Morris was escorted by armed security guards back to his office, allowed to gather some personal possessions, then escorted from the building.

Morris, an employee of Time Warner since 1978, a man who had felt for the past month that he was about to achieve the highest ambitions of his career, stood outside his office on West 54th Street, clutching a box. He had been fired for publicly unspecified causes and would not receive a dime in additional compensation from the remaining four years of his pact as chairman and CEO of Warner Music Group. Morris filed suit for $50 million a few days after his dismissal, alleging that Time Warner had refused to pay him what he was entitled to under his contract. (Morris would later be joined on the unemployment line by several senior executives, including longtime associate Mel Lewinter, who also sued Time Warner for wrongful termination. Danny Goldberg left the company in late August 1995 to "pursue other interests," according to the official announcement.)

According to the suit, Morris signed a contract with Time Warner on December 5, 1994, to serve as chairman and CEO of Warner Music U.S. until December 31, 1999. The company also issued Morris a May 15 letter that allegedly promised that he would be promoted to president and CEO of the global music division by June 25, 1995. Morris was fired on June 21, 1995.

Morris's suit claimed he was owed $50 million if fired without cause. The lump-sum payment, according to the suit, would be based on salary, benefits, bonuses, and stock options projected over a period of the next four years.

Why was Time Warner balking? Speculation centered on the embarrassment arising from the executive payouts the firm was already obligated to make. Besides Morgado's $50 million, Time Warner owed former Elektra chairman Bob Krasnow $7 million, Mo Ostin $8 million, and Lenny Waronker an unspecified large sum. If

Morris were compensated under the terms of his contract, Levin would have a hard time selling his board and stockholders on the idea of paying well over $100 million to former executives.

Fuchs mounted a media offensive to explain Morris's abrupt departure. Morris was leading a campaign to destabilize Warner Music, Fuchs claimed to the *New York Times*. The company was under pressure when Republican Senator Bob Dole claimed that the company was contributing to the decline of American civilization by its distribution of violent films like *Natural Born Killers* and so-called "gangsta" rap music, which usually features highly explicit lyrics and brutal imagery.

Morris was one of Warner Music's biggest defenders of artistic freedom, having signed 2 Live Crew to a deal at Atlantic during the height of that group's controversy, and was pushing Time Warner to invest in Priority Records, one of the leading independent labels in gangsta rap. But Fuchs insisted that affinity had nothing to do with the firing.

"When I got here, I discovered that this place was becoming organizationally dysfunctional," Fuchs said. "My decision is not just based on my observations over the past six weeks. This is a situation that has been simmering in the music group for more than a year."

The final blow, Fuchs said, came when rumors circulated in the wake of Dole's comments that Time Warner might divest itself of Interscope Records, which had a strong presence in gangsta rap, or might even sell its entire music division. The latter rumors had been planted by Interscope executives, who were hoping, in effect, to sell their company twice. Time Warner already had paid $120 million for a 50 percent stake in the company and would have to sell that stake at fire sale prices if it was perceived as desperate.

Fuchs accused Morris and his loyal executives of trying to destabilize Time Warner by spreading rumors concerning Interscope and Time Warner. Remarks by Warner Bros. Records chairman Danny Goldberg in the *Washington Post* defending gangsta rap were particularly galling to Fuchs, who ordered Goldberg to cancel an appearance on TV's *Face the Nation*, where Goldberg, former head of the Southern California chapter of the American Civil Liberties

Union, was scheduled to again defend free speech. Fuchs was determined that no executive, save him, would speak about Warner Music Group.

"It's true that Time Warner has been under intense pressure recently, but this decision had absolutely nothing to do with the lyric controversy," Fuchs insisted. "It was about chemistry inside the company, and I had to make a profound change to ensure that this organization could grow. You know what they say—when a team is not working well, sometimes you fire the manager and it shakes up the ballclub."

Fuchs, much like Morgado, had apparently decided that empowering the individual executives within the music division was not the proper way to move Time Warner forward, despite the method's history of success. "This company has a long history of feudal baronies," Fuchs said to the *Los Angeles Times*. "There were giant figures who built nation-states around themselves. There is a history at Warner Communications of fierce competition between the divisions. I mean, this was part of the culture. But this is not 1970 and I was not going to live under the old rules. This is 1995. And what used to work in the old days does not work anymore."

An internal memo sent to Warner Music Group employees made it clear that Fuchs was now in charge. "The time has come to create an environment where people can operate in a maximum efficiency and without the distraction of internal politics."

Fuchs underlined to the *Wall Street Journal* just how different the demeanor was going to be at the new, improved Warner Music Group he envisioned. "The individual takes a back seat to the health and welfare of the corporation," Fuchs said. He was not quoting the philosophy of Mo Ostin.

SWALLOWING THE WORLD

Although SBK was the most successful startup record label of
the late '80s—at least in gross volume—it was by no means the only
one. Buoyed by the wave of compact disc sales, major distributors
decided to create new recording labels at an unprecedented rate.

Many of the startup labels were created as a reward to members
of the record industry's old-boy network, as executives like Derek
Shulman (an A&R man named to helm Atco Records), Vince Faraci (a
longtime Atlantic records salesman who was given the copresidency
of EastWest America), and Terry Ellis (the Chrysalis Record cofounder
and Imago Records head) were given millions of dollars to spend by
the multinationals, based on record industry success that, in some
cases, was a least a decade old.

Labels like Giant, Def American (later changed to American
Recordings), Zoo Entertainment, DGC Records, Impact, Jive, East-
West, and the umbrella organization known as the PolyGram Label
Group (which handled office functions for several small labels)
sprouted during this period, all aimed at creating new talent-seeking
structures within the corporate monoliths. The moves seemed a tacit
acknowledgment that bigger record companies are not necessarily
better, particularly when it comes to finding and nurturing talent.
The accent within the new startups was on entrepreneurship, and the
hope of every distributor funding these labels was that at least one

band would break through in its first two years and justify the startup costs.

Unfortunately, the wave of optimism that CD sales inspired was soon tempered by the realities of the U.S. national economic recession, which engulfed the East Coast in 1988 and was a full-fledged national problem by 1991, the world market also feeling the effects during that period. Consumers, more worried about putting food on the table than music in their portables, were carefully budgeting and became more willing to turn on the radio than buy records, a fact underscored in 1991 when first-half sales were disastrous.

The results of the crimp can most clearly be seen in numbers released by the International Federation of Phonographic Industries, a world trade body similar to the domestic Recording Industry Association of America. Statistics covering the year 1991 saw unit sales dropping by 326 million, an 11.2 percent fall. However, the value of the music that was sold climbed 5.5 percent, indicating that the price inflation of compact discs was helping the music industry remain afloat even though consumers were buying less music.

General music industry consensus dictates that a startup record label generally takes five years to achieve profitability, basically because there is no track record either in executive cohesion or in the artist roster. "In the fifth year you're in your third and fourth records, and all of a sudden you're starting to see the acts develop," said one veteran executive. "And then, over the next five years, you hopefully make back your startup costs. I mean, when did Geffen Records [one of the success stories of the '80s] really happen? Seven years in. Then it really happened."

Of the major startups in the late '80s and '90s, only Interscope Records appears likely to achieve long-term profitability. Funded by department store magnate Ted Field, with producer Jimmy Iovine serving as the company's creative director, Interscope has consistently been on the cutting edge of the charts, whether through dance music (Marky Mark and Gerardo), rap (Dr. Dre, Tupac Shakur, and Snoop Doggy Dogg), avant-garde rock (Helmet and Nine Inch Nails), career revivals (Tom Jones), or soundtracks (*Bill & Ted's Excellent Adventure*).

Ironically, Iovine was turned down by many would-be capitalists before finding Field, whose deep pockets allowed Interscope to outbid other labels for available talent. Time Warner took a 25 percent position in the new company upon its January 1991 startup and by 1994 had purchased an additional 25 percent stake and was actively dickering for the remainder at a price rumored to be in the neighborhood of $400 million.

"What they did is they played the Koppelman game," said one rival record executive. "They spent. They went the high road. They spent big. The one thing about that is the company's creative vision, Jimmy Iovine, really understands the record business. He signed all the right things, even though they paid more money than anybody else."

Interscope also outspent the competition when it came to executives. "They hired people and paid promotion guys $70,000 a year that were making $40,000," said one executive familiar with the company's operations. "I mean, they said, 'We're going to be aggressive.' And they made it happen. In three years they accomplished a hell of a lot more than Virgin accomplished in six years. Virgin did it all with mirrors. They spent a lot of money but never achieved profitability. At least Interscope spent the money, and they've actually delivered."

A prominent music business attorney agreed. "They've got a lot of good will. They're a hot company on the street and artists want to be with them. So they've created, in effect, a trademark or a franchise that, unless it's screwed up, will carry them for a while longer because they have Nine Inch Nails and Primus and Helmet, so a lot of cutting-edge rock bands want to be at that label. And then what they've done with Dr. Dre and Snoop Dogg and Tupac makes them also an attractive place for rappers."

Unfortunately, the success story at Interscope was not to be repeated elsewhere. While the would-be entrepreneurs who founded the labels might have had bank accounts equal in stature to Ted Field's, their agenda was slightly stranger.

Chameleon Records is one classic case. Originally a Los Angeles–based label that specialized in a hodgepodge of blues and rock, the company was purchased in 1991 by Daniel Pritzker, the son of the family that owns the Hyatt Hotels and Ticketmaster. The twentysomething Pritzker promptly dissolved Chameleon's existing management infrastructure, dropped most of the acts from the roster, and moved the operation to New York, hiring former RCA president Bob Buziak as his label leader.

Buziak, who had built an impressive roster of alternative-music talent at RCA Records, attempted to create the same operation at Chameleon. However, Pritzker was interested in a record company for reasons beyond financial—he had his own music career to consider.

"He was a kid who deceived me about his passion and love for real, honest artistry and never played his hand until I made the deal [for distribution through Elektra Records]," said Buziak, now a Sony executive. "And once the deal was done, then he sort of changed his whole approach and his whole interest in the music. Nobody knew he had this band called Sonia Dada. He never told me that. If he had told me that, I never would have gotten involved with him."

Pritzker, nicknamed "The Kid" by company gossip, became something of a nuisance around the Chameleon office, constantly piping up about the prospects for his own act and openly smoking marijuana. Meanwhile, the label's own startup costs began to mushroom, despite a roster that included the respectable Lucinda Williams, Kyuss, and Ethyl Meatplow. By the time Pritzker's family in Chicago told him to put away his toys and come home, the company had lost close to $25 million.

In a similar vein, Savage Records in New York was funded by Ferarri heir David Mimran. Building a roster that included David Bowie, Savage hired Michael Jackson's former manager, Frank DiLeo, to run the label's operations. But DiLeo was constantly vexed by Mimran's meddling and finally exited the company just before the release of Bowie's *Black Tie, White Noise*. The album's short shelf life paralleled that of the remainder of the record company, which quickly dissolved, leaving in its wake losses that approached $20 million.

While those startup labels struggled, the imprints backed by established major record labels fared little better. Charisma Records, born in January 1990, was a Virgin offshoot designed to take advantage of the executive talent of Phil Quartararo, a promotion man. The label's roster produced hits by Enigma, Right Said Fred, and Maxi Priest, but the majority of its thirty-album release schedule was not successful. Upon Virgin's sale, Quartararo was rewarded with the presidency of Virgin Music U.S., while the majority of the label's roster and employees were bid adieu.

DGC Records, a Geffen offshoot, was more of a logo than an actual label, sharing most of its administrative functions with its parent label. DGC enjoyed the biggest single success of the 1990s, releasing Nirvana's *Nevermind*, a record that broke alternative music into the mainstream. But the world recession adversely affected Geffen, and the company decided that the workload of both labels could be handled by a single staff.

EastWest Records had an odd shelf life, falling victim to the turmoils at parent corporation Time Warner. Started in October 1990 as a home for veteran sales man Vince Faraci and rising executive Sylvia Rhone, the label made its initial mark in R&B. Volume was added when the failed Atco Records was merged into EastWest, which slowly became Rhone's label. The final result saw EastWest merged into Elektra Entertainment, with Rhone running the operation.

Other labels had mixed success. BMG's Zoo Entertainment was founded as an artist-development label using the talents of former Island executive Lou Maglia. The label broke Matthew Sweet, Tool, and Green Jelly but lost money every year since its March 1990 startup. Giant Records, funded as a joint venture between former MCA Music Entertainment Group leader Irving Azoff, had mixed success, scoring with Color Me Badd and Don Henley's charity album, *Common Thread*, but also released Hammer's embar-rassingly bad stab at gangsta rap. Giant claimed to be making money, but if that was the case, the bottom line was more attributable to Azoff's financial acumen than the label's sales tonnage.

Morgan Creek Records was among the bigger failures of the startups. It was founded by studio executive and car importer James Robinson, with day-to-day operations run by former Capitol execu-tives and copresidents Jim Mazza and David Kershenbaum. The label heads loudly trumpeted their $100 million war chest upon their 1991 startup. Immediate success fueled their ardor: The soundtrack to *Robin Hood: Prince of Thieves* hit No. 5 on the album charts on the strength of Bryan Adams's "(Everything I Do) I Do It For You."

The windfall "totally altered the business plans," according to Mazza. "We recouped very quickly any kind of startup costs and were operating in the black within six or seven months of starting the company." Unfortunately, the A&R genius began and ended with soundtracks. Despite another soundtrack hit, *Last of the Mohicans*, the label is primarily remembered for its massive spending on alternative rock band Mary's Danish, which failed to click. The label lost in the neighborhood of $10 million before being folded into Robinson's Morgan Creek Pictures as a soundtrack division.

All of these labels failed in one way or another. But none of them failed as grandly as Hollywood Records, which became the whipping boy of the record industry for its perceived strategic and artistic failures.

After years of inquiries about purchasing a record label, the cash-rich Walt Disney Co. finally took the plunge late in 1989 and created its own. Hollywood Records was announced by Disney chairman and CEO Michael Eisner, with its first official release set for December 1990.

"First, recent industry consolidation has driven the cost of record company acquisitions beyond feasibility, and this has made entrance through merger or acquisition difficult if not impossible," Eisner said. "Coupled with that, we are convinced we can create greater shareholder values through a carefully engineered startup."

The surprise choice as leader of the startup label was Peter Paterno, a young, cocky attorney who wore his New York attitude on his sleeve, a characteristic that made him the barrister of choice for such outlaws as Guns N' Roses, Metallica, and American (née Def American) recordings guru Rick Rubin.

"I had not made a secret of the fact that I wanted to go run a record company," Paterno said. "I had heard David Geffen was starting Asylum Records at the time, and I asked David if he would be interested in letting me do that. He wasn't really, I guess."

But others definitely were. Paterno's reputation as a savvy music business attorney made him an attractive commodity in an industry starved for young executive talent. Paterno was in New York on business when he checked his Los Angeles messages and found that Michael Eisner had called.

"I didn't know Michael Eisner, so I thought it was a joke," Paterno related later. It was no joke. Paterno "wasn't even clear whether he wanted me to represent him as a lawyer or what," but Eisner was a man in a hurry. Eisner wanted to meet that day for lunch. Paterno, though in New York, agreed to meet the next day in Los Angeles.

"I guess he ended up liking me," Paterno said. "He said, 'You're the guy that I would like to do this with.'"

Disney was tired of virtually giving away money by allowing other labels to distribute their soundtrack albums. "Michael said, 'Here's a $25 billion business and there's only six people that are really in it, six players,'" Paterno said. "There seems like there's room for somebody else. They were obviously very successful in film and TV. They had the theme parks and they wanted to be in the next logical business, which was the record business."

The record business may have seemed a logical fit from a business standpoint, but its generally rebellious image was something that may have raised a few eyebrows in Disney's corporate culture, known for its one-time aversion to long hair on its employees and attendees at its theme parks. So Paterno decided to immediately test the waters by presenting Eisner with the worst-case scenario.

"I gave him some of the more extreme records when we'd gotten sort of down in the process, and I said, 'I want you to take these home, listen to them over the weekend and tell me if you still want to be in the record business on Monday.'" The walls of Eisner's home likely turned blue at the sounds of Slayer, N.W.A and Andrew Dice Clay. "He came back and said, 'Is this what the record business is?' And I go, 'It's not all that it is, but it's part of what it is.' And he said, 'I can't live with all this. I could live with some of it. But we will cross that bridge when we get to it.'"

The company was destined to cross that bridge sooner than later. Paterno had made his living from bands that did not make their reputations by driving paneled station wagons and preaching the rewards of clean living. Paterno was immersed in a hard-rock perspective that ran from Metallica and Guns N' Roses through Soundgarden and Alice in Chains, and he built his label's philosophy from that base.

"My view of how you do a label from a startup as opposed to what you do when you've been around for thirty years is that you sign music that's on the outside and sort of left-of-center," Paterno said. "The music either comes to the middle because the artists get older and mature, or the audience comes to them, or a combination of the two."

In other words, forget about safe, mainstream pop stars. "Not to disparage any particular artist, but, for instance, Mariah Carey, who's very talented and great looking and a great singer—you know, I don't get it," Paterno said. "Okay? I've been in the music business a long time. There are a lot of very pretty girls who sing great and they don't make it and Mariah Carey does. But it takes a lot of money to break acts like that."

It was a wild and woolly time in the record industry, with new labels popping up seemingly every week. As a consequence, experienced employees were in demand, and their price was high. The same was true with artists, who suddenly had an explosion of talent buyers bidding for their services.

"I had never worked at a record company before. I probably had a lot to learn," Paterno admits. "My initial theory was I wanted to get a lot of young people that were enthusiastic, and obviously young equates to cheap. So I would do things on an economical basis because it's kind of the Disney way and it's kind of my way, because when you're entrepreneurial, you don't really want to be spending money on flying first class and staying in suites when you're not making money. So I figured I'd try to find young, enthusiastic people and give them chances they wouldn't have someplace else, and to some extent it worked. And to some extent, it was real disastrous."

Because of the executive bidding wars, the price of even the youngest executive talent escalated. "Also at that period of time it was a very radio-driven industry," Paterno said. "And [radio promotion] is something that I've never been very good at."

In that dance-oriented, R&B world of the early 1990s, Paterno opted for outsiders to fill out his roster. He reasoned that going against the grain of the industry's current trend and promoting something unique would pay off in the longterm. "Whereas, when you take a Michael Bolton and spend $4 million promoting him or whatever it takes, you may end up with nothing," Paterno said. "For me, I can see N.W.A and say to them, 'God, this is really different.' And then it becomes a question of whether it's acceptable to a mass audience or not."

The Hollywood Records roster would not be known for much. Such bands as Ghost of an American Airman, Edan (featuring Phil Everly's son, Edan Everly), Organized Konfusion, Sacred Reich, The Poor Boys, the Party (a group of ex-Mouseketeers), D.D. Wood, Raw Fusion, Mitsou, W.W. III, Yothu Yindi, Circle of Soul, Eleven, the Pleasure Thieves, and the Scream are little more than footnotes in rock 'n' roll history.

Hollywood Records particularly lived up to its vow to step outside the mainstream by signing rappers The Lifer's Group, a club of New Jersey state prison inmates led by a man serving a life term for murder. The group would be one of the label's few bright spots, winning a Grammy nomination for best video.

The label is best remembered, however, for its deal to acquire Queen's North American catalog. Hollywood signed Queen and acquired U.S. rights to the band's fifteen-album catalog for $10 million in 1990. Many record industry observers felt that the label overpaid for a catalog whose sales levels, coupled with Queen's inactive status, made recoupment of the investment seem unlikely.

"I had heard that Queen only owed Capitol one more album and I thought Queen was still making pretty good records," Paterno said, "and they had just been kind of lost in the United States. I had known Jim Beech, Queen's manager, for years, because when they were signed to Elektra, I was Elektra's lawyer. So I wrote him a letter. 'We're starting a new label, I hear that you're free. Would you be interested in talking to us?'" He said, 'Not only we're free, our [back] catalogs are going to be available too. Would you be interested? Here's what the price is.'"

Paterno, anxious to build a foundation for Hollywood, agreed to the terms. It was only in hindsight that he discovered he may have been too hasty.

"He came in with the price and he just said, 'This is the price,'" Paterno said of his deal meeting with Beech. "Okay? And my sense was if I hadn't said yes to that price, I wasn't going to get the deal. Jim told me there were four or five interested labels. Everybody else said after the deal closed that I was the only person that was doing the deal. You don't know. The guy who was selling it to you tells you five hundred people are interested. The guys who don't get it tell you they were never interested at all. So I don't know."

One thing Paterno did know was the medical condition of Freddie Mercury upon signing the contract. Asked whether he had heard that Mercury was afflicted with AIDS, Paterno acknowledged that he had. "Yeah. Yeah, I had heard it. And Jim Beech didn't hide the fact. He said Freddie was sick. He didn't say, you know, that Freddie had AIDS or anything like that. I don't even think he said he was sick, but [Beech] said [Mercury] would not tour. He made it absolutely clear that Queen would not tour."

Paterno was convinced, though, that illness or not, Queen was worth the risk. "Honestly, I felt the catalog was good. I thought the band was still making good music. So you sit there and you go, okay. It's something that I believe in musically and there's two possibilities: either he isn't sick, in which case maybe I can convince them to tour, which means I will sell some records; or he's really sick and he may die."

"It doesn't change the fact that the music's good," Paterno continued, "and, you know, historically...I mean, without being completely crass about it, historically when people die their records sell. So economically, it didn't seem to be a huge risk. Obviously I thought Freddie Mercury was an incredible talent. I obviously hoped that he wasn't sick. But I was willing to take the risk one way or the other because I didn't think that was the risk. The risk to me was, 'Were they capable of making good music again?'"

The first Queen back catalog released—marking the first time the titles had appeared on CD in the United States—was issued in February of 1991. Hollywood had calculated that 2.7 million records needed to be sold to break even on the overall deal.

Mercury died on November 24 of that year. Hollywood had, to that point, sold 1.1 million records. "We were putting it out in a very deliberate way, and having not had the full catalog out, we had already sold 1.1 million units when he died," Paterno said. "So it was pretty clear that over the next ten years, we were going to sell enough records that the deal was not going to lose money. And then when he died, sales accelerated to the point where it became clear that within three years we were going to get our money back." The use of Queen's "Bohemian Rhapsody" in the film *Wayne's World* accelerated the pace even further.

However, Paterno couldn't really sit back and enjoy the fruits of his coup. In December 1991, his enemies at Hollywood had leaked an eight-page memo to the press and several rival record executives. The Paterno memo detailed his five-year financial plans for the label.

Addressed to Disney executives Michael Eisner and Frank Wells, the memo attempted to justify the $25 million in losses that Hollywood absorbed in its startup year, as well as financial and stylistic choices that Paterno perhaps too candidly admitted "have been just plain dumb."

The memo lobbied Disney "to be less concerned that [it is] presiding over the *Titanic* captained by the Three Stooges" and attempted to brace the company executives for projected 1992 losses of between $22 million and $33 million.

That Paterno was under pressure from somewhere inside Team Disney is made clear by the memo, Paterno writing that he received "absolutely zero value from skeptical corporate financial people telling me where to make changes to better run my business."

While not sparing himself the lash—Paterno admitted that

signees like Dave Clark, Liza Minnelli, and Patrice Rushen were "perceived to be scrapheap material"—he also reiterated his distaste for mainstream singers like Whitney Houston and Mariah Carey, noting that he liked "hardly any of them," and underlined his point that "the safe pop music business" was "the surest road to financial ruin."

What really set off the music community, though, were Paterno's swipes at the competition. Geffen, Giant, Capitol, Virgin, and SBK Records all came in for their lumps.

One of the memo's bigger attacks was on Capitol Records. Paterno claimed that the label lost $90 million to $105 million in unspecified years in its attempts to grow its own talent and pointed out that Hollywood had managed to stay away from "the financial Waterloo to which Capitol has not only been exposed but has actually experienced.

"I have been given the mission to build you a great record label that will prosper in the long run while losing as little as possible in the short run," the memo concluded. "And I feel like I am doing a pretty good job of it considering the overall market condition in which we operate."

Paterno later said the memo could probably be summarized in four words: " 'Get off my back.' That's sort of my philosophy of the world. If you hire somebody to do a job, let them do the job. If you don't like the job he's doing, you don't sit there and tell him how to do the job, especially these guys, who had no clue. You just fire him. Which they ultimately did."

From the moment the memo was leaked to the press, Paterno was a marked man at Disney. "In general, I was not a particularly popular person at Disney with my concept of signing left-of-center bands," Paterno said. "There was a lot of, 'Why can't we have Debbie Gibson? Why can't we have Mariah Carey? Why can't we have Michael Bolton? Why can't we have Kenny G? Why can't we get somebody who wants to sign those kind of artists instead of this filth?'"

Paterno also admits to some contempt for Disney's by-the-book corporate accounting. "When you're losing $7 million a year, knowing whether it's $13.18 million, to me, it didn't seem all that crucial,"

Paterno said. "To them, they thought it was the end of the world [if they didn't know exactly]. In any event, there were certainly a lot of people that didn't want a record company at Disney. The most senior people at Disney obviously were supportive. Some of the more senior people thought maybe we should have a record company, but it shouldn't be me running it."

Jeffrey Katzenberg, in particular, was a Paterno enemy. "I think it's not a secret that Jeffrey wasn't my biggest fan," Paterno said later, acknowledging that he understood Katzenberg's position. "If you're making $500 million a year off one division and losing money out of the other division, I know who'd I'd support. But there was a lot of flack. Again, we'd sign rappers that said bad words on records. We'd sign heavy metal bands. We did a couple marketing things that didn't go over real well," referring to one incident in which a rubber knife was sent out to promote a Slayer record.

Financial people would also offer Paterno advice on how to run the label. "Which, you know, without being too pejorative, they were completely clueless."

As an example of the short-sightedness at Disney, Paterno points to an attempted deal with American Recordings head Rick Rubin, who was leaving Geffen Records because of a dispute over the content on certain releases by the Geto Boys and Andrew Dice Clay. Paterno tried to get him interested in Hollywood as a potential home.

"Rick's not anything that Michael wanted to have there, and I think the feeling was probably mutual," Paterno said. "If I'd done a better job of working the studio lot and less time thinking about how I was going to beat my competitors, I probably would have ended up doing a little bit better. Although, ultimately, you're measured by your success or lack of success. If I'd been a failure for a longer period of time, it probably wouldn't have mattered that everybody loved me in the Team Disney building. But it turns out they didn't, so that wasn't particularly helpful."

In September of 1993, after a four-year run, Disney announced that Paterno would exit when his contract expired in November. Executive VP Wes Hein was named acting executive in charge of the label. The announcement came at an odd time, with Paterno having just signed new A&R VPs Bob Pfeifer and Nick Terzo, who came to Hollywood from the highly regarded Epic and Columbia labels, respectively.

"There was intense pressure on Michael internally," Paterno explained. "I mean, again, had I solved the internal problems, he probably would have stuck with it. He was very supportive. But, it's the old analogy, you don't fire the team, you fire the manager. I don't know what I was the manager of, but it was a lot easier to fire me than to fire the twenty-five people that were senior executives that didn't want me there, especially since they made money and I didn't."

Paterno said the timing of the dismissal "was really sort of inopportune. I think he pulled the trigger at exactly the wrong time. But the sort of determining event was that my contract was up. So I think that, at that point, we were a pretty good record company with bad records." However, Paterno insists, "We probably were poised to start doing pretty well," considering the import of the new A&R executives.

Despite the change of leaders, Hollywood Records to date has not turned around. "The financial guys have wanted to pull the plug on it for years," Paterno said. "I mean, it's really Michael who's prevented it from happening. So maybe one day he'll get fed up. I mean, this chapter [of executives] doesn't seem to be any more successful than the last chapter. Noting that there were few available executives who carried enough glitter and savvy to instantly turn around the operation, Paterno pointed out that even with such an executive, the restrictions imposed by the Disney image would limit prospects for such a reversal of fortune.

"There are certain areas of music [there] you really can't deal with, and you've got to have somebody sort of entrepreneurial to run it, and yet most of the record executives now are corporate kind of guys that have no entrepreneurial bent."

Disney's penny-pinching corporate culture is also a problem, Paterno said. "If you look at Interscope, which has been pretty successful, it's not exactly been a bottom-line-oriented label. They bet big and won. But I'll tell you what: That's not a real good corporate strategy. It's a good strategy only if you're trying to build something and ultimately sell it."

Reflecting on his legacy at Hollywood, Paterno talked about Queen, the Brian Setzer Orchestra, Organized Konfusion, and the Lifer's Group. "You know, there is stuff that did well that nobody cares about. I mean, the Party ended up selling 700,000 albums. Nobody cares, but they did. You know, I felt the George Michael project was really good. We had some soundtrack albums, like *Sister Act*, that did really well."

But Paterno thought more of the things that might have been. "We came pretty close to signing Smashing Pumpkins. We came very close to signing Naughty by Nature. We came very close to signing Cypress Hill. I wish any of those had come through. I mean, three months after I started there I had lunch with Stone [Gossard] and Jeff [Ament] from Pearl Jam and I said, 'What are you guys doing?' And they said, 'Well, we got a new band called Mookie Blaylock. We got a new singer we found in San Diego.' And I said, 'Great. Well, you've both got a home here.'"

However, the deal was contingent on whether Michael Goldstone, the band's A&R representative at Mercury Records, would be able to leave his job and represent the band at another label. "We have to go where he goes," the band told Paterno. "And obviously Goldstone got out, went to Epic and took Pearl Jam there, and that's that story," Paterno said. In the end, "I knew a lot of our bands just weren't very good," Paterno said. "And also, just out of sheer numbers, if you're releasing fifteen acts a year, even if you're doing a pretty good job of picking, chances are you're not going to do as well as someone who's releasing 150 a year. Just by the sheer odds and the sheer weight. I brought in new A&R people to see if we could get a new mix of artists, and I knew that a lot of the stuff we had wasn't very good. But what do you do? There was a lot of criticism about my A&R hirings, and I can only say that you don't know that an A&R hire is bad for at least two or three years. Maybe I could have cut that corner a little quicker, brought in some people a little sooner."

In the end, Paterno said, Hollywood Records was "a pretty good record company without very many good artists. I probably should have figured out a way to get better bands and better A&R. Politically, maybe I should have figured out a way not to have David Geffen mad at me the whole time and should have figured out a way not to have the corporate structure mad at me the whole time."

While the multinational corporations were out buying almost every company in sight during the 1980s, there were markets quietly developing that were building the next wave of great independent labels. These, of course, turned out to be some of the most prolific and profitable niches of the 1990s: rap and alternative music.

The 1980s saw the birth of great rap labels like Tommy Boy, Next Plateau, Sleeping Bag, Profile, and Select, as well as alternative labels like Sub Pop and Caroline. The big difference between these labels and the Islands, Atlantics, and Virgins was that the independents of the 1980s were sold early in their lives, never expanding to the point where they would be worth billions to their builders. Among the leading independent labels of the 1980s, only Profile and Sub Pop managed to retain their original owners, at least until Sub Pop eventually cashed in late in 1994 via a deal with Elektra Records.

Because of the tremendous overhead needed when a company has more than a few employees—record companies generally figure roughly $100,000 in expenses, salary, and benefits per executive employee—the small, lean, and hungry independent will always have an advantage in discovering new talent. It can afford to take more chances, explore new genres, and generally, with a minimum of business sense, can make a profit on sales of 10,000 units or less, items that wouldn't generate enough revenue to keep the lights on at most large companies.

The independents also have the advantage of speed—while multinational corporates take months to plan, construct, and record an album, the indie can conceive of the project and have it on the street several days later. In a fast-breaking and fickle world, particularly in rap, such speed proved a key advantage.

Of course, like most popular waves, rap was at first dismissed as a passing fad. No one would pay money to hear a spoken-word recording, or so the popular refrain went in some executive suites, pointing to several attempts at generating that particular genre that had crashed and burned in the past.

But the executives and artists who were creating rap music weren't ensconsed in a corporate tower. They were tapping into light poles to power their turntables in the South Bronx, or staging parties that would rely on one microphone to provide entertainment for a roomful of people. That excitement was being translated to recordings, and it was being done from the street level where the sound was born.

Russell Simmons started Def Jam from his apartment, later adding the talents of Rick Rubin, who was working out of his New York University dorm room. Profile's Steve Plotnicki and Cory Robbins began with an investment of $36,000 borrowed from relatives. Tom Silverman launched Tommy Boy Records after working as a deejay while studying geology at Maine's Colby College, headquartering the operation in his apartment on New York's Upper East Side. He placed an ad in the *Village Voice* for a support staff, acquiring president Monica Lynch, who worked as a topless dancer to support her Studio 54 nightlife habit.

One key factor that temporarily leveled the playing field between independent labels and major labels in the 1980s was the government investigations into independent radio promotion practices, a means by which large corporations attempted to lock up radio airplay by funneling cash to contractors with strong contacts in the medium.

From 1986 until the end of the decade, the system was temporarily restrained, enabling small companies to compete against multinational might. The immediate effect was that independent records cracked the pop charts for the first time in years, including the supreme triumph of Profile Records' Run-D.M.C. becoming the first true rap crossover.

Early attempts at rap by the majors were not too successful, with most artists quickly burning out. To combat such failures, many labels turned to the video world, the new friend of rejuvenation in the music industry, pumping up the profile of artists in an attempt to generate longer-term careers.

While rap music took some time to catch on at the majors, alternative music was equally slow, becoming the province of non-commercial and college radio stations. By the end of the decade, however, the indie rock community as it existed in the mid-'80s had been picked nearly clean by the multinationals, but most of the product failed to click in its new, larger home. At least until Nirvana's *Nevermind* became the breakout album for the genre.

One of the enduring myths of the modern record industry is that the consolidation of the business into the hands of six multinational corporations is actually good news for the small entrepreneur.

The thinking goes like this: The majors really can't concentrate on the type of new, innovative music that will likely sell in small amounts during its first years of existence. Hence, independent labels will spring up to take advantage of the gap in the market, in turn creating new creative hotbeds that will grow and thrive as the Islands, Virgins, and A&Ms did.

But the theory ignores the conditions of today's marketplace. Consider that retail is growing ever more consolidated, as mom-and-pop record stores are squeezed out by competition from major record chains and other forms of entertainment that didn't exist in the '60s and '70s or were minor commercial forces, like home video, pay-per-view television, computer online services, and electronic games.

Moreover, MTV had, by the late 1980s, become the dominant mass-market source for video acceptance, its decisions basically determining the fate of any expensive video clip, which would then be cast to the bitter wind of isolated airtime on regional cable shows or scattered previews on broadcast and commercial television, both with little impact.

The theory also ignores the fact that the multinational corporations now ruling the record business have far more money and resources than they did even ten years ago, which allows them to squeeze independent releases off the remaining store shelves and MTV by out-promoting the competition. True, an occasional exception will spring out of the pack, like Epitaph Records, which scored big successes in 1994 with the Offspring and Rancid.

But both bands had built strong fans bases, and label head Brett Gurewitz was already a veteran of the punk rock circuit he was mining, having spent ten years with the band Bad Religion, which ironically released its own major debut via Atlantic Records just as Epitaph was taking off.

That lone major independent financial success story in the last few years is nothing to cheer about. The conditions that allowed Chrysalis, A&M, Island, and Virgin to grow do not exist today. Worse, the multinational corporations are devising ways to tap into the independent void they created.

By the 1990s, a new, more insidious form of major label involvement was starting to take shape in the independent community. So-called "fake indies"—small labels created and funded by a major label that try to camouflage their ties to multinational corporations by appearing to be do-it-yourself creations—began springing up. It was a tactic that had been used by consumer products for years; witness the recent spate of beers touted as created by micro-brewers that are, in fact, owned by Budweiser and Miller, or so-called natural cosmetics that come from industry giants in the pharmaceutical field.

Labels like Seed (Atlantic), Thirsty Ear (Sony's Relativity division), Vernon Yard (Virgin), and others attempted to gain street credibility by downplaying their ownership by multinational corporations. Although some of the bands on those labels are distributed through the more radical avenues of independent distribution, the money and marketing schemes used to promote the bands are similar to those used for new, lower-level acts on major labels.

Today's highly cynical Generation X record buyer has been indoctrinated by the faux rebellion sold by MTV and the Seattle music scene to believe that a band's talent is directly related to its level of struggle. Thus, the major-label marketers, realizing that a sales base has to be established among those buyers, will attempt to distance themselves in any way possible from the act. That is until the corporate decision-makers are ready to make a move with the band and lead it to mass acceptance in the so-called "alternative music" market, which has now been completely co-opted by the mainstream and resembles nothing so much as Top 40 radio, with its penchant to live and die on one catchy song and a flashy made-for-MTV video.

As independent music magazine *Maximum R&R* pointed out, music that charts well at college radio will have better odds of making it onto commercial alternative radio. Thus, the momentum built for the so-called alternative act within the underground is crucial.

Four breeding grounds to build that momentum exist: college radio, indie record stores, indie-oriented magazines and fanzines, and venues.

"A good scam indie will focus on promoting its bands via all four of these avenues," said *Maximum R&R*. "Think about that. A major-supported label channeling its resources to promote bands in the four areas that are, by tradition, anti-major and anti-commercial. (You should be feeling a little queasy by now). It's clear, then, why majors need to be covert about it."

The multinationals also attempted to appear hip by a new method of funding upstart labels that resembled nothing so much as the company store used by the robber barons of the early twentieth century, whereby workers in the coal mining industry were forced to purchase their necessities from a store run by the company, creating virtual indentured servitude because the wages earned would never equal the tab being run up at the store.

SpinArt Records, a small New York label, is one venture that opted for the major label funding, signing a deal with Sony Music. A buzz had started about the label during its early success, leading partners Joel Morowitz and Jeff Price of spinArt to explore their options.

"It was our philosophy and still is that we never say no to something before we have explored the options," said Morowitz. "There are a lot of indie labels that won't talk to majors for a number of reasons, or because it's dancing with the devil, or whatever."

Under terms of their agreement with Sony, spinArt is owned and controlled by its co-founders. "They don't control us," Morowitz said. "They have no decision over our creative day-to-day. They have no decision over anything we do, basically. They provide us with a fund, and from that fund we do up to ten full-length records a year. Each record has an all-in budget. And when we say all-in, I mean everything. Recording, manufacturing, video, promotion, for everything, of anywhere from $10,000 to $16,000, which is extraordinarily cheap."

Morowitz explained the reason for the Sony deal. "We had losses. We had worked with Monster Man and the Dambuilders, Velocity Girl, Suddenly Tammy, and Small Factory; each one of those five bands has now moved onto a major label or subdivisions of a major label."

The partners rejected an offer of a salary and health care benefits from Sony. The deal boiled down to "We give you money to do your records," Morowitz said. "Use whatever independent distribution network you want."

However, "Basically, every dollar that comes back in, we pay back to them," Morowitz admitted. "We don't see anything personally." The only way for the label to make money is through sales of its back catalog. However, small alternative bands don't have a long shelf life after their initial splash. "A year and a half later, [the records] doen't sell anymore. So how do Jeff and Joel eat?"

Answer: they buy more food at the company store, i.e., they use the Sony money to sign more bands, creating more debt, but also giving spinArt a shot at recouping its debt by finding a band that will sell millions.

That happy moment hasn't yet arrived. Basically, because all of spinArt's records did not sell enough money to recoup their recording and manufacturing fees, "It's one of those things that you constantly find yourself in debt," Morowitz said. The only hope is that one of the bands goes on to become so huge within Sony's system that the catalog becomes worth money.

Unfortunately, the contract between spinArt and Sony leaves the smaller label constantly piling on debt.

"Chronologically, we signed the Sony contract, then you go eight months getting your shit together," Morowitz said. "You put out your first release eight months later, and all of a sudden you've got eight months worth of overhead. So you've got eight months of overhead, and the first release is coming out eight months later. That record comes out and you don't get paid by any distributor from three to four months. You're talking over a year and a half before the money comes in off the first record, and we've got a year and a half worth of overhead at that point. We're not going to eat for a while."

Morowitz used the band Lotion as one example of how the system works. Sony chose to invoke its right to distribute the record, thereby changing the revenue stream. "Through independent distribution, there's a split between us and Sony," Morowitz said. "When it goes through Sony Distribution, we get paid a royalty, out of which we pay the band. We make far less than anybody else in the deal. But on the other hand, we don't take the financial risk anymore, and they can do things that we can't. That's part of the reason why we did the deal."

Despite their ties, the spinArt partners had qualms about dealing with a major label.

"A major record label is nothing more than a distributor," said Morowitz. "A distributor sells product, like soap, shampoo. In this case, they sell music. And there's something inherently wrong with taking something like music and devaluing it down to the point of product. It strips it of its inherent value, because they could give a shit what the music sounds like as long as it sells. Someone pours their heart and soul into a song and it's being treated as irrelevant and basically all that matters is the numbers of units sold. There's something wrong with that when it comes to the arts. You just can't take something that's artistic and mass produce it and not strip it of some value."

By April 1995, spinArt had grown frustrated with its Sony deal. Many of the employees Morowitz and Price had closely worked with were no longer with the company. "No one was there to champion us," Price said, adding that Lotion had seen its career particularly damaged by lack of attention from the giant corporation. The deal was over, and spinArt took its business to Giant Records, sadder but wiser in the ways corporate policy can affect developing labels.

*   *   *

While the mainstream music industry warmly embraced these new sources of revenue, they also had a tough time dealing with its subject matter. As much of America had turned a blind eye to the rampant crime and casual violence of the ghettos, so too record companies objected to the four-letter words and graphic descriptions of sexual relations previously the province of the independent community that were now being issued under the corporate banner.

It was a situation that record labels might have taken control of sooner if they had been paying attention. But their hand would soon be forced by the one thing they feared—a conservative with incredible zeal, a knowledge of the law, a religious commitment, and seemingly endless appetite for press. His name was Jack Thompson, and he was soon to turn the music world on its ear.

On June 6, 1990, in southern Florida, U.S. District Court Judge Jose Gonzalez ruled that an album by 2 Live Crew was obscene, the first time a federal court had categorized a recorded music product in that light. Although the judge's decision was effective only in three Florida counties, the impact across the country was immediate.

In San Antonio, Texas, vice squad officers cited the Florida judge's ruling when they visited some thirty local stores six days after the ruling to advise managers that selling 2 Live Crew's *As Nasty As They Wanna Be* might violate the state's obscenity laws. They asked the managers to sign a letter acknowledging that they had been informed that the Florida judge and local law officials believed songs on *Nasty* to be obscene and possibly in violation of local obscenity statutes. Police in Ohio, Indiana, Alabama, Tennessee, Florida, and Pennsylvania had already issued similar warnings to retailers based on state obscenity statutes, a tactic some observers saw as prior restraint—an unconstitutional action.

The June 6 ruling by Gonzalez sprang from a suit brought by 2 Live Crew's Skyywalker Records (owned by group leader Luther Campbell) against Broward County, Florida, sheriff Nick Navarro, known as "Nick at Nite" among locals for his propensity to show up on the local televisions news shows, seeking glory for high-profile busts. The suit asked the court to enjoin Navarro from warning local retailers not to sell the album and also asked for a ruling on whether

Nasty was obscene on constitutional grounds. Gonzalez agreed that Navarro had erred in warning retailers but added that the album was indeed obscene.

Three arrests for selling albums believed to be obscene had already taken place. Two cases were dropped, and record-store owner Tommy Hammond of Alexander City, Alabama, had his conviction reversed on appeal.

Some retailers across the nation didn't need to be warned by police. They had already voluntarily pulled the album off shelves. Others kept it behind counters, restricting sales to those who had the identification to prove they were eighteen or older.

One chain, Kentucky-based Wax Works, didn't particularly care what the contents of an album were. Before pressure from other chains forced it to back down, the chain announced that it would no longer carry in its stores product marked with the Recording Industry Association of America warning sticker that stated the recording contained explicit lyrics. Another major chain, North Canton, Ohio–based Camelot, also threatened to pull records from its mall stores, citing disruptions at several locations that could lead mall owners to pull their leases.

In Florida, a Fort Lauderdale retailer was arrested for selling the album, and three members of 2 Live Crew were also nabbed for performing the album's contents at a Hollywood, Florida, concert.

On June 8, Charles Freeman, owner of E.C. Records in Fort Lauderdale, was handcuffed and taken into custody for selling a copy of *As Nasty As They Wanna Be* to an undercover detective. Freeman had flaunted his disregard of the judge's ruling in newspaper and TV interviews immediately after the Gonzalez decision, no doubt attracting the attention of the media-conscious Navarro.

The record store owner was charged with distributing obscene material, a misdemeanor carrying maximum penalties of a year in jail and a $1,000 fine. Although later acquitted in a high-profile trial that attracted national attention, Freeman eventually lost his store, partially blaming his legal problems.

Throughout all his legal troubles, 2 Live Crew leader Luther

Campbell was apalled by the lack of support from the record industry and noted how his legal bills had piled up.

"We feel like we're isolated," he said, adding that many labels may have been afraid to draw attention to groups on their roster whose content is similarly controversial. "I wouldn't feel that way if the shoe was on the other foot, because I know sooner or later, it would happen to me. Once the party ends here, it starts at another house. And when the party starts at their house, I'll remember that nobody helped me out. I know the whole nine yards of getting banned, and I could offer to help them."

While Campbell had problems, he also had a booming record on his hands. As a result of the almost-daily national media attention, *As Nasty As They Wanna Be*, which had been at No. 83 on *Billboard*'s Top Pop Albums chart, rose five places, a significant leap in light of the fact that many stores did not carry the album or restricted its sale. Campbell later signed a distribution deal with Atlantic Records, which loudly proclaimed its devotion to free speech as the reason behind the deal, but the relationship eventually soured.

A case can be made that because of the battles that were fought over censorship in the halls of Congress and the courtrooms across the country during the 1980s, recording artists had more freedom of speech then than they do now.

In the '80s, even a letter from the Federal Bureau of Investigation did not prompt the rap group N.W.A or its label to apologize for lyrics condemning the police. While Tipper Gore and the Parents Music Resource Center managed to create enough controversy with their Senate hearings and "hit lists" of artists for the recording industry to create a parental warning sticker, it was a strictly voluntary solution that many artists and labels ignored.

The climate of acceptance of an artist's right to issue whatever they wanted was vociferously defended by the media, with 2 Live Crew enjoying particular support, even though most of the mainstream press would not print the offending lyrics in their publications. Today, reviewers for those same publications often condemn lyrics and certain stances by artists. *Billboard*, in particular, surprised many in the music industry with a strong editorial by Timothy White blasting rapper Ice Cube, which prompted the artist to retaliate in a subsequent album by noting, "Fuck *Billboard*/and the editor/cause I'm the Predator."

By the 1990s, after Ice-T had issued the album containing the song "Cop Killer," the subject of controversial lyrics was inflammatory enough to draw the Time Warner board of directors into a confrontation that ultimately led to Ice-T's exit from Warner Bros. Records, with a large contingent of hardcore rappers following him out the door. Whether Ice-T left or was dropped remains unclear.

Today, record labels scrutinize lyrics as never before, censoring particular phrases and, in some cases, entire songs. Both major labels and independents have rethought their A&R policies as a result of the attention paid to controversial artists. Sony Music even took the step of distancing itself from artist M.C. Eiht by adding an additional warning sticker to an album proclaiming that the views of the artist were strictly his own, a disclaimer that was seen by many skeptics as an attempt to profit from the artist's work while avoiding any potential liability for his controversial views.

Other labels have taken steps to avoid controversy by refusing to issue particular albums by their artists. Geffen's denial of the Geto Boys and Elektra's balk at AMG are two such instances.

Retailers were equally cowed. Some areas of the country may never know what an artist intended his recording to look or sound like. Mass merchandisers skirted controversial issues by asking for and receiving "clean" versions of the same album and/or requesting changes in lyrics and cover art. Since a good portion of the U.S. music market resides in such mainstream retailing temples as Wal-Mart, the requests were complied with, even by such cutting-edge acts as Nirvana. With an increasingly consolidated and conservative retail base being created in the United States, policies are not likely to get more liberal.

If Tipper Gore was the Christopher Columbus of anti–record industry activism, then Jack Thompson was surely its George Washington. Armed only with a phone, fax machine, and incredible zeal, the Florida attorney managed in only a few years' time to turn the record industry upside down, sending it on the run from legal officials and drawing in the wagons in fear of potential suits using the federal Racketeer Influenced and Corrupt Organizations Act.

Thompson, who feared the effect of violent and sexually explicit material on women and children, was not a member of a national organization. He was merely adamant in his belief that retailers and record companies had a public duty to recognize and restrict graphic material.

Although he had been somewhat active in southern Florida politics—losing an election for Dade County state attorney (the equivalent of a local district attorney) to future U.S. attorney general Janet Reno—his real activism took off in 1989.

Beginning his career with what he termed a "private sting" on Florida music chain Spec's, Thompson used a sixteen-year-old to purchase a cassette single of the 2 Live Crew song "Me So Horny" to show that retail stores failed to adequately monitor their products. Thompson soon became a terror to chains across the country, sending a barrage of faxes to politicians, law enforcement officials, and media, declaring where and when certain recordings were being sold. The combination of bad publicity and community pressure was often enough to force the hand of local prosecutors and law enforcement officials.

By 1990, Thompson was deeply involved in the efforts against Time Warner and its release of Ice-T's "Cop Killer," joining with law enforcement groups and the American Family Association to threaten a national boycott of Time Warner programming and properties.

Thompson capitalized on his media notoriety by embarking on a college lecture series, pitting himself against such opponents as Professor Griff, whose anti-Semitic remarks had gotten him banned from the rap group Public Enemy; and Bob Guccione Jr., the founder of *Spin* magazine.

By 1995, Thompson was back to private law practice in southern Florida, being, in his own words, a "Mr. Mom" and taking care of his two-year-old son.

"I think the 2 Live Crew thing increased by a quantum leap the hard evidence for many adults as to what was available to their children," he said. "To be able to have factual evidence that this hardcore stuff was being sold to children, preteens, was a revelation to many of them. It was to me. The liberals say all we need to do is educate people and let the parents make the decision. Fine. Then parents certainly had the right to know what someone was selling to their children, so this was an educational exercise."

Acknowledging that record labels are now far more conservative in their release schedules than they were before his campaign, Thompson notes, "I just don't think that the 'Cop Killer' [backlash] would have happened without 2 Live Crew. Ultimately, Time Warner backed down, pulled it, reconfigured the album, fell out with Ice-T and you now have the new CEO of Time Warner, Gerald Levin, saying in the *Wall Street Journal* that they learned something from 'Cop Killer.' They didn't say that at the time." (Indeed, by 1975, Michael Fuchs, the chairman of Warner Music Group, said in a speech at the Edinburgh International Television Festival that the music industry could not take an "anything goes" attitude. "Here, as in every part of the entertainment business, there must be limits.")

Nearing the five-year anniversary of Gonzalez's ruling, Thompson said Campbell, in addition to losing his distribution deal with Atlantic, has lost his southern Florida nightclubs, has been successfully sued by members of 2 Live Crew over royalties, lost a suit aimed at getting Thompson from speaking publicly about him—"it was dismissed with prejudice"—and is financially strapped. Campbell filed for bankruptcy in mid-1995.

Thompson was asked if further legal entanglements for the record industry were on the horizon.

"My feeling for a long time is that the solution wouldn't come in the political or legal sphere—meaning a prosecutor doing it—and boycotts don't work," he said. "But what we would be looking at was civil lawsuits against [record companies] for having done these marketing of defective products, harmful to individuals. It's like Ralph Nader suing for unsafe vehicles. If the tobacco industry can be successfully sued for doing something that has warning labels and is not contraband, then surely a record company that sells something illegal, the 2 Live Crew album and others, can be sued successfully for selling something harmful to some of these children."

Thompson compared the heads of record companies with John D. Rockefeller in their concern for their fellow man. "What they do not seem to appreciate is the legitimate concern that people like me have. There are a few of us out here that are not going to give up because they're bigger. Some of that underestimation is justified, because people tend to go away. They're smarter than I am and certainly know how to sell, but that is the placement of profit ahead of people. Here we have the heads of record companies that don't have the heart for the working man and the children that J. D. Rockefeller had. So it's the classic limousine liberal mentality, forgetting about the poor schmucks out there whose kids are buying those records."

Danny Goldberg, now president of Mercury Records, was the head of the Southern California American Civil Liberties Union for many years and an ardent free speech defender. While admitting that we have moved through a volatile era regarding recorded content, Goldberg said attention has merely shifted from rock to rap and from record companies to retail.

"There's a lot of retail chains that are very restricted in what they'll carry," Goldberg said. "All sorts of rock albums and rap albums are not sold at Kmart or Wal-Mart, for example, which are two very, very big chains. They just have a policy and it was pretty highly publicized that Nirvana's *In Utero*, just because it had a fetus [on the cover], seemed to freak out the buyers [at the chains] and they made some changes in the artwork. It wasn't even violent or even about an abortion or anything. It was just vaguely suggestive of a pro-choice consciousness or something."

Goldberg said retail was specifically a target for harassment because it is perceived as a "weak link" in secondary markets. "In the major markets there's such diversity of outlets for music that if one store doesn't carry it, another one will. But in the smaller markets, where the economy can't support several different stores and in some instances there's not even a record store—people go to a department store and see a record department—there's a much more limited set of choices."

Ultimately, artists face a choice: They have to choose whether they want to be in those stores and realize that if they're not, they won't make as much money. While artistic freedom is, in part, protected by the capitalist even on the retail side, Goldberg contended, "I think it's very wise to remain vigilant and concerned about attempts to blame popular culture for social ills. And I think that that vigilance is part of why there's a reasonably good atmosphere, and if you drop the vigilance, the slippery slope is real and threatening."

Bob Chiappardi, head of Concrete Marketing, which specializes in the unique hybrid of hard rock and heavy metal known as hard music, said that concessions are inevitable. "I mean, my attitude whenever I get into this is to say, 'Hey, look. There are a million street corners in Manhattan. You can do anything you want on that street corner up to a certain point. But you can't drop your pants and play guitar either.' No matter what you do, there's going to be some kind of restraints. Is the music going to be any better because Mick Jagger smokes a cigarette or drinks a drink [in a video]? Is the song going to be any better or any worse? So if it's not going to compromise the music, to me, what's the deal?"

Other individuals in the music industry had, in the preceding decades, posed much the same question as Chiappardi, but in a different context. Instead of caring about the verity of music's content, they didn't see anything wrong with manipulating the record charts to serve their own purposes.

NINE

BUY ME A WASHING MACHINE

Artie Mogull, a veteran record executive who now is a semiretired consultant, took a draw on his tenth cigarette of the interview and gave his views on the new method of determining the record charts that run each week in *Billboard* magazine.

"I hate—what do they call it—SoundScan? I hate it. It's too honest. In the old days, you could fuck around with the charts. That was the music business. I liked that better."

Albums used to sit atop the *Billboard* charts for weeks, giving the impression that they were selling tons of records. The truth was sometimes far different. Albums could, in fact, be off as much as twelve places in actual rank. Not that this was any surprise to record labels—they knew the game, and they were aggressively playing it.

In some cases, albums were held aloft by promotional monies paid out to retail stores, which were reporting the albums as selling even when they were not. Free goods, cocktail parties, and concert tickets were as much the cause of an album's perpetual reign atop the charts as any public popularity. But by the late 1980s, it was clear that the music industry was ready for some rules of order. The corporate way of doing business had emerged, and balance sheets that once could be overlooked as an inconvenience to the overall operations were suddenly coming under greater scrutiny.

In the old days, most of the machine was fueled by hype. Mike

Shalett, one of the founders of SoundScan, recalls a particularly revelatory moment. "I don't think I'm telling a tale out of school when I tell you about one of the people that we showed the SoundScan system to before our existence in 1990. We went down to the bar in the Mirage Hotel, and he said to me, 'Boy, I can't wait till we start doing this. Then I can stop buying washing machines.' I said, 'What are you talking about?' He said, 'I'm having to buy washing machines for accounts. I want a No. 1 one report for that record, I've got to buy him a washing machine. He's even naming his brand.'"

Today, the only way to make a record go higher on the charts is to sell more copies. "So I would think there's a greater return on the dollar," Shalett said. "There's no value to washing machines, dollars spent on trips, or whatever kind of greed was going around."

The washing-machine era of the record industry gave birth to a war that pitted *Billboard* magazine, the industry bible whose name is synonymous with record charts, against two guys from upstate New York. In a move that was the music industry equivalent of stealing the formula for Coca-Cola, Mike Shalett and Mike Fine managed to beat the big boys at their own game, out-hustling the 800-pound gorilla of music industry charts and taking over an operation that *Billboard* had controlled for over half a century.

Shalett was a veteran radio-station DJ and record company promotion man who started his own marketing company, the Street Pulse Group, in the early 1980s.

"The concept was fairly straightforward," Shalett said. "I saw that in record companies when you went to do the marketing plan for the next record, whether it was Ronnie Milsap or Shalimar, it was literally the same marketing plan. It was like you opened one file drawer and you took out the same marketing plan for everything."

This game had been played for as long as the modern record industry had existed, according to Shalett. A business that had been birthed by street hustlers and record store clerks couldn't shake the lessons of its roots. "It was, 'You push this guy and he plays the record, and then if he plays the record, we play this game, and it goes up the chart,'" Shalett said.

But something was changing in the record industry. Business

standards were starting to be adopted, most significantly affecting the concept that records could be shipped by the distributor and then returned by the retailer for full credit. Shalett recalled, "If I shipped you 100,000 records, most likely you'd give me 10,000 free on that 100,000. So now you ship me 110,000, I've got an invoice for 100,000. But if I return 100,000, guess what I get credit for? 110,000. I saw that maybe there was a need for people to do things in a more businesslike way."

Shalett's Street Pulse Group began expanding the types of information it would offer the record industry. "In 1987, I was getting more sophisticated at what I was doing," he said. "I changed computer systems, and, in changing, I needed tabulation software." Shalett asked his repair people for a contact, and they introduced him to Mike Fine, whose firm had run the Gallup poll for years.

Together, the two started Sound Data, a company that did consumer research for record companies. "So now we were starting to see an inkling of people getting into research," Shalett said, research that would be used to make presentations at various industry trade conventions.

It was at just such a trade convention that Shalett was given the inspiration to pursue his own chart system. *Billboard* held a meeting at the National Association of Recording Merchandisers' (NARM) convention, held in 1989 in New Orleans, to explain its plans to develop a new chart that would calculate record standings based on point-of-sale information. The company had been planning the strategy for years but had delayed its implementation because the majority of the nation's retailers were not computerized and were thus unable to electronically read the bar codes of packages and accurately tabulate sales.

The morning of the *Billboard* presentation, Shalett went to breakfast with Tommy Boy Records chairman Tom Silverman. "He asked if I was going to the meeting," Shalett recalled. "I said I wasn't on their 'A' list of invitees, and besides, it was a closed, by-invitation-only meeting."

Silverman fished a dollar out of his pocket and promptly hired Shalett as his consultant. He could now attend the meeting.

The meeting did not go well for the *Billboard* executives assigned to detail their plans for a point-of-sale system. "How much money are you planning to pay us for this data?" asked one agitated retailer. *Billboard* executives were adamant. "*Billboard* has never paid for data and never will," said one of the panelists, setting up a round of grumbling.

After the meeting, which was plagued by microphone feedback, Shalett said he was approached by several disgruntled retailers and encouraged to take his own stab at point-of-sale information systems. But as he discussed the situation with his partner, Mike Fine, the obvious questions came up: Why would a retailer leave the *Billboard* system and report to them? And could they successfully compete?

The solution the team came up with was simple: Because, in the increasingly consolidated retail world, most of the data was in the hands of mega-retailers like Trans World, Musicland, Wherehouse Entertainment, and others, convincing the largest retailers to join the revolution while offering to pay for the data would likely turn the tide.

"At that point, our approach didn't differ from [that of] SoundScan," said Howard Lander, the publisher of Billboard. "It just came down to a situation of who was willing to pay the most, and it got to be a difficult situation because one thing the industry wanted to avoid was two conflicting systems. *Billboard* always had its own system, and we wanted to control the destiny of the charts. We said it was in the best interest of the industry if there was one chart."

That chart, of course, was *Billboard*'s. As trustee of the chart that the public perceived to be the chart of record for decades, the company scoffed at the notion that Shalett and Fine could compete. Shalett said that attitude served him well.

"I think that when you become an institution like *Billboard*, you can become placid, complacent, arrogant, which is a lesson we should all be well served with," Shalett said. "I got a phone call from John Babcock Jr., who was the publisher of *Billboard* at the time. He said, "I hear that you're out on the street trying to put together this point-of-sale thing. Well, let me tell you something: That's *Billboard*'s. We're gonna do that. And if I were you I wouldn't waste my time.""

After he got off the phone, Shalett went to his computer and printed out a sign that said DON'T WASTE YOUR TIME, put it in a frame, and placed it on his desk. "That was one of those things that was a reminder to me in that entire struggle to get accounts."

Both sides set out to develop a system that would take actual sales figures from retail sources and devise a ranking. Although not every sale from every store in the country would be tabulated, the store sales that were used would be taken and extrapolated, so that a picture of the total sales in the country could be calculated. It was not a perfect system, but it was far better than the previous methods, which relied on estimates from store clerks, with most of those reports highly susceptible to manipulation.

Under both systems, retailers would be paid for their information (using funds obtained from record companies and other parties interested in the data) on the basis of their number of stores. As of 1994, that amounted to $40,000 per market share point at SoundScan; in other words, if Musicland's stores in a particular market have a ten-point market share, they get $400,000. Record companies provide SoundScan with a list of their key customers (the stores that are buying their products), and then the stores are weighted by their purchasing power in relation to the size of the record distribution company.

From that fateful day at the NARM convention in the spring of 1989 until shortly after Labor Day of that year, Shalett and Fine began visiting retailers. They soon discovered that retailers were playing *Billboard* against SoundScan, hoping to eke out a progressively better deal.

In the fall of 1990, Shalett and Fine's SoundScan announced exclusive deals with accounts that represented 30 percent of the business. The partners added that they would go on-line with the information on January 1, 1991.

At that point, *Billboard* and SoundScan briefly tried a reconciliation. "I thought we had made a deal and we would work together," Shalett said. "That was on a Wednesday before a long weekend. By the time the long weekend was over, we didn't have a deal."

Shalett had mortgaged his home to finance the new venture

and was running low. But his computer software people had met a self-imposed January 1, 1991, deadline to have a system up and running, and SoundScan was ready to start.

Even though its chart system was missing various key players, such as industry giant Musicland, with over a thousand stores, *Billboard* continued to publish its rankings, resulting in a chart that was skewed toward the industry's smaller players and didn't accurately reflect sales activity.

SoundScan, although holding a healthy advantage, hadn't won yet. Record labels, which would ultimately determine which system would win because they would be the ones paying for the information, had not yet signed up. The ultimate test would come at the 1991 NARM convention, when both *Billboard* and SoundScan would outline their point-of-sale systems for the industry.

Shalett was having lunch with Joe Mangione from *Billboard*'s marketing group at a restaurant near the magazine's offices when they saw Joe Wallace, who was heading *Billboard*'s own attempt to create a point-of-sale system.

"I was gonna walk across to see a client," Shalett recalled, "and I said to Joe [Wallace], 'Can I talk to you for a second?' So we're walking toward Broadway, and I say, 'You know, I can't believe you guys. You're playing high stakes poker. I know that you've got to go to the National Association of Recording Merchandisers' convention, and I've put a pencil to paper and know you're in a miserable position. You walked away from a deal last November. I can't believe you will let this boat sail.'"

They didn't. By the time Shalett returned to his office, the magazine had called. A few meetings later, a deal was struck. *Billboard* would now use SoundScan information as the basis for its retail charts.

Billboard publisher Howard Lander conceded that SoundScan had the upper hand. "We felt SoundScan had a very good basis for their chart, they had Musicland, did a deal with some racks, they may have had Wherehouse Entertainment. We had others." However, regarding the charts *Billboard* ran in the interim after losing stores to SoundScan and before adopting the system, he notes, "If we had waited too much longer, I don't know what would have happened. I prefer not to think about it. We felt it would be better to let them gather the information."

Now came the hard part. Record labels, which ultimately would pay for the information, had to get used to a new way of doing things. They were not eager for the change. "It was almost like what we were doing was playing around before," Shalett said. "And now that it had become reality, it scared the shit out of some people at the labels."

The reason for the panic was that the old smoke and mirrors that kept albums aloft for weeks was about to vanish. "Before, if *Billboard* sent out their [inquiries] on Monday night, you could, say, 'Fix it' before the cement got too hard," Shalett said. "Any record executive would say, 'Oh, make whatever phone calls you have to, do whatever you have to do, but get it done.'"

The charts were so volatile at one time that labels were actually warned with an advance chart before the final results were in. When the pre-chart chart arrived, "then the radio guy at the record company would see it, [make a phone call], and come Friday that wasn't the chart," said Shalett. "It was an early warning system that really played right into the hands of the whole corrupt system."

Labels were given eight weeks' notice before *Billboard*'s new chart system was installed—certainly fair warning. Although there were still questions about which record labels would ultimately sign up for the new system, there was no stopping it. Ultimately all six major record distributors signed up for the SoundScan system.

While *Billboard* was looking to expand into point-of-sale systems, it also created a way to more accurately reflect the way radio airplay was monitored. The company it turned to was Broadcast Data Systems (BDS), which, much like SoundScan, had devised a system that remotely monitored actual airplay rather than relying on the often-inaccurate verbal reports from station representatives.

Thus, like SoundScan, the system was designed to eliminate much of the hype that allowed radio stations to claim they were playing songs when they actually were not.

BDS, launched in 1989, placed computerized monitors in each

market to listen to radio stations and identify which songs were playing and how often. Records were submitted to the firm's Kansas City headquarters, there to be fed into a machine that would record the data so that it could later electronically recognize each song that was being monitored on the radio.

Virtually overnight, record companies began to determine a record's progress by the number of plays it received rather than by its ranking in any number of radio tip sheets. In some cases, record labels felt that BDS's electronic monitor failed to provide accurate results. MCA Records went so far as to take out an ad in the trade magazine *Hits* to proclaim that 15 percent of Meat Loaf's radio airplay on the song "Objects in the Rear-View Mirror" had somehow eluded BDS monitoring, causing it to go down when it should have headed in the opposite direction.

"The problem is with people who interpret BDS as gospel," said Bruce Tenenbaum, MCA senior vice president of promotion. "We're telling people that they should consider many sources of information, not just one." BDS later rectified its apparent error, issuing a memo to radio programmers admitting to the under-detection. Whatever its faults, the BDS system, like SoundScan, was allowing the big multinationals that ran the music industry to spend their money on music rather than washing machines.

The system, however, was still fine-tuning itself, as *Billboard* itself may have tacitly admitted when it announced in 1994 that it was committing $5 million to install a whole new BDS system that would be in place sometime in 1995.

Finally, the big day came for the *Billboard* album chart changeover to SoundScan data. While everyone knew the *Billboard* 200 chart would be different, no one was prepared for the amazing results that followed. With the first chart, SoundScan's data collection had an instant impact: country music, specifically Garth Brooks, rapidly ascended to the top of the chart, while new and developing artists virtually dropped off.

Henry Droz, the president of WEA, the distribution arm for

Atlantic, Elektra, and Warner Bros. Records, the largest U.S. label group, neatly summed up the reaction of many in the industry to the new chart: "In one single day, you ruined ninety years of *Billboard*."

With Garth Brooks reaching No. 1 on the test chart issued the week before, most record labels were warned. But many feared the reaction if Brooks was the first artist to top the chart under the new system. It was unusual for a country artist to be that high on the charts; having him lead it would make the system appear nutty.

"Thank god for Michael Bolton," said Shalett. "He was the first No. 1 artist when *Billboard* began using the SoundScan chart. But it wasn't really long before Garth Brooks jumped back into the No. 1 slot."

"I remember that the industry overall [was] pretty positive," said *Billboard* publisher Howard Lander. "There were some pockets of resistance, where they felt the SoundScan panel was not deep enough. Tower was not part of it at the time. The industry felt it was heavily weighted toward the rackjobbers [large department stores, which sell more mainstream types of music]. Certain labels had hoped we would wait until we had the chart in better shape, with more independent retailers."

That notion, however, flew in the face of an old philosophy developed at the inception of SoundScan, Shalett said. "Mike Fine was insistent on the idea that if we said to the record labels we were going to be up on January 1, 1991, we didn't give a shit if we were operating with one indie store. We said we would be there, and we were. *Billboard* said on many occasions, 'We will be going to the point-of-sale system,' and they would always postpone it. Mike Fine, who had done polls for years for the government, said he couldn't call the government and postpone elections."

Developing artists are the equivalent of research and development projects at major record labels. To have those acts vanish off the charts would mean labels had wasted millions of dollars in marketing and promotion to achieve that chart position. Atlantic Records was one of the labels not pleased by the vanishing act. It reacted to the new chart by pulling all of its subscriptions and ads from *Billboard*.

But, eventually, record labels came to realize that the truth now reflected in the charts was not something to fear but rather something that had real business advantages.

Shalett said the difference between the old charts and the new SoundScan system is simple. "I say to people, you look at the right side of the chart where it shows Tim McGraw is selling 130,000 pieces per week. That's a million-three [in revenue]. The difference between No. 1 and No. 10 is not the image or nine positions. You can build touring on that. You can sell T-shirts on that. You've got an artist. Before, I think there was just so much that was ethereal. It was gaseous."

Yet floating around the industry were all sorts of rumors about the manipulation of the system.

"I remember going to a pig roast, and I met the guys from SoundScan," said one prominent artist manager, who requested anonymity. "Sony thought that EMI was buying hits. I remember standing there with the SoundScan guys and I talked to them. The guy denied any [manipulation]. But it actually came out that it was delayed by six weeks because SBK had already found a way to pervert it. Something with the computers. Something at source where they can get numbers punched in, you know, and they found a way to do it economically."

Shalett denies the SBK rumor and notes that several other tales were making the rounds at SoundScan's inception.

"There was one tale where record companies allegedly would give candy bars to the stores that they could sell for a nickel, and the bar would have the universal product code [UPC] for a record on it," Shalett said. "Except most of the guys do not use UPCs on their scanners. They use stock keeping units [SKUs]. It's when they send data to us that it's in UPCs. Some of these tales were hilarious and only pointed out the lack of knowledge on the part of certain individuals in nonsales positions who didn't understand how the retailer systems work."

Still, the human factor couldn't be entirely avoided. Record companies now worked hard to make sure an artist debuted near the top of the charts, stroking buyers at major retail chains, radio personnel about early singles, and press to whet the public appetite before an album went on sale. From Meat Loaf to several obscure rappers, the strategy paid off. However, the race for the top had a downside as well: When an artist started sinking on the charts, even though his or her recordings were still selling, the perception remained that a record was over.

"You can't deny what we say now," Shalett said. "We're practically collecting every sale. You can't deny what BDS says, because they're in every major market listening to every major radio station."

While accuracy had at last come to the charts, truth was not necessarily breaking out all over the record industry. At least at EMI Music, corporate politics still ruled at the Capitol Tower.

SHELL GAME

By 1995, EMI was in deep trouble in North America. At Grammy time, traditionally a point when the state of a company's affairs comes into focus at major record labels, the chart share of EMI's CEMA distribution was dead last among the Big Six.

Worse, the company's big artists of the moment were Frank Sinatra, at age seventy-nine unlikely to be turning out albums for many more years; the Beatles, who were revived by decades-old BBC recordings; Garth Brooks, whose greatest-hits package was being released for a limited time; and Bob Seger, who hadn't had a major artistic success in years yet was on the comeback trail courtesy of a greatest-hits collection.

Despite the morass, the bottom line for the company still looked good. Part of that was the marketing genius of Charles Koppelman, who risked traditional entertainment retailer wrath by taking the bold step of being the first major record executive to tie in with McDonald's and its enormous ability to tap into the American mainstream. In the fall of 1994, EMI had offered music from Roxette, Garth Brooks, and Tina Turner for sale through the hamburger chain, moving over 9 million units in North America. The fig leaf used to cover the experiment with alternative retailing was a token $1.00 contribution to Ronald McDonald House for every unit sold.

Koppelman claimed that retailers had gotten over their initial anger at the McDonald's experiment when they saw the spillover business that bought the McDonald's music and then went to the record stores to purchase other albums by the artists. He also predicted further experiments with unusual marketing and hinted at the possiblity that fans may be able someday to buy new albums with a side order of fries at some fast-food outlet.

But the overall prospects for EMI's North American operations were dim. The various labels had few promising new artists, and, coming off a year when many of the label's big guns had delivered less-than-successful records, it looked as if the company were set for a long downward spiral.

Even Capitol Records, where Koppelman had installed Gary Gersh, was not working well. EMI was still doing record numbers, but as Fifield himself admitted to a former employee, "It's getting harder and harder to pull it out."

It had gotten to the point where many in the industry wondered how much time Koppelman had left to turn the operation around. Under terms of his original buyout on SBK Records, Koppelman and Bandier had signed management contracts that carried through 1995. Whether he had signed a new deal had not been revealed in the first half of 1995, leading to widespread music industry speculation that a decision was still being made by EMI upper management on whether to renew his contract.

The bleak outlook was taking some of the glamour away from Charles Koppelman's high-flying image.

"They sold [EMI chairman] Colin Southgate a bill of goods," said one executive intimately familiar with the machinations at the company. "[EMI executives] loved the idea of a guy with a jet that flies all over the world and entertains. The bloom is off the rose now, and people realize that it's bullshit. Every once in a while, if they have tons of press and media, the Koppelman business methods can have some effect. But on a day-to-day basis, it doesn't work that way."

There was new speculation that EMI Music was merely pumping itself up for a sale. After all the spending to acquire record labels and changes in the executive teams, the company was ice cold on the charts. Yet the stock price remained solid: the company could trot out an impressive number of big names on its artist roster to any potential buyer, and, if EMI were interested in selling, it could argue that there were only six major record distribution companies in the world.

Late in the summer of 1995, EMI's Southgate revealed that the company was considering splitting its music division off as a separate entity from its other interests. The immediate speculation was that the music division would be sold or Thorn EMI would sell a majority interest in the division to any number of interested parties. The decision on whether to split the company was to be decided early in 1996.

As further proof that a sale of the company might be possible, industry insiders noted that Fifield and Koppelman—executives whose bonuses were based on the company's performance and who probably held stock options that would enrich them wildly upon any sale—had likeiy done all they could to exploit the company's back catalog, and were having little success at developing major new artists, the financial lifeblood of any record company. It would benefit them to seek buyers before the financial picture began to change.

The sales rumors were denied by Thorn EMI executives. And there were still some in the business who believed EMI would continue to make its numbers.

One executive familiar with the system agreed that things were likely to remain stable. "I will guarantee that around October or November of 1995 they will put out the Beatles album with the three surviving Beatles, and will start putting out the great shit that the Apple/EMI battles kept off the shelves," the executive said. "They have enough other little goodies that they are able to repackage."

"I hope that by the time I'm finished EMI Records Group North America becomes the preeminent music company," Charles Koppelman said, reflecting on his career from his thirty-seventh-floor office in Manhattan. Koppelman did not hesitate to blame his predecessors for the difficulties faced by his company. "We've got a long road to go, and we started real late. There's been about twenty years between the Beatles and now where not a lot has been done with these companies here in North America, where they had an opportunity and really let it slip away."

To get EMI Records Group North America to the lofty goals he envisioned, the Charles Koppelman of 1995 seemed to have embraced a new style. The master of radio-driven promotion now looked to albums and artist development for his salvation.

"One of the things we're thinking about is to not even put out singles on artists such as Jon Secada or Joshua Kadison or Richard Marx or maybe even a Bonnie Raitt," Koppelman said. "Maybe just put a single out for the first release from the album and then not put out singles so that we don't have our energies spent on trying to fake retail sales in order to go up a chart that only speaks to single sales, when these artists are in the marketplace selling humongous amounts of albums."

Koppelman's new choice to head EMI Records Group, Davitt Sigerson, also indicated that he was out to change the way business had been done at EMI. Patience was in; hits by instant artists (Koppelman's past style) was out.

"I wish that Vanilla Ice showed up tomorrow morning, as does every guy that I know that runs a record company," Koppelman countered. "I think Davitt's point about not looking for hits is going to be looking for artists that we hope will have more longevity. Now, having said that, one never quite knows, and if a Vanilla Ice shows up and you can sell ten million or twelve million albums...one really doesn't know that the next Vanilla Ice isn't going to be successful. I mean, we always get a great benefit with hindsight."

Hindsight was something that made the picture at SBK look a lot better for Koppelman. "The misnomer was that at SBK we always spent a lot of money to promote our acts," he said. "That's not true. We always spent about what everyone else spent. But I think we spent it more efficiently. I think we made use of press very well, as with Jon Secada and Wilson Phillips. We got the press interested in the stories of these artists so that we would continually be getting news stories on television, and print media." Jealousy was the reason the rumors about SBK's spending were spread throughout the music industry, Koppelman contended.

As for SBK's long-term catalog, it is "probably not there. How could it be there? We were in business three years. I mean, the mission for me when I started SBK Records was to sell a lot of records. You only know if they end up being long-term artists if they become long-term artists. Do you know whether Snoop Doggy Dogg is going to be here five years from now? Is Dr. Dre going to be relevant five years from now? I don't know that. Maybe Nine Inch Nails is going to be what's really relevant five years from now. Is Interscope a great success? Absolutely. On any measuring stick you want to measure it. SBK? We broke Jesus Jones, an alternative act. Technotronic, a dance act. Wilson Phillips, a pop act. Vanilla Ice, a rap act. What other measuring stick could someone have for a three-year-old record company that started without one employee, without one artist signed? Would one look better at it if I sold a quarter of the sales?"

If he had continued running SBK rather than selling the company and graduating into his jobs as head of EMI Records Group and then EMI Records Group North America, Koppelman felt, the company would have broken new artists and sustained the careers of others. "SBK Records was a unique moment in time," he said. "I don't know very many companies that can look in five years at those kinds of successes. I mean, David Geffen is the first one to tell you that for the first ten years he didn't make a dime. Now it's a different kind of company. So maybe longevity gives you that. Maybe had I stayed at SBK, you know, we'd be looking back and have a whole different kind of scenario."

As the music business becomes more corporate, the case can be made that consumers, musicians, and, ultimately, culture are damaged.

Music as art is certainly a victim. While critics tend to dismiss the changes in the industry over the last ten years as no different than the '50s, '60s, and '70s, when a flood of imitators greeted every pop success, the relentless mainstreaming of every niche market in the last decade has invariably taken the avant garde and reduced it to its lower common denominator.

One has to look no further than the co-opting of the term

"alternative music" to see the danger in the herd mentality that has come with the advent of big business in the record business. The artistic work that used to develop and flourish in the underground now becomes as disposable as pop music. Recording artists who might have quietly developed the stability necessary for a long-term career wind up strangled in their cradle by the voracious competition created by the hits-driven system.

The bands themselves are also victimized by this process. Van Halen spent seven years playing Los Angeles nightclubs before they signed their first major label recording deal in the 1970s. By 1994, Veruca Salt signed a deal that included a non-recoupable bonus estimated at anywhere from half a million to a million dollars after playing a handful of club dates, while Mary Lou Lord was the object of a frenzied bidding war by recording labels after previewing a few original songs and performing a live set consisting mainly of songs popularized by other artists.

The need to sell hundreds of thousands of records in order to justify these huge expenditures leaves most acts with a shortened shelf life. Where once bands could expect to have at least two albums to work out their direction, it is not unusual today for an act to be dropped after its first record.

SoundScan illustrated how the system that now exists, with its huge economies of scale, needs hits to survive. In a three-year study of over 90,000 song titles sold at retail, 67 percent sold 1,000 units or less and only 3 percent accounted for 72 percent of sales. Thus, record companies can't afford to nurture—they must have hits. In the process, they are creating a system that will inevitably cannibalize itself. Absent the type of catalog—the Beach Boys, Rolling Stones, Beatles sort—that can keep a record company afloat for long, dry periods between hits, the financial bottom line will ultimately suffer.

The homogenization of the culture—not limited to music, but including films and television—not only hurts consumers aesthetically, it also has an impact in their wallets. Compact disc prices can't be lowered because they have to support the infrastructure and keep quarterly profit reports squarely in the black. Foreign consumers are particularly gouged, paying two times the U.S. price for compact discs simply because it's a price their markets will bear.

Some observers argue that this increased corporatization and consolidation of the recording industry will inevitably spawn a backlash. The argument neglects to mention that the distribution and promotion of recorded music has changed so fundamentally in the past decade that it will be virtually impossible to achieve the levels of success previous independent record labels have attained.

Where once there was a thriving network of independent record distributors and regional radio, today most distribution is attached to the six multinational distributors; radio is controlled by national consultants; mom-and-pop record chains are being driven into bankruptcy by mega-chains like Musicland and electronics retailers like Circuit City and Best Buy that purchase in mass quantities and offer huge discounts that can't be matched by small stores. The cost of doing business as a record label has also risen enormously, resulting in small record labels' being pressured to license their material to the Big Six distributors or otherwise affiliate with them in order to achieve any level of success. Thus, the risk-taking attitude that used to mark some of the best creative decisions in this street-oriented business is increasingly being determined by corporations whose decisions are not based on sentiment, love of music, or regional affiliation.

Of course, the people in charge at the record companies have an entirely different view. EMI CEO Jim Fifield insists that the growth of corporate culture inside the music business is attributable to a changing world, one in which most businesses have adopted more sophisticated methods. Fifield likened his job to "running a global empire. I don't do what Joe Smith ever did or what Mo Ostin ever did. It's a different business, because it is a business. It's bigger, with more needs."

Consolidation, according to Fifield, was the result of entrepreneurs' seeking new ways to grow their business, and realizing that they could not expand beyond a certain plateau without the aid of a larger partner. Dealing with a variety of distributors and manufacturers in various parts of the world is much more expensive than having one company that controls all of those functions in all territories, he said. "So you'll see all sorts of other labels come up and then they're going to hit that wall, $20 million in sales or whatever. When they get to that point, they're going to need a global partner. And the evolution will just continue."

Even if artists are satisfied with their record labels, there is another downside to their careers. Although business practices have become more sophisticated and global, many artists still have as much trouble getting a fair and accurate accounting of their royalties as the artists of the 1950s.

While most of the biggest acts in the world are British and American artists, the situation is worse when it comes to "local repertoire," which is industry parlance for music produced by the people of the country in question. Particularly in Latin America, most of the deals signed are with production companies, which in turn hire the singers and performers and control most aspects of production and payment.

As a result, many artists are paid a flat fee for their contributions, see no royalties, and watch as their work goes on to generate millions of dollars in revenue for multinational corporations, which, incidentally, charge exorbitant prices for compact discs in overseas markets simply because, in the grandest business tradition, they can get the high price they are asking. Thus, there is little to separate the music company from automobiles, pharmacy, tire makers, sneaker makers, all of whom exploit Third-World labor.

But even in the best-case scenarios, artists must often resort to hiring outside auditors in order to claim their fair share of the income generated by their work.

Steven Ames Brown is a San Francisco–based attorney specializing in artists' rights enforcement. His high-profile cases have included royalty issues for Motown's Mary Welles, Martha Wash versus C + C Music Factory, and, most prominently, Yvette Marine's losing battle to have a court declare her the co–lead singer on Paula Abdul's multimillion-selling debut album.

Brown, who first became involved in artists' rights in 1979, feels that the rock 'n' roll business "is built on unpaid talent. Small companies become big companies by cheating. Period. And the cheating is so institutionalized that people will really look at it and think of it as being legitimate. And it goes back to the earliest royalties agreements which developed a concept which is unique in any industry. Name the business where the employee or independent contractor is responsible for paying the employer's expenses."

Brown suggested that a record company's attitude is akin to "'After we recoup it, we'll start paying you. We'll take a hundred percent of our costs and charge them against your ten-percent income so that we will recoup that money ten times before we pay you any money.'

"Now," Brown said, "that is the standard. So what they're saying is that by creating the standard, they've institutionalized the rape. And now people speak about recoupment as if it's a sacrosanct right of a record company. It's preposterous."

"For every Michael Jackson, there are a thousand recording artists who are not compensated accordingly," Brown said. "What you need to remember is that if there are ten people performing on a record, meaning all the side artists and background musicians and singers, there may be one, two or three people who are paid a royalty or who at least have a contractual right to a royalty. Whether they actually get one is a separate issue. If a record remains popular for decades and somebody created something that's viable, why is it that if anybody's getting compensation, it's only one person out of ten, while the record company, of course, continues to reap the profits?"

Music and publishing industry consultant Thomas A. White agrees with that assessment. "I think the system of compensation has a lot of inequities built into it," he said. "One of them is that there is no duty to exploit by the record company. Record companies use their sole discretion. Occasionally there is a marketing commitment, but for the most part, record companies use 'their best judgment,' the theory being that the same judgment that would propel a record company or an artist to perform well also propels a record company to spend where it feels it can make money. The problem is that an album is vital to the success and the future career of an artist. For the record company, it's one of many."

Brown, who pursues money from record companies for artists, argues that he has "never heard of anybody working in a royalty department who was disciplined for making an error in favor of the company. The second point is it's a waiting game and a difference in economic base between individual artists and record company. It costs money to sue a record company. The fact is that most people won't make that investment."

Brown notes instances of apparent out-and-out fraud in his dealings with the new breed of multinational record companies, practices that quite resemble the old shoebox accounting methods of some of rock 'n' roll's forefathers.

"Whenever you concentrate the power, basically 90 percent of the market, in the hands of five or six companies, if you have to deal with those people, you simply lose leverage," Brown said. "People think of the big rock stars as being rich. They keep forgetting that seven out of every ten recording artists aren't even contractually entitled to royalties. And of the three out of ten who *are* entitled to them, most of them are never going to see anything because they're almost always in a negative position with the record company because of the way the economics work. Since this is so unique to just the record business, you can't break that tradition. If it's firmly entrenched in the five or six companies that control 90 percent of the market, it's not going to change and it's not healthy for artists. Consolidation is not good for them. It's worse."

Jim Fifield may be correct in his theories of the benign benevolence of the modern corporate record entity. But the most crucial dissent to his theory comes from the lifeblood of the industry—recording artists. Over the past decade, artists like Don Henley, Prince (or TAFKAP), Ice-T, Metallica, and Graham Parker contend today's music industry is not friendly to creative people with their own ideas about lyrics, marketing, promotion, and release schedules.

Although some of the complaints undoubtedly had more to do with business gamesmanship than with battles over the creative process, there still remains a legacy of interference that raises questions about the real agenda of the Big Six distributors.

George Michael's suit against Sony in the United Kingdom in 1993 was the most noteworthy attempt at breaking a contract over creative differences. The suit, which industry insiders contend came about after Michael overhead a slur about his personal life from a senior Sony executive, sought to break Michael's fifteen-year, eight-album contract with Sony, which Michael contended had changed into a soulless electronics corporation during his time at the company.

Michael lost his suit but maintained that the battle was fought because musicians have no rights under their deals with major record companies. "Even though I both created and paid for my work, I will never own it and have any rights over it," Michael said after the U.K. court's decision against him. "I have no control or say in the way that my work is exploited. In fact, I have no guarantee that my work will be released at all.... Perhaps most importantly, I have no right to resign. Effectively, you sign a piece of paper at the beginning of your career and you are expected to live with that decision, good and bad, for the rest of your professional life."

The result according to Michael, was akin to "professional slavery." Fortunately for him, in August 1995, Michael found an overseer willing to buy his way out of the Sony deal. DreamWorks SKG, the label helmed by David Geffen in conjunction with Jeffrey Katzenberg and Steven Spielberg, initiated a settlement that reportedly included future payments on Michael's albums to Sony.

Despite his problem, George Michael at least enjoyed a successful career before his legal misfortune, having sold millions of albums with Wham! and during his own solo career. But consider the plight of yet another musician further down the food chain.

Although Motorhead is acknowledged by many musicians as an inspiration for their faster, stronger, louder approach to music, the band has not had the type of career that will allow its members to retire. A good deal of its problems had to do with record companies that could not get a handle on its artistic sensibility.

In his keynote address to the 1994 Concrete Foundations Forum, an annual convention of record industry personnel in the hard rock/heavy metal genre, Ian "Lemmy" Kilmister, the bassist and lead singer of Motorhead, detailed in his own inimitable style his experience with the corporate machine. It is a speech that should be required reading for every band and every record executive in today's music industry.

By way of background: Motorhead had produced its second major-label album for Epic Records. The most promising song, the band felt, was "I Ain't No Nice Guy," which had guest appearances from Ozzy Osbourne and Guns N' Roses guitarist Slash.

The band, according to Lemmy, went to the head of the promotion department at Epic and tried to convince him that the track could be promoted in several different radio formats. The answer they received was that promotion had already tried to push the track, but no one wanted it.

Lemmy and Motorhead didn't believe it. The band "hired a guy and gave him a telephone and said, 'You can have your trousers back when we have a hit,' and locked the door," Lemmy related. "One month later, we were on eighty-two stations coast to coast."

So it was back to the promotion office, this time seeking funding for a video. Lemmy said, "'Well, we're No. 10 on the radio charts, so can we have a budget for a video? Ozzy and Slash have both agreed to be in the video, and Ozzy's on Epic too.'" They said no.

The band shot its own video, admittedly ramshackle, at a cost of $8,000. "Most video shoots pay that for security," Lemmy said. "Having made the video, we went back to the great man's office. 'MTV?' we inquired. 'No,' he said. And he was as good as his word." The video was also held up for six weeks because a release signature had not been obtained, Lemmy said.

"It's not that we are the only ones that this sort of miserable, shameful shit happens to," Lemmy said. "It happens every day, and mostly to young bands who aren't even confident enough in themselves to fight it. But I'm not that young anymore. The only reason I can think of for destroying a hit on your own label that was handed to you, all expenses paid, is 'tax loss.' Either that or a fit of pique because it wasn't your idea. It came from the band, God forbid, the band got up on its hind legs and dared to differ with your opinion. Bad dog! Bad dog, back in that box!"

The slight on budgets wasn't the only problem the band encountered. "Perhaps I should have realized that we weren't exactly flavor of the month at the label when I went to New York after being nominated for a Grammy and the head of the label didn't even see fit to grant me an audience," Lemmy said. "I thought a Grammy nomination might have merited a quick handshake and 'Glad to have you aboard,' or something. But no. Three or four months later they dropped us. That is fucking disgraceful. The word is not out of context—we got fucked."

Lemmy continued, "'The Business,' to coin a phrase, is very confused by people that they haven't been told by their grassroots pollers and market overview experts is the next big thing. I mean, being told that we wanted to get our own artist to do the *1916* [a Motorhead album] cover because their ideas were not quite what we had in mind, their reaction was (a) disbelief and deep unreasoning hatred, and (b) disbelief and deep unreasoning hatred.

"They got the sleeve wrong fourteen times. It's still wrong. They showed us a thing or two, right?

"The trouble is, when a company does something 'wrong'— that is to say, inferior to win a political points decision in the corridors of power, there are serious ramifications. The public [who pay all the bills] is getting less than the band originally gave, for the ego of some jumped-up art department head who doesn't like the band anyway because we enjoy ourselves too much.

"Also, it is a catalog of mistakes, incompetence and out-and-out spite that has no place in rock 'n' roll. The record companies have managed to convince us that it is necessary in all things that they must oversee everything from the album sleeve, work contained therein, and even the words themselves on one or two occasions.

"'The Business' is a bunch of self-serving, spiteful, petty-minded people who seem to think that as long as the books are into the black every month, we're doing the right kind of music. Nothing to do with rock 'n' roll. Rock 'n' roll is joyful music. It makes you shake your ass! It makes you feel so good that you dance to it alone in your room! Well, if the business has its way with it, all that nonsense is over. The business is now run by accountants whose job it is, in all fairness, to make the books balance. The problem comes when making the books balance is the only criterion involved. I mean, whoever heard of anyone falling in love to the sound of a good fiscal year?

"Fight it. Fight it to the death, for that is what it brings. Death. Death to spontaneity. Death to 'off-the-wall.' Death to surprises. Death to interaction between bands and companies on ideas on promotion, message, and music. If the business had been right, we would never have had Buddy Holly, Elvis Presley, Little Richard, the Beatles, the Rolling Stones, Nirvana, Iron Maiden, the MC5, the Stooges, The Who, Jimi Hendrix, or Motorhead. The business gave us Bobby Rydell, Brian Hyland, Bobby Vinton, the Strawberry Alarm Clock, The 1910 Fruitgum Company, the Archies, the Monkees, David Cassidy, and Leif Garrett.

"Be not afraid of these people in suits. Most of them are trying to hold on to their jobs so desperately you can forget any kind of fair deal from them. If you want fair play, go watch *The Partridge Family*.

"Oh, and if you still don't believe me, try to imagine a record executive going to his boss and recommending that the band should have a say in their latest video, the album sleeve, the promotion for it, the tracks on it. See what I mean?

"But, and this is the strength we have against those adding machines wearing suits—you don't have to. Speak up. Get fired. Get dropped. Get a bad name in the business.

"But don't play music you hate for money. Don't get sold short.

"And don't die ashamed."

INDEX

A&M Records, 78–79, 100, 101
Abbo, 116–17, 153
Abbott, Gregory, 63
Adams, Bryan, 170
Advertising, 37–38
Aldon Music, 52–53
Alexander, Linda, 41
Alpert, Herb, 79
Alternative music, 42–43, 123, 134, 150–51, 182–84, 210–11
Anderson, Ray, 110
April Blackwood Music, 56, 57, 67
Ariola, 93
Arista Records, 93
Arrested Development, 142–45
Arthur, Brooks, 32, 52–53, 56, 57
Arthur, Marilyn, 52, 56
Artist development, 38–39, 149–54, 203, 209
Artist royalties, 46, 61, 62, 213–15
As Nasty As They Wanna Be, 187–89
Asylum Records, 171
Atco Records, 169
Atlantic Records, 78, 148, 155, 157–58, 189, 203
ATV Music, 63–64, 67
Ayeroff, Jeff, 88
Azoff, Irving, 25, 139, 169
Azzoli, Val, 158, 159

Babcock, John, Jr., 198
Bandier, Martin, 57–60, 62, 63–74, 102–9, 118, 120, 207
Baumstein, Ken, 143, 145
Beatles, the, 15, 17, 83, 206, 208
Beech, Jim, 174
Beghe, Francesca, 115

Berkowitz, Artie, 51–52
Berman, David, 129, 130
Berry, Ken, 89, 91
Bertelsmann Music Group, 80, 89–90, 93–96, 99
Big Six distributors, 5–8, 150, 212, 215
Billboard, 190, 195–203
"Billy Jean," 40
Black artists, 39–40
Blackwell, Chris, 75–78
Blessid Union of Souls, 128
Blood Sugar Sex Magik, 124
BMG. *See* Bertelsmann Music Group
"Bohemian Rhapsody," 175
Bolton, Michael, 203
Born in the U.S.A., 33
Bowen, Jimmy, 85
Bowie, David, 168
Branca, John, 45
Branson, Richard, 86–92
Broadcast Data Systems (BDS), xi, 201–2
Bronfman, Edgar, 98
Brooks, Garth, 202, 203, 206
Brown, Steven Ames, 42–43, 213–15
Buggles, the, 35
Bust It Productions, 135
Buziak, Bob, 168

Cages, the, 133
Camelot, 188
Campbell, Luther, 188–89, 192
Capitol-EMI Music, 3–4, 9, 14–20, 83, 129, 130–40
Capitol Records, 9, 14–15, 20–22, 54–55, 85, 125, 176, 207
Capitol Tower, 9, 137